新东方雅思(IELTS)考试指定辅导教材

CAMBRIDGE IELTS 4

剑桥雅思考试全真试题解析4 精讲

周成刚 ◎ 主编

群言出版社

图书在版编目(CIP)数据

剑桥雅思考试全真试题集（4）精讲 / 周成刚主编.
北京：群言出版社，2005
ISBN 7-80080-507-7

Ⅰ. 剑...　Ⅱ. 周...　Ⅲ. 英语—高等学校—入学考试，

国外—解题　Ⅳ. H319.6

中国版本图书馆 CIP 数据核字(2005)第 076160 号

责任编辑　孙春红
封面设计　王　琳
出版发行　群言出版社
地　　址　北京东城区东厂胡同北巷 1 号
邮政编码　100006
联系电话　65263345　65265404
电子信箱　qunyancbs@dem-league. org. cn
印　　刷　北京朝阳新艺印刷有限公司
经　　销　全国新华书店
版　　次　2005 年 7 月第一版　2006 年 12 月第 4 次印刷
开　　本　787×1092　　1/16
印　　张　16
字　　数　350 千字
书　　号　ISBN 7-80080-507-7
定　　价　28.00 元

New IELTS Preparation Package
New Learning Experiences
——丛 书 序

Why Us

我们了解雅思

我们了解中国的英语学习者

我们更了解准备参加雅思考试的人

Why This Book

目前市面上的雅思辅导书林林总总，良莠不齐。国人所编之书多有拼凑之嫌，质量不高；国外引进之书科学性强，但水土不服，无法适应中国考生实际需要。作为国内最大的雅思培训基地，新东方教育科技集团集其8年雅思教学经验精华和众多雅思教学专家之长，隆重推出这套全方位、学习型的雅思辅导丛书——“新东方雅思(IELTS)考试培训教程”系列丛书。该丛书分为预备级、进阶级和飞越级，囊括了雅思考试的各分项测试及留学指南，满足了不同层次的读者的全方位需求。

What to Expect

- **最权威的选材来源——我们提供权威解读！**

无论是最基本的词汇，还是听力、阅读习题，丛书的素材均紧密结合最权威、最新的雅思真题出版物和近两年来的雅思考试，时效性极强。中外专家联手，保证了丛书在国内雅思培训类图书中的颠峰地位。

- **最有效的应试技巧——我们知道症结所在！**

本套丛书的作者均为在新东方任教多年的优秀雅思教师，我们对雅思考试有着最权威的分析和应对策略，我们了解中国考生在备考雅思和雅思实战过程中经常出现的问题，并能为他们提供最有效的应试技巧。

- **最实用的学习方法——我们想考生之所想！**

雅思成绩的最终提高有赖于语言实力的长进。本系列丛书与同类出版物的一个很大不同，就在于我们在提供应试策略的同时，也为中国考生提供了真正提高听、说、读、写能力的切实可行的方法，让读者在体验雅思的同时，也获得对各种技能的习得的全新认识。

- **最全面的学习体验——我们为您量身定做！**

本套丛书自成体系，以词汇始，听、读、说、写齐头并进。书后还附有为期90天的学习规划，为中国考生备考雅思提供了详实丰富的学习套餐，使得备考雅思的过程成为一种全方位、整合式的英语学习体验。

- **最友好的互动答疑——我们为您指点迷津！**

本套丛书为其使用者提供了一个新的起点，在考生前行的过程中，我们的团队始终伴随左右。考生在使用本书的同时，可以登陆新东方的BBS(http://bbs.tol24.com)，然后进入“出国留学”的“留学考试”，最后进入“IELTS考试”一栏。通过这个平台，考生可以了解最新的雅思考试动向，并就学习过程中的问题与我们进行交流。

新东方雅思名师团队

Preface 前　言

备考雅思，真题的重要性不言而喻。由新东方教育科技集团于2005年独家引进并奉献给广大考生的《剑桥雅思考试全真试题解析4》(*Cambridge IELTS* 4)，收录了包括2004年在内的4套学术类真题和2套移民类真题。有了最新的真题对于考生来讲无疑是一种福音，但是有了真题该如何去利用？是不是仅用于考前模拟？是不是光做一遍题然后核对答案即可？如果是这样的话，那么真题的价值便没有真正被发掘出来。

为了帮助考生更好地使用《剑桥雅思考试全真试题解析4》，揭示雅思出题规律，分析雅思考试所涉及题型，新东方教育科技集团集近十年雅思教学经验精华和众多雅思教学专家之长，隆重推出《剑桥雅思考试全真试题解析4·精讲》。

本书特点：

★ 新东方雅思专家亲笔撰写，洞悉雅思考试出题规律

本书编写团队由新东方资深雅思教学专家组成。他们长期从事雅思第一线教学，对雅思考试的出题规律有精到的见解。编写者均多次参加雅思考试，几乎每次都取得总分8.5分。我们演奏业内实力最强音！

★ 针对中国雅思考生的特点和需求，分题型全面破解

针对雅思考试出题模式，我们分题型给出了最切实有效的解题方法。针对中国雅思考生的总体水平和特点，我们对剑4中听力测试部分的难点进行分析，阅读部分增加了阅读背景知识介绍和题型解析，写作部分从不同角度给出了写作范文，口语部分则提供了完整的口语8分答案。我们详细破解最新真题！

★ TESTING与LEARNING的完美结合，超越纯粹应试

我们在讲解题型的同时，也给出了解决考试之苦的最根本途径——学习方法，帮助考生将应试训练和语言能力的提高结合起来。此外，雅思考试内容丰富，语言测试

的背后蕴涵着丰富的社会生活背景、文化内涵和自然、社会科学知识，有鉴于此，本书提供了相关领域的背景材料，以开拓考生的视野。Teaching not just testing！我们助您真正提高语言实力！

★ 附赠光盘，雅思专家与你亲密接触，面授机宜

为了让广大考生能够面对面地聆听雅思专家对备考雅思的建议，以及如何最大化利用雅思真题的价值，我们特意制作了这张光盘，免费赠送给广大考生。各位雅思专家分别就雅思考试的听力、阅读、写作和口语部分的最新测试趋势及备考策略进行了深入剖析和总结，使考生在领略各位雅思专家风采的同时，能够对如何备考雅思做到心中有数，有的放矢。免费赠送，物超所值！

希望我们的读者能够妥善利用剑 4 及本书，也祝愿你们能够早日实现飞越重洋的梦想。本书在资料收集、编写、校对的每一过程无不力求审慎周全，但恐仍有疏漏之处，尚祈读者不吝指正。你们的支持，就是我们前进的动力。

编　者

Contents 目　录

Test 1

LISTENING

SECTION 1

篇章结构

题　　型：笔记填空、表格填空
考查技能：听出具体信息
场　　景：旅游+咨询

场景背景介绍

在这个旅游讨论场景中，学生就英国某学校组织的旅游活动一事向校方负责人进行咨询。为帮助国际留学生更好的感受英国的文化，英国大学通常为他们提供类似的旅游活动，游览地点多为英国的著名城市和名胜古迹，如本题中提到的伦敦塔Tower of London以及Salisbury平原上的史前巨石柱Stonehenge。校方(通常为国际留学生办公室International Office)会将游览的安排事先公布，学生提前报名，并交纳低廉的费用。学校会负责游览当天的来回交通，学生可以自行活动，也可参加有导游的游览。若想了解更多的旅游信息，www.visitbritain.com是个不错的网站，这样前往英国学习的同学可在出国前就订下自己的旅游计划清单了！

本节必备词汇、词组

cancel	*v.* 取消	vary	*v.* 变化，不同
coach	*n.* 长途汽车	guided tours	有导游的游览
confirm	*v.* 确认	in advance	提前
departure	*n.* 出发	notice board	公告栏
reserve	*v.* 预定	places of historical interest	历史古迹
(full) refund	*n.*（全额）退款	sixteen-seater minibus	16座小巴
schedule	*n.* 时间表		

旅游场景词汇拓展

arrival	*n.* 到达	package tour	跟团旅游
hiking boots	旅行靴	round-trip	往返
itinerary	*n.* 行程，路线	sleeping bag	睡袋
one-day pass	（公共交通）一天的通票	souvenir	*n.* 纪念品
one-way ticket	单程车票	travel agency	旅行社
opening hours	开放时间	tourist attraction	游览胜地

文本及疑难解析

1. P130. "Yes, we **run** five every month: three during weekends and two Wednesday afternoon trips." 是的，我们每个月组织5次。其中有3次是在周末，两次是在周三下午。run在此当"组织、运营"来讲，相当于前文中提到的"organize"。类似的例句还有He runs a drug counseling service in London. 他在伦敦提供戒毒咨询服务。

2. P130. "Well, obviously it **varies**, but always places of historical interests..." 很明显他们是不一样的，但肯定都是历史古迹。vary做不及物动词时是雅思考试中的高频词汇。常见搭配有：vary from...to..., 如The heights of the plants vary from 8 cm to 20 cm. 树高从8厘米到20厘米不等；或者vary in, 如Tickets vary in price.票的价格不等。

3. P130. "...because we're able to say that all our visits are less than **three hours drive**." 我们所有的游览地都不超过3个小时的车程。three hours drive是常见的表示路程的表达方式，也可以写成a three-hour drive。同类的表达方式还有 a five-minute walk 五分钟步行

4. P130. "Again it varies — between five and fifteen pounds **a head**," 价格同样不等——在每人5镑到15镑之间。 a head相当于题干中的per person，一般用来指每人花多少钱。当然，类似的词组还有per capita，不过这个词组常用在商业报表或政治、经济学范畴里。

5. P130. "Oh, and we **do** offer to arrange special trips if..." 我们的确也可以提供特别行程。do用在动词原形前表示强调。

6. P130. "We **figure** it's best to keep the day fairly short." 我们觉得最好把一天的行程控制的短一点。figure在此当"考虑、认为"讲，多用于口语。还有一个很好用的词组figure out，指"想出问题的答案或理解某事"，如It took him a couple of days to figure out what had happened.他花了好几天才弄明白到底发生了什么。

7. P130. "If you can just give some idea of the weekend ones so I can, you know, **work out** when to see friends, etcetera." 如果你可以告诉我周末游览的情况的话，我就可以安排跟朋友见面或其它事情的时间了。work out在此当"仔细考虑并计划"讲，类似例句如I had it all worked out.我把一切都考虑到了。在日常口语中work out的另外一个重要意思是"锻炼"I like to work out on weekends.我喜欢周末健身。

8. P131. "we'll have only sixteen places available '**cos** we're going by mini-bus." 我们只有16个名额，

因为届时我们将乘坐小巴。'cos=because，为英式英语中的口语用语。

9. P131. “we’ll be taking a medium-sized coach so there’ll be forty-five places on that” 到时可以有45个名额，因为我们会乘坐一辆中巴。将来进行时多用于口语中，表示将来的打算。

（图一）

10. P131. “We’re going to **Salisbury** on the eighteenth of March and that’s always a popular one because the optional extra is Stonehenge.” 3月18号我们去Salisbury，这条路线总是很受欢迎，因为走这条路还可以去史前巨石柱。Stonehenge（史前巨石柱，见图一）位于Salisbury平原，其主体是由一根根巨大的石柱排列成几个同心圆，石阵的外围是直径约90米的环形土岗和沟。公元前2300年左右，这些世界著名的巨石被竖立起来，有来自附近马尔伯勒的重达20吨的砂岩漂砾巨石，也有来自英国西部威尔士的4吨胆矾巨石。至于胆矾巨石是如何辗转380公里来到此处，至今仍是个谜。本节中提到的许多景点都是英国文化和历史的遗产，如伦敦塔Tower of London（图二），S.S. Great Britain号涡轮驱动船（图三），都是去英国学习不可错过的参观内容。

（图二）

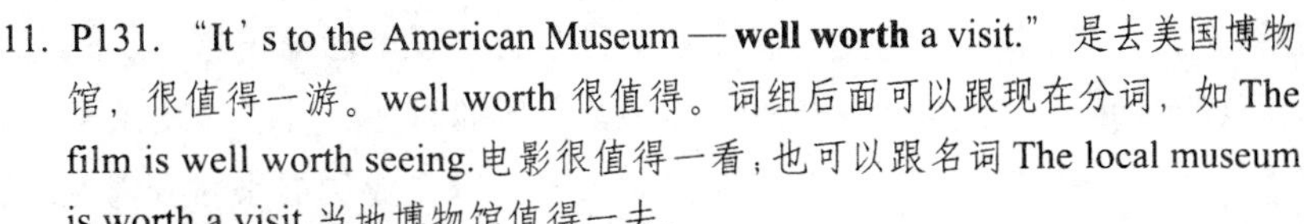

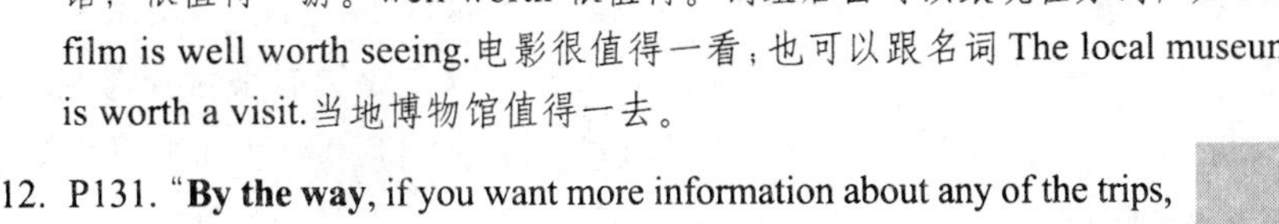

11. P131. “It’s to the American Museum — **well worth** a visit.” 是去美国博物馆，很值得一游。well worth 很值得。词组后面可以跟现在分词，如 The film is well worth seeing.电影很值得一看；也可以跟名词 The local museum is worth a visit.当地博物馆值得一去。

12. P131. “**By the way**, if you want more information about any of the trips, have a look in the student newspaper.” 对了，如果你想了解更多有关游览的事，可以看看学生报纸。by the way 在雅思听力中中是重要词组，虽然只是“顺便一说”，但后面往往跟着考点。

（图三）

题目解析

1－4题为笔记填空题，笔记中的黑体字均为该学生提问问题的关键词，而答案均出现在校方负责人的回答中。做题时应抓住这些黑体字及题干中的关键词，依次写出所听答案。5－10题为表格填空题，顺序原则是解题关键。题干中有很多英国的城市名和名胜名称，所以考生在平时应对英联邦国家的常见地名有所掌握，如英国的Bristol, Bath, Brighton, 和澳大利亚的Brisbane, Canberra等。

SECTION 2

篇章结构

题　　型：完成句子、地图标记
考查技能：听出具体信息
场　　景：导游介绍游览地点

场景背景介绍

景点介绍场景是雅思听力中的常见场景，通常出现在第二部分，形式为导游或组织者的个人独白。雅思中所介绍的景点似乎特别偏爱 industrial village，agricultural park，澳洲的 zoo 以及新西兰 Christ Church 的南极科考站。该场景中经常会出现地图标记题，所以考生对各种方向、方位词要熟练掌握。本节中导游介绍了英国某个工业村庄，所以涉及到了工业化的历史以及机械制造中的一些词汇，但雅思听力考试向来不会以专业词汇来考查考生，题目答案通常都是基本词汇，因此即使考生对制造业中的某些词汇感到陌生，也不必紧张，只要把握要领，照样可以把题目做出。

本节必备词汇、词组

a brief account	简要介绍	steam engine	蒸汽机
roam	*v.* 闲逛、漫游	plan	*n.* 在地图题中指平面图
manufacture	*v.* 制造	entrance	*n.* 入口
availability	*n.* 可用性	Ticket Office	售票处
raw materials	原材料	Gift Shop	售纪念品处
mineral	*n.* 矿物、矿石	Showroom	陈列室
iron ore	铁矿石	on display	展出
abundance	*n.* 充裕	grind	*v.* 打磨
fuel	*n.* 燃料	furnace	*n.* 炉子
coal	*n.* 煤	smelt	*v.* 冶炼
craftsman	*n.* 工匠	cast	*v.* 铸造
iron forge	铁匠铺	antique	*n.* 古物
the bend in the river	河流的转弯处	cottage	*n.* 村舍
water mill	水磨		

场景词汇拓展

Information desk	咨询处	in front of	在…前面
Reception desk	前台	ahead of	在…前面
Car park	停车场	opposite	在…对面
Café	咖啡店	across ... from...	隔着…与…正对着
heritage	*n.* 遗产	in the middle	在中间
toilet	*n.* 厕所	at the top	在顶端
lounge	*n.* 休息室	in the top right-hand corner	(面对地图)在右上角
on the right/left	(面对地图)在右边 / 左边	to the left/right /east/west	在…的左边 / 右边 / 东边 / 西边
at the bottom	下面		

文本及疑难解析

1. P131. "Now, from where we're standing you've **got a good view** of the river over there" 从我们站着的地方看去，那边河流的美景尽收眼底。"get a view" 在景点介绍场景中很常见，类似的例句还有From the top you get a panoramic view of the city.站在最高点，你可以看到城市的全景。

2. P132. "...and many of these continued to operate **well** into the nineteenth century." 这其中的很多一直到19世纪还在运转。well在此能够表达出一种惊讶和赞许的情感，而类似用法在口语中很常见，如The amphitheatre is well worth a visit.圆形剧场绝对值得一看。

3. P132. "...and **immediately** to our right is the Ticket Office." 售票处就在我们的右边。immediately在此指"空间上紧挨着"，类似的用法有the seat immediately behind the driver紧靠着司机后面的那个座位。

4. P132. "...**just past** it are the toilets" 过去一点就是厕所。just past指"过去一点"。类似的用法有There are parking spaces over there, just past the garage.车库过去一点有停车位。

5. P132. "that building with bigger windows is the Showroom, where samples of all the tools that were made through the ages are on display." 在景点介绍场景中常出现类似的结构，相当于中文中的"那个有着大窗户的建筑物是陈列室，那里摆放着几个世纪以来所有制作过的工具的样本"。

6. P132. "These were built for the workers towards the end of the eighteenth century and they're still furnished from that period so you can **get a good idea of** ordinary people's living conditions." 这些(村舍)是在18世纪末为工人们建造的，它们依然保持着那个年代的装修风格，因此你可以很好的了解当时普通人的生活条件。get/have an idea of...指"对…所了解"。类似的用法有Don't worry if you don't understand it right now — you'll get the idea.现在不懂没关系，以后你会理解的。

7. P132. "Across the yard from them, you can see the stables where the horses were kept for transporting the products." 穿过院子跟他们(村舍)相对的是马厩，那里放着用于运输产品的马。类似的用法有Across the street from where we're standing, you can see the old church.穿过马路跟咱们正对着的就是那个古老的教堂。

8. P132. "If you' d like to **come along**, this way please, ladies and gentlemen." 先生们，女士们，如果你们想跟着一起，那咱们走这边吧。come along 意指"跟着一起"，类似的用法如 It should be good fun. Why don' t you come along? 应该很好玩，为什么不一起来呢？

题目解析

1. 11－13题为完成句子题。由于前半部分涉及很多跟工业制造相关的单词，而且在介绍历史时涉及较多时间，因此题目难度较大。考生在做题时首先需要紧紧把握住题干中的关键词，如11题中的"fuel"，13题中的"water mills"和"the eighteenth century"。还要进行必要的预测，如12题中肯定填某些人群，而前半部分中提到的人群只有"local craftsmen"，13题的答案应该是数字，而前半部分材料中除了时间外只出现了一个数字"a hundred and sixty"。最后，考生也要把握必要的同义结构，如11题中"such as"相当于原文中的"like"，13题中的"over"相当于原文中的"more than"。

2. 14－20题为地图标注题，考生在解题时切记紧跟题目顺序，同时迅速反应出原文中的关键方向、方位词。本部分中虽然出现了某些专业词汇如"grinding"，"stable"等，但他们都被设计成了已知信息，答案中用词均为常见词。

SECTION 3

篇章结构

题　　型：选择题，匹配题，标注图表题
考查技能：听大意和辅助性信息
场　　景：师生间就作业展开的讨论

场景背景介绍

学术、学习讨论是雅思听力第三部分的常见场景。该场景中会有2～4人就学习、学术或科研话题进行讨论。本节中就是一位学生和她的导师之间的对话，主要讨论的是作业延期和参考书目的使用。在国外学习的过程中，如果在完成作业或论文时遇到很大的问题，可以去找导师商量延期交作业。一般来讲，在导师看来只有两个理由是可以接受的：病假或家人病重或去世（compassionate leave）。当然，其他原因如果合情合理，也会得到导师的理解的，比如本节中学生没有借到参考书目，导师便给了她两个礼拜的时间。在国外读书的时候，写作业或论文之前要先阅读大量的文献，如果同一专业的同学人数众多的话，图书馆的藏书自然供不应求，因此凡事先下手为强。但导师提供的参考书目也并非本本都读，有的要详读，有的要略读，而有的只要读某个章节即可，正如本节中所讨论的那样。

本节必备词汇、词组

assignment	*n.* 作业	journal	*n.* 期刊
due	*adj.* 到期	relevant	*adj.* 相关的
extension	*n.* 延期	essential	*adj.* 实质性的
medical or compassionate	疾病或亲人病重或	bar graph	柱状图
reasons	去世等原因	photocopy	*n.* 复印件
reference	*n.* 参考书目	indicate	*v.* 指出
submit	*v.* 提交(作业、论文)	proximity	*n.* 临近
research methodology	研究方法论	tenant	*n.* 房客

场景词汇拓展

office hour	上班时间	tutorial	*n.* 辅导
tutor	*n.* 导师	presentation	*n.* 发言、陈述
plagiarism	*n.* 抄袭	attendance	*n.* 出勤
paper	*n.* 论文	word limit	自述限制
essay	*n.* 作文	deadline	*n.* 最后期限
dissertation	*n.* 硕士/博士论文	draft	*n.* 草稿

文本及疑难解析

1. P132. "and it's **due** in twelve days" 12天后就得交了。due指"到期"，后面通常跟in或者on，如The final results of the experiment are due on December 9.实验的最终结果将于12月9号揭晓。

2. P133. "I'm also having — been having — trouble getting hold of the books." 我一直借不到书。现在时是口语中的常用时态，该学生说话时将现在进行时改为完成进行时，意在指出问题一直存在。

3. P133. "Sounds like you should have started borrowing books a bit earlier." 听上去好象你应该早点开始借书。对过去的虚拟，语气中略带批评。

4. P133. "I got eighty-seven percent." 我得了87分。国外的评分体系中70%便是A或者"优秀"了，60%便是"良"。87分的确是非常高的分数了，难怪导师对这为学生的态度有所改变。

5. P133. "the one by Roberts says very relevant things, **although** it's not essential." Roberts的文章跟这次作业关系密切，当然了，也并非不读不可。在口语中although的这种用法比较常见，跟在主句后面对前面的论断进行转折限定。同样的例句You can copy down my answers, although I'm not sure they're right. 你可以把我的答案抄下来，尽管我也不知道他们到底正确与否。

6. P134. "Bar two is to **do with** the people living nearby disturbing them," 第二栏跟附近的人影响他们有关。have/be to do with somebody/something 关于某人/某物。类似的例句This question doesn't have anything to do with the main topic of the survey.这个问题跟调查的主要话题毫无干系。

题目解析

1. 21－22题为选择题，考查的是考生对大意的把握和抗干扰能力。21题中的解题关键是原文中的"another course"，选项B和C均为断章取义。22题原文中的"medical or compassionate reasons"被替换成了选项中的"personal illness or accidents"，类似的替换在选择题中或任何有选项的题型中屡见不鲜，因此考生在处理类似的题型时对题干中关键词的同义、近义词要敏感。最后考生也可把这个考点当常识来记住，以便在国外学习时合理安排时间。

2. 23－27题为匹配题，解题时要紧抓住题目的顺序，在解答这样的题型时，考生应尽量将选项通读一遍，但选项中的字眼很可能跟原文的有所出入，因此做题时也可以当笔记题一样来解答，最后再根据原文在选项中的同义词来最终确定答案。

3. 28－30题的解题思路跟前面一样，只要注意选项中的字眼在原文中的替换词即可，如选项中的“uncooperative landlord”、“noise neighbours”和“environment”在原文中的对应分别是“the owner is not helpful”、“people living nearby disturbing them”和“attractive neighbourhood”。

SECTION 4

篇章结构

题　　型：笔记填空
考查技能：听出具体信息和大意
场　　景：关于树木对城市地貌影响的讲座

场景背景介绍

有关生态环境的讲座在雅思听力的第四部分很常见，这体现出雅思考试在选材方面对环保以及人与环境问题的关注。在本节中，演讲人就城市中树木与气候以及树木与噪音的关系做了介绍，其中包含了许多关于气候的词汇。

本节必备词汇、词组

urban	*adj.* 城市的	property	*n.* 特性
landscape	*n.* 地形	exploit	*v.* 开发、利用
vegetation	*n.* 植被	filter	*v.* 过滤
significant impact	重大影响	considerably	*adv.* 相当地
as a whole	总体上	gust	*n.* 阵风
humid	*adj.* 湿润的	built-up areas	建筑物密集的区域
inland city	内陆城市	intensify	*v.* 加强
on the local scale	在局部范围内	a belt of trees	林带
shady	*adj.* 多荫的	vehicle	*n.* 车辆
internal	*adj.* 内在的	surrounding	*n.* 周围环境
mechanism	*n.* 机制	frequency	*n.* 频率
temperature	*n.* 温度	canyon	*n.* 峡谷
regulate	*v.* 控制	high-rise	*adj.* & *n.* 高楼
evaporate	*v.* 蒸发	enclose	*v.* 装入
humidify	*v.* 使潮湿		

场景词汇拓展

environmental problems	环境问题	solar energy	太阳能
population explosion	人口爆炸	deforestation	森林采伐
water resources	水资源	acid rain	酸雨
underground water	地下水	air pollution	空气污染
in short supply	短缺	carbon dioxide	二氧化碳

文本及疑难解析

1. P134. 讲座的开头开门见山，指出本次讲座的主题，非常符合西方lecture的风格。第一段中“...how we can better plan our cities using trees to provide a more comfortable environment for us to live in”我们如何利用树木来更好地规划我们的城市，以便为大家提供更舒适的生活环境。

2. P134. “**Well**, the main difference between a tree and a building is a tree has got an internal mechanism to keep the temperature regulated”一棵树和一幢楼的主要区别在于树有一个内在的机制来对自己的温度进行控制。在讲座中，“well”可以用来引出新的话题，所以要想跟上讲座的顺序，对这样看似不重要的词要格外关注，类似的词汇有“Right”，“OK”等。

3. P134. “The temperature of a building surface on a hot sunny day can easily be twenty degrees more than our temperature”炎炎烈日下，一幢建筑物的表面温度很容易就比我们的体温高出20度。

4. P135. “**The reason that** high buildings make it windier at ground level **is** that, as the wind goes higher and higher, it goes faster and faster”高楼的存在使得其地表附近风大的原因在于，随着风越升越高，风速也就越来越快。“the reason that...is...”表示“某事发生的原因在于”，be动词后面既可以加从句(如本句)，也可以加不定式短语，如The reason I called was to ask about the plans for Saturday.我打电话的原因是询问周六的安排。

5. P135. “Some of it goes over the top and some goes around the sides of the building, **forcing** those high level winds down to ground level”有一部分风上升至建筑物的顶部，也有一部分绕到两边，迫使高空的风下降到地表。现在分词作状语表结果，很地道的语法结构。

6. P135. “Low-frequency noise, **in particular**, just goes through the trees **as though** they aren't there.”特别是低频噪音，依然能穿过树木带，仿佛那些树木根本不存在一样。“in particular”相当于“especially”。“as though/as if”均可译为“仿佛、好像”，如例句Mrs Crump looked as if she was going to explode. Mrs Crump看上去好像要大发雷霆了。

7. P135. “There is not a great deal you can do if you have what we call a street canyon—a whole set of high-rises enclosed in a narrow street.”如果遇上了我们所说的“街道峡谷”的话——一幢幢高楼挤在狭窄的街道两旁——那你也没有很好的办法了。

题目解析

1. 31－40题为笔记填空题，笔记的顺序完全遵照讲座的顺序，因此考生要跟得上节奏，并把握住笔记的主体框架（即处于很明显位置的7个词组）。31－33题不难，原文中“on the local scale”一个信号之后便给出了34题的答案，35题的答案离34稍远一点，但也是清晰可辨的。讲完树木的影响后，说话人又通过一个“well”转入了对树木和建筑物的比较，36题答案明显，37题要紧抓住“level”一词，38题有好几个可能的答案，哪个答案的拼写熟悉就写哪个。39题中的“frequency”是关键词，第40题的答案在最后跟“water”和“sunlight”一起给出。整个section并没有太多的生僻词汇，难度适中。

READING

READING PASSAGE 1

篇章结构

体裁 说明文

主题 孩子对热带雨林的错误观点

结构 第一段：孩子对热带雨林容易产生错误观点　第二段：孩子们的错误观点产生的原因
第三段：在孩子中展开研究的目的　第四段：研究方式及问卷的前两个问题
第五段：问卷的第三个问题　第六段：女生与男生的差异
第七段：问卷的第四个问题　第八段：孩子对热带雨林被毁原因的普遍误解。
第九段：问卷的最后一个问题

必背词汇

第一段

confront	*v.*（与with连用）使面对；使面临	equivalent	*adj.*（常与to连用）相同的；同等的
loss	*n.* 损失；丧失；毁灭		
tropical	*adj.* 热带的	duration	*n.* 持续时间；期间
graphic	*adj.* 图解的；图形的，生动的	vivid	*adj.* 鲜明的；生动的
illustration	*n.* 例子；图表；插图	coverage	*n.* 新闻报导（范围）；报导
readily	*adv.* 无困难地；容易地	endanger	*v.* 危及；危害
relate	*vt.* & *vi.*（与to连用）认同；欣赏；领略	independent of	不依赖；独立于
		tuition	*n.* 指导；教导
estimate	*n.* 估计；推测	mistaken	*adj.* 错误的；误解的

第二段

harbour	*v*. 持有或抱有（某种特殊的思想或感情）*n*. 海港；藏身之处；避难所	component	*adj*. 合成的；作为一个组成部分的
		erroneous	*adj*. 错误的；由错误得出的
misconception	*n*. 误解；错误想法	robust	*adj*. 强壮的；健壮的；
pure	*adj*. 理论的；免除经验要素的	accessible	*adj*.（与to搭配）易受影响的
curriculum	*n*. 课程	modification	*n*. 更正；修改；修正
isolated	*adj*. 隔离的；孤立的	develop	*v*. 逐渐形成；逐渐拥有；获得
multifaceted	*adj*. 多方面的；	absorb	*v*. 吸收；吸纳
conceptual	*adj*. 概念的；概念上的	re-express	*v*. 重申
organized	*adj*. 有条理的；有组织的	refine	*v*. 使完善；使高雅；提炼
incorporated	*adj*. 合成一体的；一体化的	peer	*n*. 同辈；同等的人；同学
framework	*n*. 框架；基本结构		

第三段

extensive	*adj*. 广泛的；大量的	available	*adj*. 可用的，可获得的
coverage	*n*. 新闻报道；新闻报道量	strategy	*n*. 策略；对策
destruction	*n*. 破坏；毁灭；消灭	displace	*v*. 替换；取代

第四段

survey	*v*. 调查；勘查	damp	*adj*. 潮湿的
questionnaire	*n*. 调查表；问题单	geographical	*adj*. 地理的；地理学的
open-form	*adj*. 开放式的	location	*n*. 地点；地方
description	*n*. 描述	equator	*n*. 赤道
self-evident	*adj*. 不言而喻的；不言自明的		

第五段

dominant	*adj*. 主要的；占优势的	habitat	*n*. 栖息地；
raise	*v*. 提出	indigenous	*adj*. 本土的；当地的

第六段

observation	*n*. 言论；评论；观点	sympathetic	*adj*. 同情的；怜悯的
consistent	*adj*. 与…一致的；和谐的	intrinsic	*adj*. 本质的；内在的
conservation	*n*. 保护；保存	non-human	*adj*. 非人类的；不属于人类的

第七段

encouragingly	*adv.* 令人鼓舞地	refer to	*v.* 谈到；提到；打听；查阅
identify	*v.* 确定；认为	specifically	*adv.* 明确地；清晰地
personalize	*v.* 使个人化	logging	*n.* 伐木业

第八段

acid rain	酸雨	atmospheric	*adj.* 大气的
proportion	*n.* 比例	oxygen	*n.* 氧气
embrace	*v.* 包含；包括	incompatible	*adj.* 不和谐的；无法共存的

第九段

survive	*v.* 生存；活着	considering	*conj.* 鉴于；考虑到；顾及
contribute to	*v.* 导致；引起		

第十段

predominate	*vi.* 占优势；占绝大多数	climatic	*adj.* 气候上的；与气候有关的
ecosystem	*n.* 生态系统；生态环境		

第十一段

volunteer	*v.* 自动说出	acquire	*v.* 获得；得到
appreciate	*v.* 鉴别；觉察；领会	value	*v.* 尊重；重视
appreciation	*n.* 鉴别；估价；评价	evaluate	*v.* 对…评价；对…鉴定
complexity	*n.* 复杂性；复杂度	conflicting	*adj.* 不一致的；矛盾的；冲突的
indication	*n.* 表示；迹象	arena	*n.* 活动场所；舞台
range	*n.* 范围；广泛	essential	*adj.* 必不可少的；绝对必要的
encouragement	*n.* 鼓励；起鼓励作用	decision-maker	*n.* 决策人

难句解析

1. For example, one graphic illustration to which children might readily relate is the estimate that rainforests are being destroyed at a rate equivalent to one thousand football fields every forty minutes — about the duration of a normal classroom period.

参考译文：打个比方，孩子们很容易就能理解这样一个图例，即平均每四十分钟，也就是一节课的时间内，世界上就会有相当于一千个足球场大小的热带雨林遭到破坏。

语言点：relate to 的用法

(1) relate 做不及物动词时，有“发生共鸣；欣赏；领略；认同；理解”的意思，下面是一些相关例句：

① He is trying to create an image that average voters could relate to.
他在试图打造一个普通选民能够认同的形象。

② I know he feels upset, and I can relate to that. 我知道他很难过，我能理解他。

③ Group work helps children learn to share things and relate to each other.
集体活动可以教会孩子们分享东西，并且帮助他们互相理解。

(2) relating to 有关；关于；涉及

a legislation relating to motor vehicles 一项有关机动车的法令

2. These misconceptions do not remain isolated but become incorporated into a multifaceted, but organised, conceptual framework, making it and the component ideas, some of which are erroneous, more robust but also accessible to modification.

参考译文：这些误解不是孤立存在的，而是组成了一个尽管多层面却十分有条理的概念体系，这一点使得该体系本身及其所有的组成观点更加难以攻破，有些观点本身甚至就是错误的，但是也正是这样，它们反而更容易被改动。

语言点：现在分词做结果状语

but organised 是插入语，用来修饰conceptual framework,在翻译句子的过程中要注意由两个逗号或双破折号隔开的部分。

making it ...是现在分词做结果状语，在其中又插入了由which引导的非限制性定语从句，关于现在分词做结果状语的情况可以参见下列例句：

① Her husband died three years ago, leaving her with three children.
她丈夫三年前过世了，留下她和三个孩子相依为命。

② The face of the Moon is changed by collisions with meteoroids, causing new craters to appear. 月球表面经过流星的撞击，形成了新的火山口。

另外现在分词还可以做时间、条件、让步、伴随、原因等状语。

3. The aim of the present study is to start to provide such information, to help teachers design their educational strategies to build upon correct ideas and to displace misconceptions and to plan programmes in environmental studies in their schools.

参考译文：所以，目前这项研究的目的就是要给教师提供这样的信息，帮助他们设计自己的教学策略，以便帮助学生构筑正确的观点，置换他们的错误概念，并在学校中展开环保研究项目。

语言点：不定式做表语，to start to provide...

不定式做表语。例如，

① The duties of a postman are to deliver letters and newspapers.

邮差的职责就是送信送报纸。

② The best thing would be for you to make a formal application.

你最好提交一份正式的申请。

另外不定式还可以做主语。例如，

To err is human; to forgive, divine. 凡人皆有过，宽恕则是神。

为了避免头重脚轻，有时候用 it 来做形式主语，真正的主语则在后面，例如，

It is not easy for me to answer this right here right now.

想让我一下子马上回答出这个问题不容易。

4. This is surprising considering the high level of media coverage on this issue.

参考译文：鉴于媒体对这个问题长篇累牍的报道，这样的结果真是有点出人意料。

语言点：considering (that) 的用法

(1) considering that 或 considering 用来引出真实或肯定的事，但主句表述的往往是令人吃惊或对照鲜明的事情。例如，

Considering that they are such an important part of undergraduate courses, lectures are often presented in a remarkably poor manner.

鉴于演讲课在本科课程当中的重要地位，现在的授课水平可谓十分之差。

(2) 另外请区别如下几个条件连接词：

a. on condition that 强调事先认可的条件。例如，

He was released on bail on condition that he did not go within half a mile of his mother's address. 他只有保证不接近他妈妈家附近半英里的范围，才得以保释。

b. providing that 的用法与 if 相似。例如，

You can borrow the car, providing I can have it back by six o'clock.

如果你六点之前能把车还回来的话，我就借给你用。

c. assuming that 的意思是说如果一件事是真实的，那么第二件事也是真实的，例如，

Assuming I convince you, you can convince your father in turn.

假设我说服了你，接下去你就可以说服你父亲。

d. given that 则表示第一件事已经被确知是真实的，例如，

I don't see what I can do for you, given that you have no evidence.

鉴于你没有证据，我不知道如何帮你。

e. suppose that 相当于 let us suppose，因此整个句子带有设想成分。例如，

Suppose you buy a lottery ticket and win a big prize. What will you do?

设想一下你买彩票中了大奖，你会做什么？

试题分析

Questions 1—8

- 题目类型：TRUE/FALSE/NOT GIVEN
- 题目解析：

1. The plight of the rainforests has largely been ignored by the media.

参考译文	热带雨林的困境基本上被媒体所忽视了。
定位词	media
解题关键字	plight / largely / ignored
文中对应点	第一段：In the face of the frequent and often vivid media coverage... 第三段：Despite the extensive coverage in the popular media of the destruction of rainforests, frequent/vivid/extensive/coverage 等词都说明媒体对于热带雨林的现状十分关注并做了广泛报道
答案	FALSE

2. Children only accept opinions on rainforests that they encounter in their classrooms.

参考译文	孩子们只接受课堂里所学到的有关热带雨林的观点。
定位词	children / classroom
解题关键字	only
文中对应点	第二段：These ideas may be developed by children absorbing ideas through the popular media. 这句话证明学生也从大众媒体中吸取有关热带雨林的观点，而并不是只从课堂中得到相关知识。 TIPS：题目中有ONLY，大多数情况选FALSE
答案	FALSE

3. It has been suggested that children hold mistaken views about the 'pure' science that they study at school.

参考译文	许多研究表明孩子们对于在学校里学到的科学知识心存误解。
定位词	"pure"
解题关键字	suggested / mistaken / pure

文中对应点	第二段: Many studies have shown that children harbour misconceptions about 'pure', curriculum science. 本题的重点是理解harbour一词所包含的"包含；心怀"等意思，比如I think he's harbouring some sort of grudge against me.我认为他对我怀有怨恨。
答案	TRUE

4. The fact that children's ideas about science form part of a larger framework of ideas means that it is easier to change them.

参考译文	孩子们的科学观点构成了一个更为庞大的理论体系，这一事实使得我们更容易去改变这些观点。
定位词	framework
解题关键字	framework / easier
文中对应点	These misconceptions do not remain isolated but become incorporated into a multifaceted, but organised, conceptual framework, making it and the component ideas, some of which are erroneous, more robust but also accessible to modification. accessible to 的意思是易受影响的
答案	TRUE

5. The study involved asking children a number of yes/no questions such as 'Are there any rainforests in Africa?'

参考译文	研究包括问学生很多是非题，比如"非洲是否有热带雨林？"
定位词	Africa
解题关键字	yes/no
文中对应点	第四段：Secondary school children were asked to complete a questionnaire containing five open-form questions. Open-form 指简答题，与yes/no直接矛盾，
答案	FALSE

6. Girls are more likely than boys to hold mistaken views about the rainforests' destruction.

参考译文	女生比男生更容易对热带雨林的毁坏持有错误观点。
定位词	girls / boys
解题关键字	more likely than
文中对应点	第五段：More girls (70%) than boys (60%) raised the idea of rainforest as animal habitats.

文中对应点	第六段：Similarly, but at a lower level, more girls (13%) than boys (5%) said that rainforests provided human habitats. 虽然这两句话也拿女生和男生做了比较，但是所比较的事物却不是对热带雨林毁坏的错误观点，所以此题属于典型的并不存在的比较关系。
答案	NOT GIVEN

7. The study reported here follows on from a series of studies that have looked at children's understanding of rainforests.

参考译文	本文所报道的研究是从一系列调查孩子对热带雨林了解程度的研究之后继续开展的。
定位词	a series of studies / children
解题关键字	follow on from
文中对应点	第六段：These observations are generally consistent with our previous studies of pupils' views about the use and conservation of rainforests... "previous"一词是先前的意思，证明在此研究之前，人们也就学生对热带雨林的看法做了研究，因此本文所提到的调查是在这些研究之后进行的。
答案	TRUE

8. A second study has been planned to investigate primary school children's ideas about rainforests.

参考译文	人们已经计划展开第二个研究，调查小学生们对热带雨林的了解。
定位词	primary
解题关键字	primary / second
文中对应点	文中直到最后只字未提这项研究是否会有续篇，因此这是一个典型的续貂式的NOT GIVEN。
答案	NOT GIVEN

Questions 9—13

- 题目类型:MATCHING
- 题目解析:

题号	定位词	文中对应点
9	What was the children's most frequent response when asked where the rainforests were?	Street Business Partnership部分第一点第四段：The commonest responses were coninents or countries: Africa (given by 43% of children)...

题号	定位词	文中对应点
10	What was the most common response to the question about the importance of the rainforests?	第九段：...the majority of children simply said that we need rainforests to survive.
11	What did most children give as the reason for the loss of the rainforests?	第七段：...more than half of the pupils (59%) identified that it is human activities which are destroying rainforests,...
12	Why did most children think it important for the rainforests to be protected?	第五段：The dominant idea, raised by 64% of the pupils, was that rainforests provide animals with habitats.
13	Which of the responses is cited as unexpectedly uncommon, given the amount of time spent on the issue by the newspapers and television?	第九段：Only a few of the pupils (6%) mentioned that rainforest destruction may contribute to global warming. This is surprising considering the high level of media coverage on this issue.

Question 14

- 题目类型: MULTIPLE CHOICE
- 题目解析:

第一段当中提到：孩子对热带雨林容易产生错误的理解，因此本文重点应该放在孩子对热带雨林遭破坏状况的观点上，因此要选择一个带有孩子的标题。

答案：B

参考译文

无论大人还是孩子都经常会遇到这样的报道，那就是热带雨林正在以惊人的速度消失。打个比方，孩子们很容易就能理解这样一个图例，即平均每四十分钟，也就是一节课的时间内，世界上就会有相当于一千个足球场大小的热带雨林遭到破坏。面对媒体频繁且生动的报道，也许不需要任何正规的教育，孩子们就能够形成一系列有关热带雨林的观点：比如说雨林是什么，位置在哪里，为什么如此重要，又是什么在威胁它们等等。当然，这些观点也很有可能是错的。

许多研究表明孩子们对于在学校里学到的科学知识心存误解。这些误解不是孤立存在的，而是组成了一个尽管多层面却十分有条理的概念体系，这一点使得该体系本身及其所有的组成观点更加难以攻破，有些观点本身甚至就是错误的，但是也正是这样，它们反而更容易被改动。这些错误观点正是由于孩子们从大众媒体上吸收了信息而形成的。有时连这些信息本身都是错误的。学校似乎也没能够给他们提供一个再度阐述自己观点的机会，因此老师及其他学生也不能帮助其检验及纠正这种错误观点。

尽管媒体对于热带雨林所遭受的破坏做了大量的报道，但是有关孩子相关观点的信息却少之又少。所以，目前这项研究的目的就是要给教师提供这样的信息来帮助他们设计自己的教学策略，以便帮助学生构筑正确的观点，置换他们的错误概念，并在学校中展开环保研究项目。

该项研究调查了孩子有关热带雨林的科学知识以及态度。研究要求一些中学生填写一份包含了五个简答题的调查表。对于第一个问题，最常见的解答就来自“热带雨林”这一名称所附带的不言自明的含义。有些孩子把雨林描述成一个又潮又湿或闷热的地方。第二个问题是关于雨林的地理位置的，大多数答案都提到了国名或洲名：百分之四十三的孩子写了非洲；百分之三十写了美洲；还有百分之二十五的人认为热带雨林主要分布在巴西。有些孩子给出了如“赤道附近”这样更为宽泛的答案。

第三道题目问及了热带雨林的重要性。百分之六十四的学生认为雨林为动物提供了栖身之所。较少的学生回答说雨林是植物的生长地。更少的学生提到了雨林中的土著居民。其中，有百分之七十的女孩子认为雨林是动物的家，而男孩子中只有百分之六十的人执此观点。

相似的是，有百分之十三的女生认为热带雨林为人类提供了居所，而男生中有此想法的人只占百分之五。这些观点与先前就学生对热带雨林的开发及保护状况所做的研究的结果基本一致，该结果表明女生更容易表现出对小动物的同情，其观点也更容易将内在价值观基于动物而非人类生命上。

第四个问题问到了热带雨林遭到破坏的原因。值得庆幸的是，过半的学生(百分之五十九)都认为是人类的行为导致了这一破坏，有人甚至用“我们”这样的字眼将问题与自身联系起来。大概有百分之十八的学生将这一破坏归咎于滥砍滥伐。

百分之十的学生错误地认为是酸雨导致了雨林的破坏，还有百分之十的学生觉得污染才是罪魁祸首。看来学生们是将热带雨林所受的破坏与上述因素对西欧森林的毁坏混为一谈了。百分之四十的学生认为热带雨林为人们提供了氧气，在某种程度上，这样的答案也包含着一个误解，那就是认为热带雨林的消失会减少大气中氧气的含量，最终导致地球上的大气不再适合人类呼吸。

在被问及雨林保护的重要性时，大部分学生只是认为人类离开雨林就无法生存。只有寥寥百分之六的人提到热带雨林的消失会导致全球变暖。鉴于媒体对这个问题长篇累牍的报道，这样的结果真是有点出人意料。还有些学生认为保不保护雨林根本无关紧要。

研究结果表明，在学生们对雨林的观点中，某些观点明显占上风。在有些问题上，比如说热带雨林是植物、动物及人类的栖息地以及天气变化与雨林破坏之间的关系等，学生们的回答又表明了他们在一些基本科学知识上的误区。

学生们给出的答案并不能够表明他们了解热带雨林所遭受破坏的原因的复杂性。换言之，没有任何迹象表明他们了解热带雨林对人类来讲到底如何重要以及那些破坏行为背后所潜藏的复杂社会、经济及政治因素。然而，值得欣慰的是，其他类似环保研究的结果表明，大孩子们已经具备了鉴赏、理解以及评价矛盾观点的能力。而环保教育正是为这些能力的养成提供舞台，这一点对于孩子们成为未来的政策制定者是至关重要的。

READING PASSAGE 2

篇章结构

体裁 说明文

主题 鲸鱼和海豚的感官

结构 第一段：鲸鱼和海豚的嗅觉及味觉　第二段：鲸鱼和海豚的触觉
第三段：鲸鱼和海豚的视觉　第四段：眼睛的位置与视力的关系
第五段：栖息地与视力之间的关系　第六段：鲸鱼和海豚的听觉

必背词汇

标　题

cetacean	*n.* 鲸类动物，鲸	porpoise	*n.* 海豚，小鲸
mammal	*n.* 哺乳动物	comprise	*v.* 包含，由…组成

第一段

sense	*n.* 官能；感觉	*blowhole*	*n.* (鲸等的)呼吸孔；喷水孔
terrestrial	*adj.* 陆生的；在陆上生长或繁殖的；非水生的	migrate	*v.* 移动；移往
		neural	*adj.* 神经系统的；神经中枢的
reduced	*adj.* 减弱的；减轻的；削弱的	pathway	*n.* 路径；神经纤维链
absent	*adj.* 缺乏的；不存在的	sacrifice	*v.* 牺牲；献出
toothed	*adj.* 有牙齿的	*taste bud*	味蕾
baleen	*n.* 鲸须	degenerate	*v.* 退化；衰退
functional	*adj.* 有功能的；起作用的	*rudimentary*	*adj.* 未完全发育的；未成熟的
speculate	*v.* 推测；猜测		

第二段

captive	*adj.* 被俘虏的；被束缚的；此处引申为人工饲养的	free-ranging	*adj.* 自由放养的
		calf	*n.* 幼崽
dolphins	*n.* 海豚	subgroup	*n.* 亚群；副族
remark on	评论；评价	contact	*n.* 接触；触碰
responsiveness	*n.* 敏感度；敏感性	maintain	*v.* 维持；维护
rub	*v.* 摩擦；擦	order	*n.* 秩序

stroke	*v.* 抚摸	sensitive	*adj.* 敏感的；灵敏的
courtship	*n.* 求爱；求偶	object to	*v.* 抱反感；不喜欢
ritual	*n.* 仪式；典礼；礼节		

第三段

close	*adj.* 封闭的；包围的	film	*v.* 拍成电影
quarter	*n.* 地区；区域	track	*v.* 跟踪；追踪
captivity	*n.* 囚禁；监禁	moderately	*adv.* 一般地；有限地
right whale	露脊鲸，特征为头部硕大、嘴边长有鲸须而无背鳍	restrict	*v.* 限制；约束
humpback whale	座头鲸：一种有圆背和长而多节的鳍状肢的须鲸。座头鲸复杂而与众不同的歌声可以使它们互相识别，且在求偶过程中起重要作用	stereoscopic	*adj.* 有立体感的；体视镜的
		stereoscopic vision	立体视觉；体视

第四段

freshwater	*adj.* 淡水的；内河的	interface	*n.* 分界面；界面
upside down	肚皮朝上；颠倒	preliminary	*adj.* 开头的；初步的
comparison	*n.* 比较；对比	experimental	*adj.* 实验性的；实验的
bottlenose dolphin	宽吻海豚	accuracy	*n.* 精确度；精确性
keen	*adj.* 敏锐的；敏感的	leap	*vi.* 跳跃；跳起
airborne	*adj.* 飞行中的；在飞行的	anecdotal	*adj.* 轶事的；趣闻的
flying fish	飞鱼	to the contrary	相反地
fairly	*adv.* 相当地；相当		

第五段

variation	*n.* 变异；变化；变更	*boutu*	亚马逊海豚
with reference to	关于；就…而论	beiji	白鳍豚
habitat	*n.* 栖息地	*Indian susu*	印度河中的一种小海豚
inhabit	*v.* 居住；栖息	slit	*n.* 裂缝；狭缝
turbid	*adj.* 混浊的；脏的	intensity	*n.* 强度；强烈
plain	*n.* 平原		

第六段

deteriorate	v. (使)恶化	utterance	n. 说话方式；发声；吐露；表达
compensated	v. 抵消；弥补	employ	v. 采用；使用
well-developed	adj. 发达的	spectrum	n. 光谱；频谱
acoustic	adj. 声学的；有关声音的	sperm whale	抹香鲸：生活于热带及温带海洋中，巨大的脑袋中有一个含鲸油及鲸蜡的空腔，而长长的肠子则经常含有龙涎香，也作 cachalot
vocal	adj. 声音的；歌唱的	monotonous	adj. 单调的；无变化的
forage	n. 觅食	high-energy	adj. 精力充沛的；活跃的
echolocation	n. 回声定位法	click	n. 喀哒声
primarily	adv. 主要地；根本上	complicated	adj. 复杂的；难懂的
frequency	n. 频率	communicative	adj. 易于沟通的；爱说话的
repertoire	n. 全部本领；全部功能	speculation	n. 沉思；遐想；猜测；推断
notable	adj. 显著的；值得注意的	solid	adj. 充分的；正确的；有根据的
chorus	n. 合唱		
bowhead whale	北极露脊鲸，弓头鲸：生活在北冰洋的一种有鲸须的鲸鱼，具有大的头部和拱形的上颚		
haunting	adj. 萦绕心头的；难以忘怀的		

难句解析

1. Trainers of captive dolphins and small whales often remark on their animals' responsiveness to being touched or rubbed, and both captive and free-ranging cetacean individuals of all species (particularly adults and calves, or members of the same subgroup) appear to make frequent contact.

参考译文：训练人工饲养海豚和小鲸鱼的人常常会评论他们的小动物对于触碰和抚摩的敏感度。而无论是人工饲养还是放养，几乎所有种类的鲸鱼个体之间都会进行频繁的接触，特别是在成年鲸鱼和幼鲸之间或同一亚群的成员之间。

语言点：to 做介词

to 做介词的用法：

(1) to 做介词的时候，后面要带名词或动名词

be used to doing sth. / be accustomed to doing sth. 习惯于做某事。例如，

She was a person accustomed to having eight hours' sleep a night.

她是那种每晚睡八个小时的人。

(2) be addicted to 沉溺于某事，例如，

My son's addicted to computer games — he hardly ever comes out of his room.

我儿子迷恋计算机游戏——他几乎不出门。

(3) be confined to 局限于，例如，

He was confined to a wheel chair after the accident.

经过那场事故后，他就离不开轮椅了。

(4) be opposed to 反对，例如，

Most people are opposed to the privatization of the city’s public transportation system.

大部分人反对城市公共交通系统的私有化。

后面可以搭配to的形容词			
accustomed	adjacent	allergic	central
comparable equal	equivalent	essential	fundamental
identical	immune	impervious	indebted
inferior	irrelavent	married	paralleled
proportional	sensitive	similar	subordinate
superior	susceptible	unaccustomed	used
useful	vital		

2. By comparison, the bottlenose dolphin has extremely keen vision in water. Judging from the way it watches and tracks airborne flying fish, it can apparently see fairly well through the air-water interface as well.

参考译文：相反的是，宽吻海豚在水中视力就很敏锐，而从它观察及追踪空中飞鱼的方式来看，它在水天交界面的视力也相当好。

语言点：现在分词做原因状语

现在分词做状语的时候要注意以下几点：

a. 主语要一致：分词短语的逻辑主语与句子主语要一致

b. 独立分词结构：有时候分词的动作与谓语动作不是同一主语发出的，这时分词可以带上自己的逻辑主语，就形成了“名词/代词 + 分词短语”的结构，即所谓的独立分词结构。例如，It being so nice a day, we go out for a walk.

有时候在分词的逻辑主语前还可以加上 with / without，例如，

The old man often takes a walk after dinner with his dog following him.

在有些情况下，分词的逻辑主语与句子的主语不一致，但是已经约定俗成，因此也是正确的例如，generally speaking, strictly speaking, judging from, allowing for, talking of

3. Although the senses of taste and smell appear to have deteriorated, and vision in water appears to be uncertain, such weaknesses are more than compensated for by cetaceans' well-developed acoustic sense.

参考译文：尽管鲸鱼的味觉和嗅觉严重衰退，在水中的视觉又不那么确定，然而这些缺陷完全可以被它们那高度发达的听觉系统所弥补。

语言点：more 的用法

(1) more than 的用法

a. 在口语当中，more than 通常表示“极其；非常”。例如，

They are more than willing to accept our offer.

他们非常乐意接受我们的帮助。

b. 另外 more than 还有“超出；超过”的意思。例如，

Some of the stories were really more than could be believed.有些故事实在离谱。

(2) more 的其他用法：

a. all the more 更加；越发。例如，

This puzzled him all the more. 这越发让他迷糊了。

b. and what is more 而且；更有甚者

You are late for school, and what’s more, you have lost your books.

你迟到了，而且，你还把书弄丢了。

c. more of 更大程度上的…。例如，

Viewers want better television, and more of it. 电视机迷想在更大程度上看更好的电视。

d. more...than...与其说…倒不如说

She is more mad than stupid. 与其说她愚蠢，还不如说她疯狂。

e. no more than 至多；不超过；同…一样不。例如，

She’s no more able to read French than I am. 她和我一样读不懂法文。

f. not more than 不比…更。例如，

The big one is not more expensive than the small one. 大的那一个不比小的更贵。

4. Some of the more complicated sounds are clearly communicative, although what role they may play in the social life and ‘culture’ of cetaceans has been more the subject of wild speculation than of solid science.

参考译文：有些复杂的声音显然具有交流作用，然而想要搞清楚它们在鲸鱼的社会生活及文化中到底起何作用，与其说是严谨科学研究的对象，不如说是丰富想像力的结果。

语言点：主语从句的用法(1)

(1) 如果一个完整的句子来充当整个句子的主语，这类句子就叫做主语从句，what role they may play 就是一个完整的句子，此时谓语动词要用单数。

(2) that 引导主语从句。例如，

That they are still alive is a consolation. 他们还活着令人欣慰。

(3) Whether 引导主语从句。例如，

Whether we shall stay remains uncertain. 我们是否呆在这里仍不确定。

注意：此时的 whether 不可以用 if 替换

① what / who / whom / whose / which / whatever / whoever / whomever / whichever / whosever 也可以引导主语从句，含有疑问意思。例如，Who will head the department has not yet been decided. 谁将领导这个系还没定下来。

② where / when / why / how / wherever / whenever / however

也可以引导主语从句，但是它们都不能够被省略，例如，

Why he refused to work with you is still unknow. 他为什么拒绝与你工作还不清楚。

试题分析

Questions 15—21

- 题目类型：TABLE COMPLETION
- 题目解析：

题号	定位词	文中对应点
15	Taste	第一段： Similarly, although at least some cetaceans have taste buds, the nerves serving these have degenerated or are rudimentary.
16	vision not/stereoscopic	第三段： However, the position of the eyes so restricts the field of vision in baleen whales that they probably do not have stereoscopic vision.
17	dolphins and porpoises	第四段： On the other hand, the position of the eyes in most dolphins and porpoises suggests that they have stereoscopic vision forward and downward.
18	forward and upward	第四段： Eye position in freshwater dolphins, which often swim on their side or upside down while feeding, suggests that what vision they have is stereoscopic forward and upward.

题号	定位词	文中对应点
19	bottlenose dolphin	第四段： By comparison, the bottlenose dolphin has extremely keen vision in water. Judging from the way it watches and tracks airborne flying fish, it can apparently see fairly well through the air-water interface as well.
20	most large baleen	第六段： Large baleen whales primarily use the lower frequencies and are often limited in their repertoire.
21	song-like	第六段： Notable exceptions are the nearly song-like choruses of bowhead whales in summer and the complex, haunting utterances of the humpback whales.

Questions 22－26

- 题目类型：SHORT ANSWER QUESTIONS
- 题目解析：

题号	定位词	文中对应点
22	mating	第二段： This contact may help to maintain order within a group, and stroking or touching are part of the courtship ritual in most species.
23	upside down / eating	第四段： Eye position in freshwater dolphins, which often swim on their side or upside down while feeding...
24	follow / under the water	第四段： By comparison, the bottlenose dolphin has extremely keen vision in water. Judging from the way it watches and tracks airborne flying fish, it can apparently see fairly well through the air-water interface as well.
25	habitat / good visual ability	第五段： For example, vision is obviously more useful to species inhabiting clear open waters than to those living in turbid rivers and flooded plains.

题号	定位词	文中对应点
26	best / cetaceans	第六段： Although the senses of taste and smell appear to have deteriorated, and vision in water appears to be uncertain, such weaknesses are more than compensated for by cetaceans' well-developed acoustic sense.

参考译文

鲸鱼的感官

鲸目动物（包括鲸、海豚、鼠海豚等哺乳动物）的感官功能测试

对我们人类以及其他的陆地哺乳动物来说，有些感官是与生俱来的，然而对于鲸鱼来讲，这些功能要么已经衰退或彻底消失，要么就无法在水中正常发挥作用。比如说从齿鲸的大脑结构来看，它们是嗅不到气味的；而须鲸虽然有与嗅觉相关的脑部结构，可是我们却无法判断这些结构是否起作用。据推测，由于鲸鱼的气孔进化并最终移到了头部的正中，所以掌管嗅觉的神经纤维几乎全部不见了。同样，尽管有些鲸鱼也有味蕾，但这些味觉器官要么已经退化，要么就根本没有发育。

有人认为鲸鱼的触觉也不发达，不过这个观点很可能是错误的。训练人工饲养海豚和小鲸鱼的人常常会评论他们的小动物对于触碰和抚摩的敏感度。而无论是人工饲养还是放养，几乎所有种类的鲸鱼个体之间都会进行频繁的接触，特别是在成年鲸鱼和幼鲸之间或同一亚群的成员之间。这种接触有助于维护同一种群内部的秩序，而且对大多数鲸鱼而言，抚摸和触碰也是求偶仪式的一部分。 气孔周围的部分尤其敏感，一旦被触碰，人工饲养的鲸鱼就会有激烈的反应。

不同种类的鲸鱼，视觉发达程度也各不相同。通过研究一只被人工饲养了一年的小灰鲸，以及通过对阿根廷和夏威夷沿海所放养的露脊鲸和座头鲸的研究及拍摄，人们发现在封闭水域中的须鲸显然可以利用视觉来追踪水下的物体，而且它们无论在水中或空气中视力都相当好。但是眼睛的位置如此严重地限制了须鲸的视野，以致于它们可能不具备立体视觉。

从另一方面来看，大多数海豚和江豚眼睛的位置表明它们是拥有向前及向下的立体视觉的。淡水海豚经常侧游，或是在吃东西的时候肚皮朝上游泳，这就表明眼睛的位置使它们拥有向前及向上的立体视觉。相反的是，宽吻海豚在水中视力就很敏锐，而从它观察及追踪空中飞鱼的方式来看，它在水天交界面的视力也相当好。尽管之前的实验证据表明，海豚在露天环境中可能是睁眼瞎，然而，它们能够从水中跃起很高，并且能够准确地吃到训练员手中的小鱼，这就有趣地证明了上述观点是错误的。

当然，这些变异可以通过这些品种所生长的环境来解释。比如说，对于宽广清澈水域中的鲸鱼来说，视觉显然就有用的多；而对于那些住在混浊的河流或水淹的平原上的品种来说，视力显然就没什么大用。比如，南美洲亚马逊河中的江豚以及中国的白鳍豚视力都相当有限，而印度河中的江豚根本看不见东西，它们的眼睛已经退化成了两条窄缝，除了感知一下方向和光的强度几乎没什么作用。

尽管鲸鱼们的味觉和嗅觉严重衰退，在水中的视觉又不那么确定，然而这些缺陷完全可以被它们那高度发达的听觉系统所弥补。尽管鲸鱼们音域不同，但是大多数鲸鱼都很会“唱歌”，而且还能用回声定位法来觅食。大个子须鲸只能用低频发声，除此之外就黔“鲸”计穷了。当然也有些著名的例外：比如夏天里北极露脊鲸歌曲般的合唱，还有座头鲸那复杂的。令人难以忘怀的低语。与须鲸相比，齿鲸们可以更多地利用频谱，发出多种声音，当然，抹香鲸只会发出一系列单调激烈的喀哒声。有些复杂的声音显然具有交流作用，然而想要搞清楚它们在鲸鱼的社会生活及文化中到底起何作用，与其说是严谨科学研究的对象，不如说是丰富想像力的结果。

相关背景

关于文中出现的几种海豚：

*Indian susu

This species inhabits the Indus river in Pakistan from Kotri, Sind, to Jinnah, northwestern Punjab and is also known as *Blind River* Dolphin or Side-Swimming Dolphin.

The Indus River Dolphin has a long beak which thickens toward the tip, revealing the large teeth; the mouthline curves upward. The body is stocky with a rounded belly, the flippers are large and paddle-shaped, and there is a low triangular hump in place of a ‘true’ dorsal. The forehead is steep and the blowhole is on the left of the head, above the tiny, poorly-seeing eye. The tail flukes are broad in relation to the body size. Indus River Dolphins are grey-brown in colour, sometimes with a pinkish belly, and measure between 1.5 and 2.5m in length, weighing a maximum of 90kg.

*boutu

The boutu has a strong beak studded with short bristles and a mobile, flexible head and neck. Most boutus have a total of 100 or more teeth. Their eyes, although small, seem to be more functional than those of other river dolphins. Boutus feed mainly on small fish and some crustaceans, using echolocation clicks to find their prey. Boutus live in pairs and seem to produce young between July and September.

READING PASSAGE 3

篇章结构

体裁 议论文

主题 盲人能否理解视觉符号

结构 第一部分：盲人能否理解具体的图形

第一段：惊奇的发现：盲人可以画出运动线

第二段：针对盲人理解视觉符号的实验

第三段：实验方式及过程

第四段：实验结果

第五段：进一步的实验结论

第二部分：

第一段：盲人对抽象符号的理解

第二段：相关实验

第三段：实验结论：盲人能够理解抽象符号

必背词汇

第一部分 第一段

appreciate	*v.* 评价，欣赏；充分意识到	trace	*v.* 勾画…的轮廓；描绘
outline	*n.* 提纲；略图	curve	*n.* 曲线，弯曲 *v.* 弄弯，弯曲
perspective	*n.* 设想；透视图	circle	*n.* 圆；圈子；周期 *v.* 环绕，围绕…画圈
describe	*v.* 描绘，描写；形容，把…说成		
arrangement	*n.* 排列，整理；安排，准备	take aback	惊吓，迷惑
surface	*n.* 平面；表面	illustration	*n.* 说明；例证，插图；举例说明
literal	*a.* 文字(上)的；字面的	note	*v.* 指出；特别提到；表明
representation	*n.* 陈述；表现	trend-setting	*a.* 引导潮流的
initiative	*n.* 主动的行动；倡议；首创精神；进取心	cartoonist	*n.* 漫画家
		virtually	*adv.* 事实上，实质上
spin	*v.* 旋转	figure	*n.* 外形；人物；形象
motion	*n.* (物体)运动；动作		

第二段

subject	*n.* 对象	somehow	*adv.* 以某种方式；从某种角度
rendition	*n.* 处理；表演；译文	indicate	*v.* 表明；暗示
appear	*vi.* 显现、出现	indicator	*n.* 指示物；指示者
repeatedly	*adv.* 再三，一再；多次	broken	*a.* 破的；断断续续的
spoke	*n.* （车轮上)幅条	wavy	*a.* 波浪形的，起伏的
curved	*a.* 弯曲的	apt	*a.* 恰当的；聪明的
metaphorical	*a.* 隐喻的，比喻的	idiosyncratic	*a.* 特质的，异质的，特殊的
suggest	*v.* 建议，提议；表明，暗示	sighted	*a.* 眼睛看得见的；有视力的
majority rule	*n.* 多数决定原则	interpret	*v.* 说明；理解；诠释
device	*n.* 设计，手段；装置；图案		

第三段

search out	寻找到	assign	*v.* 派给，分配；选定，指定(时间、地点)
raised	*a.* 书脊棱带	wobble	*n.* 摆动,动摇,不稳定,变度
depict	*v.* 描绘，描写，描述	steadily	*adv.* 稳定地
bent	*a.* 弯曲的	jerk	*vi.* 颠簸；震摇
dashed	*n.* 虚线	brake	*n.* 闸，刹车，制动器 *v.* 刹(车)
extend	*v.* 延伸，延长；伸出，伸展	control group	试验时的参照组
perimeter	*n.* 周(边)，周长		

第四段

distinctive	*a.* 特别的；独具一格的	consensus	*n.* (意见等的)一致，共识
Sign	*n.* 符号；象征；征兆	unfamiliar	*a.* 不熟悉的
assume	*v.* 设想，假定	evidently	*adv.* 明显地，显而易见
signify	*v.* 表示，意味着	figure out	*v.* 搞清楚；领会到
favored	*a.* 有利的，受惠的，幸运的	come up with	*v.* 提出；想出
instance	*n.* 例子，事例，实例	frequently	*adv.* 时常，频繁地

第二部分　第一段

visual	*a.* 视觉的；可见的	symbol	*n.* 象征，符号，标志
metaphor	*n.* 隐喻；象征	explore	*v.* 勘探，探险；调查
as well	倒不如，还是…的好	symbolism	*n.* 象征主义，符号论

第二段

term	*n.* 术语；词汇	square	*n.* 广场；正方形
telate to	和…相关	go with	伴随，与…相配

第三段

deem	*v.* 认为，相信	resemble	*v.* 与…相似
ascribe to	归于	score	*v.* 得胜；得分；获得好评
reveal	*v.* 显示，显露；泄露，揭发	pair	*v.* 使成双，使配对
respectively	*adv.* 分别地	abstract	*a.* 抽象的，不具体的

难句解析

1. All but one of the blind subjects assigned distinctive motions to each wheel.

参考译文：除了一个人，其他所有的盲人都将具体的动作与车轮搭配了起来。

语言点：

(1) all but 的用法

a. 除了…都，相当于 all except。例如，

the 34 delegates (all but four women) 三十四名代表中，除了四位，其余都是女性

b. 几乎；差不多。例如，

The fridge is all but empty.冰箱几乎快空了。

c. 几乎完全的。例如，

all but freedom 几近彻底的自由

(2) 另外一些关于 all 的词组搭配

a. all along 始终，一直；一贯。例如，

We know all along that he is going to make it. 我们一直认为他会成功的。

b. all in all 总之。例如，

All in all, his health has improved. 总的来说，他的健康状况改善了。

c. all for (口)完全赞同；支持。例如，

If he can turn the company around, I' m all for it. 如果他能使公司扭亏为盈，我全力支持。

d. all too 非常；很。例如，

In these conditions it was all too easy to make mistakes. 在这种情况下，犯错误太容易了。

e. that's sb. all over (口) 以典型的态度或行为；典型地。例如，

He was late of course, but that's Tim all over! Tim 又迟到了，这对他来讲太典型了。

f. not all that 不太…；不很…。例如，

I don't think it matters all that much. 我认为这没有那么重要。

2. Evidently, however, the blind not only figured out meanings for each line of motion, but as a group they generally came up with the same meaning at least as frequently as did sighted subjects.

参考译文：然而，很明显，盲人不仅能够搞清楚每种运动线所代表的意义，而且作为一个团队，他们达成共识的频率也不比普通人低。

结构分析：这句话将盲人的表现与普通人的表现进行了比较，come up with the same meaning 可以等同于 have consensus on sth. 在…方面达成一致。

语言点：关于比较状语从句

(1) as...as...，例如，

① They want peace as much as we do. 他们和我们一样渴望和平。

② I didn't finish as large a part of the work as he did. 我完成的工作没有他完成的多。注意在这个例句中，不可以把冠词 a 放在 large 前面。

(2) (just)as..., so...结构表示类比，当意为正如…，所以…也时，so 后面的结构可以使用倒装。例如，

① As you sow, so will you reap. 种瓜得瓜，种豆得豆。

② As food nourished the body, so do books enrich the mind.
食物滋养身体，书本丰富精神。

③ As it is the mark of great minds to say many things in a few words, so it is the mark of little minds to use many words to say nothing.
大智者寥寥数语，即能达意；寡智者口若悬河，仍言而无物。

(3) not so much A as B 与其说是 A，不如说是 B，例如，

The great use of a school education is not so much to teach you things as to teach you the art of learning. 学校教育的意义不在于教会了你什么，而在于教你学习的方法。

3. In fact, only a small majority of sighted subjects — 53% — had paired far and near to the opposite partners.

参考译文：实际上，也只有刚刚过半—— 53% ——的普通受试者认为圆形代表远，而方形代表近。

语言点：这句话应该和上一句连起来看才能准确翻译。上文说到有个先天失明的人做得极好。他的选择只有一个与众不同，那就是把“远”与方形联系起来而把“近”同圆形联系起来。显然，从作者的口气上来看，这个选择显然有些错误。Opposite partners 在这里可以理解为相反的选择。In fact, among the sighted subjects, only 53% had matched far with circle and near with square.

试题分析

Questions 27—29

- 题目类型：MULTIPLE CHOICE
- 题目解析：

题号	定位词	文中对应点
27	first paragraph	第一段： From a number of recent studies, it has become clear that blind people can appreciate the use of outlines and perspectives to describethe arrangement of objects and other surfaces in space.
28	surprised / blind woman	第一段： To show this motion, she traced a curve inside the circle (Fig. 1). I was taken aback. Lines of motion, such as the one sheused, are a very recent invention in the history of illustration.
29	Part 1/ found	第一部分最后一段： Evidently, however, the blind not only figured out meanings for each line of motion, but as a group they generally came up with the same meaning at least as frequently as did sighted subjects.

Questions 30—32

- 题目类型：PICTURE NAMING
- 题目解析：
  1. 用方框里的词回文中定位，定位点在第一部分的第三段和第四段。
  2. 准确翻译方框中的单词
  3. 看懂图画，尤其是 32 题

题号	文中定位点	题解
30	第一部分 第四段： Subjects assumed that spokes extending beyond the wheel's perimeter signified that the wheel had its brakes on...	图中的直线延伸到了圆的外面，正好符合文中的叙述，因此要选择 E (use of brakes).
31	第一部分 第四段： ...and that dashed spokes indicated the wheel was spinning quickly.	这道题目是整篇文章中最难的一道题目，关键点在于认识dashed line这个词，在这一部分第二段出现的 broken lines 也是虚线的意思。
32	第一部分 第四段： Most guessed that the curved spokes indicated that the wheel was spinning steadily；	文中提到了三种曲线：大曲线，小曲线和波浪线，其中 curved lines 代表稳定地转动，bent lines代表不稳定地转动，wavy lines代表颠簸。

Questions 33－39

- 题目类型：SUMMARY
- 题目解析：

对于带有词库的 summary，按照常规步骤解题的同时，应该先看看词库中的单词，本题可以利用词库中单词的词性来填出某些空。

题号	定位词	文中对应点	题解
33	Part 2 / a set of word	第二部分第二段： We gave a list of twenty pairs of words to sighted subjects...	此空要求填一个名词，而词库中只有 associations, pairs, shapes, words 四个词是名词，从意思上判断，words 和 shapes 显然不太合适，最后只能填 pairs.
34	abstract	第二部分第三段： Thus, we concluded that the blind interpret abstract shapes as sighted people do.	Abstract 是形容词，空里要求填个名词。从上面剩下的名词中我们可以挑选一个，最合适的就是 shapes.
35	circle / soft/ hard/ square	第二部分第三段： All our subjects deemed the circle soft and the square hard.	虽然在这句话中没有出现sighted这个词，但是根据上文推测，此处的 subjects 指得是 sighted subjects.

题号	定位词	文中对应点	题解
36 & 37	51%	第二部分第三段： And only 51% linked deep to circle and shallow to square. (See Fig. 2.)	同上
38	repeated / volunteers	第二部分第三段： When we tested four totally blind volunteers using the same list, we found that their choices closely resembled those made by the sighted subjects.	此空要求填一个形容词，在词库中，sighted 和 blind 是反义词，也就构成了一对 twins 选项，而 sighted 已经选过了两次，不大可能再选，因此此处只能选 blind.
39	choices	第二部分第三段： He made only one match differing from the consensus, assigning 'far' to square and ‘near’ to circle.	Consensus 是共识的意思，从这句话我们可以知道盲人们对如何搭配基本可以达成一致意见.

Question 40

- 题目类型：MULTIPLE CHOICE
- 题目解析：

定位点	题解
文中最后一句话： Thus, we concluded that the blind interpret abstract shapes as sighted people do.	根据文中最后一段话可知只有选项 B 最符合题意。

参考译文

盲人与视觉符号

第一部分

最近的几次研究表明，盲人可以理解用轮廓线和透视法来描述物体排列及空间平面的方法。但是，图画不只是表面意思的体现。在研究中，一名盲人女性自发地画出了一个转动的车轮，这就引起了我对上述事实的极大关注。为了展示这样一个动作，她在圆圈中画了一条曲线(见图 1)。我大吃一惊。像她所使用的这种运动线是插图史上最近的发明。实际上，正如艺术学者 David Kunzle 指出的那样，Wilhelm Busch，一名引领潮流的 19 世纪卡通画家，直到 1877 年才开始在其最流行的人物身上使用运动线。

当我要其他接受研究的盲人对象画出转动中的车轮时，一种特别聪明的画法反复出现了：几个人把车条画成了曲线。当被问到为什么要用曲线的时候，他们都说这是暗示运动的一种带有隐喻意味的方法。多数原则会认为从某种角度来讲，这个图案充分地表示了运动。但是就此而言，曲线是不是比，比如说虚线，波浪线或者其他任何一种线条，更能说明问题呢？答案是不确定的。所以我决定测试一下，不同的运动线是否就是表现运动的恰当方式，而或它们只是一些特殊的符号而已。进一步而言，我还想找出盲人和普通人在诠释运动线时的不同之处。

为了找出答案，我用凸起线条做出了五幅有关轮子的画，车条被画成大曲线，小曲线，波浪线，虚线以及超出车轮的直线。然后，我让18名盲人志愿者抚摩这些轮子，并且将它们分别与下列运动中的一个搭配：不稳定地转动，飞速转动，稳定地转动，颠簸和刹车。参照组则是由来自于多伦多大学的18名普通大学生组成的。

除了一个人，其他所有的盲人都将具体的动作与车轮搭配了起来。大多数人猜测被画成大曲线的车条表示车轮正在稳定地转动；而他们认为波浪线车条表示车轮在不稳定地转动；小曲线则被认为是车轮正在颠簸的象征。受试者推测，超出车轮边缘的车条代表车轮正处在刹车状态，而虚线车条则说明车轮正在飞快地旋转。

另外，在每种情况下，普通人喜爱的表达与盲人喜爱的基本一致。更有甚者，盲人之间的共识几乎与普通人的一样高。因为盲人不熟悉运动装置，因此这个任务对他们而言相当困难。然而，很明显，盲人不仅能够搞清楚每种运动线所代表的意义，而且作为一个团队，他们达成共识的频率也不比普通人低。

第二部分

我们还发现盲人同样可以理解其他的视觉隐喻。有个盲人女性在心形中画了个小孩儿——她说选择心形是为了表示这个孩子周围充满了爱。于是，我和刘长虹，一名来自中国的博士生，开始探索盲人对如心形这样含义不直白的图形的象征意义，到底理解到了何种程度。

我们给普通受试者一张有二十对词的单子，并且要求他们从每一对词当中挑一个最能代表圆形的词以及一个最能代表方形的词。举个例子，我们会问："哪个形状和柔软有关？圆形还是方形？哪个形状表示坚硬？"

所有的受试者都认为圆形代表柔软，方形代表坚硬。高达94%的人将快乐归给了圆形，而没有选悲伤。但是在其他词组上，不同意见就出现了：79%的人分别认为圆是快的而方是慢的，圆是弱的而方是强的。只有51%的人将深与圆形相连，将浅与方形相连(见图2)。当我们用同样的单子去测试四个完全失明的人时，他们的选择几乎与普通受试者的一模一样。有个先天失明的人做得极好。他的选择只有一个与众不同，那就是把"远"与方形联系起来而把"近"同圆形联系起来。实际上，也只有刚刚过半53%的普通受试者认为圆形代表远，而方形代表近。因此，我们可以得出结论，盲人同普通人一样能够理解抽象的图形。

WRITING

WRITING TASK 1

考官范文

The table gives a breakdown of the different types of family who were living in poverty in Australia in 1999.

On average, 11% of all households, comprising almost two million people, were in this position. However, those consisting of only one parent or a single adult had almost double this proportion of poor people, with 21% and 19% respectively.

Couples generally tended to be better off, with lower poverty levels for couples without children (7%) than those with children (12%). It is noticeable that for both types of household with children, a higher than average proportion were living in poverty at this time.

Older people were generally less likely to be poor, though once again the trend favoured elderly couples (only 4%) rather than single elderly people (6%).

Overall the table suggests that households of single adults and those with children were more likely to be living in poverty than those consisting of couples.

(154 words)

分析

雅思的图表作文是写作 Task 1 的必考项目（Task 2 是议论文）。图表通常分为两大类。一类是数据图，包括曲线图(graph/ line chart)，柱状图(bar chart/ column chart)，饼状图(pie chart)和表格(table)。另一大类是示意图 (diagram)。目前在雅思考试中主要出现的是数据图。

对于数据图来说，首先要仔细审题。审题包括看文字说明以及图表。文字说明部分一般提供了有关这个图表的最基本信息，如所涉及的时间地点和研究的对象。对于图表部分，我们需要仔细考查，找出值得描述的总体趋势(overall trends)和不规则变化(irregularities)。

图表作文通常应该分成三部分。第一部分介绍图表基本事实性信息。我们通常可以把题目进行改写。对比题目和范文：show — give, proportion — breakdown, type — category, who were living — living。其实就是使用同义词替换和语法改写。

第二部分是图表作文的主体。其中最关键的是分析并描写趋势。很多考生可能会草率地直接从上往下逐一描述，这样的结果就是一个流水账，而不是对于信息的处理和总结。在这个表格里，应该先描写黑体字(表示强调)的总量(all households)中贫困家庭的百分比。然后，描述表格中最突出信息(the most obvious feature)，也就是贫困家庭百分比最大的19%和21%的single, no children和sole parent群体。得出单身群体，无论是有没有小孩，生活在贫困线以下的比例较高。接下来，可以进行对比，与这两个群体形成鲜明对比的是7%和12%的couple, no children和couple with children群体。得出的趋势是成年人中，无论是有小孩的，还是没有小孩的，夫妻要比单身的不容易陷入贫困。最后，描述一下6%和4%的single aged person和aged couple群体，老年人最不容易生活在贫困之中。

第三部分是图表的结论。通常应该对图表进行总结或者把图表中最明显的趋势再次加以说明。当然，考生要注意的是在用词上不要照抄，要进行改写。

值得指出的是，考生在写作图表时，不仅要内容完整，结构清晰，还要用词准确多样，句子有变化才能获得高分。在范文中，大家可以学习用词：在第二段第一句中用了comprise，在第二句就改用了consist of，意思一样(“组成”)，但避免重复。同样表示“贫困人口”概念，在文中分别使用了poor people和people living in poverty。在句型上，同样表示百分比大小的比较，分别使用了lower...than, higher than, less likely to, favour...rather than, more...than等等。在语法结构的多样化上，文中用了定语从句，插入语，形式主语句，状语从句和宾语从句等等。

WRITIGN TASK 2

题目要求

Compare the advantages and disadvantages of three of the following as media for communicating information. State which you consider to be the most effective.

comics, books, radio, television, film, theatre

题解

这篇文章要求从六种媒体（连环漫画、书籍、广播、电视、电影、戏剧）中选出三种来加以比较，比较它们在传达信息方面的优点和缺点，并且指出哪种媒体最有效。

值得注意的是：题目中一共有六种媒体可供选择。考生所需要做的是从中选出自己有把握写好的三种。通常说来，大部分考生都会选择书籍、广播和电视，因为这三种媒体最为人所知，和大家的关系也最为密切。考生最好也是要选择自己熟悉的话题，不要为了过分追求与众不同而写自己不了解的内容。另外，需要引起考生注意的是，如果泛泛比较这三种媒体的话，很有可能会由于审题不清导致失分。本题要求的是比较三种媒体在传达信息方面的优缺点，要围绕这个方面展开。

范文一

Books, radios and films, as different media of communication, vary considerably in the delivery of information and thus in the results produced.

Books boast the longest history compared with radio programs and films. Books can have a touch upon almost all the aspects of our life. Therefore it is no exaggerating to say that the history of books is also the history of human development. But books usually tend to be somewhat slower than the time depicted in them. That may disappoint those who want to acquire the latest information.

Films can be the most artistic among the three forms of media as it combines audio, visual and sometimes even special effects. They can get people involved in a more colorful and real world. But unlike books that can be read in the couch or on the bus, movies will not be available without a ticket to the cinema and are shown only once a time.

In comparison with books and films, radio can provide the fastest source of information. Radio programs offer weather forecast and domestic and international developments in the fields ranging from presidential election in the U.S. to reform in the banking system in China to protests against humans' mistreatment of animals in Europe. Radio is also easier to carry compared with the other two. But in terms of the depth of information carried in it, it is no match for books and films.

In conclusion, books make people think, movies let people enjoy and radio helps people live.

分析

这篇范文开头简洁有力，指出书籍、广播和电影在传递信息以及产生的效果方面有不小差异。注意，本开头没有照抄题目，而是用了同义表述。题目中使用的communicate information在这里转化成了delivery of information.

文章的主体段落分别论证书籍、广播和电影的优缺点。在第二段，作者指出书籍与广播和电影相比历史悠久，涉及面广，涵盖人类发展过程的方方面面。同时指出，书籍的时效性较差，不利于获得最新的信息。在第三段，作者分析了电影的优缺点。一方面，电影由于综合了视觉、听觉，甚至特殊效果，产生的艺术性最好，从而可以有效地传达信息。另一方面，书本可以随意阅读，而电影只能在电影院观看，而且不像书籍可以反复阅读，只能一次看一场。第三段，作者指出，和前两种媒体相比，广播传递信息的速度最快。在这里还用了举例的论证手法。其次，广播携带方便。但是，广播在信息处理的深度方面不如书籍和电影。

在结尾部分，作者指出，书本有助于我们思考，电影让我们娱乐，而广播则便利我们的生活。作者好像没有直接回答题目中的“哪种媒体最有效”这个问题，但是通过指出三种媒体各自的有效性，从而间接回答了这个问题。也就是说，这三种媒体各有所长，分别在不同的方面体现各自的有效性。

范文二

Of the six types of media listed above, three are to be chosen — largely because of their being representative — to look at their advantages and disadvantages in relation to communicating information: books, radio and television.

As the oldest media form, books are still of great influence in recording information and spreading knowledge. Almost all information in history and most information at present are stored and conveyed in books. However, in comparison with other technology-assisted media, booksi' shortcomings are also apparent: they cannot sustain long-time storage and are comparatively lagging behind the time in delivering information.

Radio might be one of the earliest technological media. Its biggest advantage lies in its convenience because of its portability. With radio, people may listen to the up-to-minute information anytime and anywhere only if the radio signal is available. Of course, people sometimes complain that with visual pictures, it would be much better, and which, as known to all, results in what we call TV set, rather than radio.

In television, people see the best integration of both visual and acoustic effects. Furthermore, people more watch TV for leisure in addition to obtaining information because of the sensual enjoyment it provides. On the contrary, television has always been facing the fiercest criticism of its side-effect that information is delivered in such a passive way as to kill the audiences' creativity.

Agree with it or not, television is the most effective in communicating information. Currently, most households have TV set and some have even more than one. No other media parallels with it in terms of audience coverage. Besides, a big variety of information is available in television, such as news, documentary, music and movie, to meet preferences of different audiences. What is particular of television lies in its unmatched magic of live broadcast. Among others, these features suffice to draw the conclusion that television is the most powerful in spreading information.

分析

本文开头直接有力，指出想探讨的三种媒体是书籍、广播和电视。在句子上，使用了有一定复杂性的句型，还使用了插入语。

文章第二段直接写出主题句，指出书籍作为这三种媒体里最古老的一种，依然在记载信息和传播知识方面发挥重要作用。第二句话进行原因论证，表明历史上几乎所有信息和现代的绝大多数信息都是用书籍记载和传播的。第三句话笔锋一转，指出书籍的弱点，那就是，和其他技术相对先进的媒体相比，可能不耐储存，并且难以做到同样的时效性。

第三段话写广播。广播是较早的电子媒体。最大的优势就是便携。接下来用了解释说明的论证手法，只要有信号，就可以随时随地获得信息。然后，让步一下，指出广播只能听得到声音，没有图像。而有声音有图像的就是电视了。这一句话起到了承上启下的作用，引出下一段话。

第四段话的主题句指出电视是视觉和听觉效果的最佳综合。同时指出人们看电视经常是用来娱乐而不仅仅获得信息。而且，看电视过多可能会导致创造性萎缩。

文章结尾回应了题目的第二个问题，指出电视在传递信息方面是最有效的。电视覆盖范围广泛，家家户户都有电视，而且，信息可以以各种各样的形式在电视节目中得以体现。而且，电视还可以进行实况转播。最后一句话很好地总结了全文：电视在传播信息上是最强有力的。

SPEAKING

E=Examiner C=Candidate

E: Good morning. Take a seat. Right, and please give me your full name.

C: Wang Ailin.

E: Do you have an English name?

C: Yes. Eileen. An English friend said it suits me, and it sounds like my Chinese name.

E: It does. And where are you from, Eileen?

C: I was born in Shanghai, but now I'm studying in Beijing.

E: Where do you live now?

C: Now I live in Beijing, on campus sharing a dormitory with three other girls.

E: Do you like Beijing?

C: Yes. The city has a very good academic atmosphere, especially in and around Zhongguancun, where my university is. And I love some of the historic sites in Beijing, like the Great Wall and the Temple of Heaven. They fascinate me.

E: Anything about the city that you don't like?

C: It's too crowded. And the air pollution is getting more and more serious. Too many cars.

E: So will you stay in Beijing after you graduate?

C: I'm not sure, I guess it all depends on what I decide to do. I hope to go to Australia to do my Master's, but will probably have to do it in Beijing if I don't get a scholarship.

E: Have you applied?

C: Not yet, because I won't graduate for another two years.

E: Well, you said you both like and dislike Beijing. What do you like doing in your spare time? Do you like films?

C: Oh, I love movies. I've got lots of DVDs.

E: What kind of film do you like most?

C: Comedy, I guess, especially when I am under great pressure with schoolwork.

E: How often do you watch films?

C: Usually two or three times a week.

E: Do you like to watch alone or with your friends?

C: Well, I like to hang out with friends, but I usually prefer to watch films by myself. Because sometimes I identify with the characters so much that I can't stop crying or laughing: That really makes me seem crazy.

E: Do you prefer to watch films in the cinema or at home?

C: Both have advantages. You always get a better sound effect in a cinema, and the screen is so much bigger. But watching a film at home is much cheaper. I usually watch films on my laptop in the dormitory. My parents gave me he laptop for my birthday.

E: That's a nice present. How important are birthdays in China?

C: Quite important, I think. Birthdays are like milestones in one's life, and very meaningful.

E: What kinds of present do Chinese children get on birthdays in your country?

C: Toys, I think, just like in the West. And kids must also get some noodles, like children in the west have a birthday cake.

E: What is the most important birthday celebrated in China?

C: It's the 88th birthday. In Chinese it's called "Mi Shou". In ancient China, scarcely anyone could live to that age. So, if a family has a member aged 88, it's a real jubilee that's worth celebrating.

E: Good. Now I'm going to give you a topic. I'd like you to talk about it for two minutes. Before you talk, you have one minute to think about what you're going to say. You can take some notes. Here is your topic.

Describe an interesting historic place.

You should say:

What it is
Where it is located
What you can see there now
and explain why this place is interesting.

E: All right, remember you have two minutes. I'll tell you when time is up. You can speak now.

C: The Temple of Heaven is one of the interesting historic places I have ever been to. Located in the southern part of Beijing, it is China's largest existing complex of ancient sacrificial buildings. Believe it or not, it is three times the area of the Forbidden City. There you can see The Altar of Prayers for a Good Harvest, standing on a round foundation built with three levels of marble blocks. There is also the famous Echoing Wall enclosing the Imperial Vault of Heaven. One interesting place is the Center of Heaven Stone that echoes when a visitor speaks loudly when standing on the stone. Nearly every one who visits The Temple of Heaven likes to try it. I think it is an interesting historic place because the design of the temple reflects the mystical ancient Chinese perception of things. For example, because the number nine was considered the most powerful digit, many things are designed in multiples of nine. The Temple of Heaven is where the Emperor came every winter to worship heaven and to pray for a good harvest. A bad harvest could be interpreted as his fall from heaven' s favor and threaten the stability of his reign. Now the temple is a place where many people do exercises in the morning. This is a great change of role for The Temple of Heaven.

E: How do people in your country feel about protecting historic buildings?

C: People have begun to realize the importance of protecting historic buildings. Historic buildings are precious heritages of significant historic value that reflect the culture of a people with a 5,000 history. People feel the necessity to protect historic buildings be cause they are tired of the identical, block-like, unfriendly concrete skyscrapers.

E: Do you think an area can benefit from having an interesting historic place? In what way?

C: Sure. I believe an interesting historic place passes on the culture of its people. It inspires people' s interest in history. People learn history while visiting these places. It also serves as a good example to promote people's consciousness of the need to protect historic places. Historic sites are also good resources for tourism. Local people can benefit a lot economically if it a site attracts many tourists. But the premise is that people have to protect it.

E: What do you think will happen to historic places or buildings in the future?

C: As our country is under large-scale construction, many historic places or buildings may be torn down. Some may disappear due to neglect of protection and repair. Though some people have begun to realize the importance of protecting historic places, it is still not an issue that draws great attention from the general public. In addition, we have little policy support or enough money for the protection of heritage sites. When people realize what they have lost, it is too late.

E: You mentioned history. How were you taught history when you were at school?

C: History was a subject that we had to learn because there were history examinations to pass. We just read lots of books and listened to the teacher. This is mostly a passive way of learning. We were told to remember historic figures, events and other facts. We learnt mechanically, though we were not really interested in those numerous facts. And we were given little chance to analyze what lay behind historical events.

E: Are there other ways people can learn about history, apart from at school?

C: The Internet is a quick and convenient way to access abundant information, and also vivid pictures, but the information may not be well organized. People feel at a loss dealing with too much information. I think one good way to learn about history is watching serious historic newsreels. Visual images can inspire people's interest in learning. Historic places and cultural relics are things that can teach us a lot about history. People often feel they gone back in time when they visit historic places.

E: Do you think history will still be a school subject in the future?

C: I guess so. But I hope it's taught in a much more interesting way than it is nowadays, and isn't just the boring and compulsory reciting of historic facts. It is going to exist as a school subject because the younger generation should know something about what hap pened to our nation and the world in the past. They observe present reality better if they learn about history. There are many other ways to learn history, but we have to admit that school is the place where history can reach the largest number of young people. The sub ect should inspire interest in the past, not stifle it.

Test 2

LISTENING

SECTION 1

篇章结构

题　　型：选择题、选择填空题、句子填空题
考查技能：听出具体信息
场　　景：讨论旅游行程

场景背景介绍

由于国外节假日比较多，而学校里的假期更是频繁，如圣诞节(Christmas holidays)、复活节(Easter holiday)和暑假等，度假和旅游成为海外老百姓生活和校园生活极为常见和重要的一部分。反映到雅思考试上，有关度假和旅游的讨论在第一部分频频出现。说话人多讨论目的地的选择、住宿方式、游览行程等内容，因此考生对上述话题所涉及的词汇和文化背景应有所掌握。

本节必备词汇、词组

guidebook	*n.* 旅行指南	architect	*n.* 建筑师
chilled	*adj.* 冰镇的	snack	*n.* 小吃
mineral water	矿泉水	sightseeing	*n.* 观光
cash	*v.* 兑现	cathedral	*n.* 大教堂
travellers cheque	旅行支票	castle	*n.* 城堡
exchange rate	汇率	Hang on!	(英式英语口语)稍等
teller	*n.* 出纳员	art gallery	美术馆
temporarily	*adv.* 临时地	botanical garden	植物园
transaction	*n.* 交易	church services	教堂礼拜仪式

charge	*n.* 收费	picnic	*n.* 野餐
spectacular	*n.* 壮观	swan	*n.* 天鹅

场景词汇拓展

cash point	取款机	credit card	信用卡
backpack	*n.* 背包旅行	Visa Card	维萨信用卡
B & B	只提供早餐和住宿的旅馆	Master Card	万事达信用卡
Youth Hotel	青年旅馆	American Express	美国运通卡
motel	*n.* 汽车旅馆		

文本及疑难解析

1. P135. “You’ve been **ages.**” 你去了那么长时间。ages 多出现在英式英语口语中，指“a long time”很长时间。其他例句如 Simon! I haven’t seen you for ages. 西蒙，好久不见！

2. P135. —— **What would you like to drink?**
—— **I’d love** a really chilled mineral water or something.
日常生活中极其常用的句型，问对方喝点什么。

3. P135. “The waitress will **be back in a moment**” 服务员一会儿就回来。

4. P135. “...they told me the computer system was temporarily **down**, so they couldn’t do any transactions.” 他们说计算机系统出现暂时故障，因此无法进行交易。down 多指计算机出现故障。

5. P136. “I really want to spend some time in the Art Gallery, because they’ve got this wonderful painting by **Rembrandt** that I’ve always wanted to see.” 我很想去美术馆看看，因为那里有我一直想一睹为快的伦勃朗的画。

6. P136. “...they only open on Thursdays” 他们仅在每周四开放。open 既可当形容词用，也可像这里一样用做动词。表示固定时间“每周一/二…”时，日期后加 -s 用复数形式。

7. P136. “The view is supposed to be spectacular” 据说景色壮观极了。be supposed to do/be something 有“据说、被很多人认为”的意思，类似例句如：*Dirty Harry* is supposed to be one of Eastwood’s best films. Dirty Harry 被很多人认为是伊斯特伍德最出色的电影之一。

题目解析

1－5 题为选择题，解题关键在于迅速读题，并且由于有选项存在，考生在听时要对原文措辞和选项措辞之间可能发生的替换尽快做出判断。五个答案依次出现，但选项中的正确答案都对原文中的字眼做了改动，如第一题中原文中的 “chilled mineral water” 成为答案中的“a cold drink”。第二题中的A选项是干扰选项，选项C才是对原文中“the computer system was temporarily down” 的正确替换。

3－5题较简单，如果能抓住“New York”、“bus system”和“a snack and a drink”，题目就迎刃而解了。

6－8题为选择填空题，难度较大，但是紧抓住关键词“all day”、“Mondays”、“free entry”可以帮助考生跟上原文的进度，从而知道答案可能出现的位置。解第8题时，原文中的“except”是很重要的提示词。

第9题原文中没有直接提到目的地，只讲了要去看“painting”，如果考生对前面的谈话有印象，可以知道伦勃朗的画是在美术馆，如果考生不记得了，也可以通过常识猜测出答案，因为画通常放在美术馆里。

第10题答案直截了当，比较容易辨别出来。

SECTION 2

篇章结构

题　　型：选择题
考查技能：听出具体信息和大意
场　　景：介绍学校咨询服务的讲座

场景背景介绍

在国外大学学习的过程中，学生难免会遇到各种各样的问题，如学习、感情、钱等等，而国际留学生可能遇到的麻烦会更多。为了帮助学生解决这些问题，国外大学都设有一些机构来为学生提供咨询和帮助，如本节中的Counselling Service(咨询服务处)就是一个很有代表性的一个例子。考生在作题的同时，也可以了解一下他们到底都可以提供什么服务，这样一旦在国外遇到类似的难题，就可以向学校的援助机构寻求帮助了。除了这样的机构外，学生还可以向学校里的International Office或Oversea Student Office(国际留学生办公室)，或者自己的tutor(导师)寻求帮助。

本节必备词汇、词组

counselling service	咨询服务	social contacts	交往的人(如熟人、家人、朋友等)
arise	*v.* 出现		
chase up	提醒某人尽快做某事	trigger	*v.* 引发
tutor	*n.* 导师	interrupted personal relationships	中断的个人关系
feedback	*n.* 反馈		
stress	*n.* 压力	break off	中断，断绝
adjust	*v.* 调整	unmotivated	*adj.* 没有动力的
mounting pressure	日益增加的压力	concentrate	*v.* 集中
deadline	*n.* 最终期限	resident	*adj.* 常驻的
creep up on sb.	某事不期而至	chaplain	*n.* (军队、团体、医院里的)牧师
cope with	应付		
social network	社会关系网	drop out	放弃
anxiety	*n.* 焦虑	self-esteem	*n.* 自尊

resit	*v.* 重考，补考	musical instrument	乐器
anthropology	*n.* 人类学	Welfare Service	福利服务
sympathetic	*adj.* 同情的	staff cuts	裁员
dietary problems	饮食问题	appeal	*n.* 要求，诉请
to one's liking	合乎某人的喜好	launch	*v.* 发起
upset	*v.* 使不适	on behalf of	代表
dietician	*n.* 饮食专家	understaffed	*adj.* 人手不足的
low-interest loan	低息贷款		

场景词汇拓展

self-access language center	语言自学中心	campus	*n.* 校园
computer center	计算机中心	coordinator	*n.* 协调人
common room	师生共用的休息室	auditorium	*n.* 大礼堂
cafeteria	*n.* 助餐厅	sports center	体育中心
administration building	行政楼		

文本及疑难解析

1. P136. "**Let's take** academic counseling." 我们先谈谈学业方面的咨询。Let's take...(for example)是个很常见的举例句型，如 Not everyone is doing so well. Take Sheryl, for example — she's still looking for a job.并不是每个人都很顺利。比如说 Sheryl，她还在找工作呢。

2. P137. "If you are confused about subjects or how to combine them in your degree, then we can advise you and discuss the career you are aiming for, so that you can **see** it all **in context**." 如果你对课程感到困惑，或者不知道如何把他们融入到你的学位中去，我们可以为你提供建议，并讨论你的职业规划，这样你就可以把这样的问题放到一个大的环境下去考虑了。see something in context 在相关的环境中去看待某事。

3. P137. "But **it's not the end of the world** if you don't pass an exam — I had to resit First Year Anthropology, so I can certainly offer you **a sympathetic ear**!"考试没过也不是什么世界末日——我大一学人类学时也曾补考过，所以(如果你们遇到这样的问题)，我会很乐意倾听你们的遭遇。a sympathetic ear 愿意倾听别人诉说他们的遭遇。类似例句有 We hope always to provide a friendly sympathetic ear. 我们希望总能够成为一个友善的听众来倾听别人的问题。

4. P137. "You may also **be off** your food..." 你可能不再有胃口。be off 不再喜欢，类似的例句有 Toby's been off his food for a few days. Toby 整整好几天没有胃口。

5. P137. "...we won all **but** just one of the twelve appeals that we launched on behalf of students." 在以学生的名义发起的对校方的 12 项要求中，除了其中一个没有成功外，其他均得到校方采纳。but 在这里当介词 "except" 讲。

题目解析

11－20题均为选择题，个别题目难度较大。

11题题干中的关键词是“tutor”，此词在原文只出现了一次，即答案之所在。就像其他的选择题那样，本题中的正确选项也对原文中的原始信息做了同义替换，“(getting) proper feedback”被替换成“inform”，“how you' re getting on in your subject”被替换成“progress”.

12题难度较大，选项A和C均是干扰选项，虽然“teach(er)”和“unfamiliar”在原文中的确出现，但不是指“新老师”和“课程不熟悉”，而是“学生要对他们可能不太熟悉的教学和学习方法做出调整”，原文中紧接着出现的“mounting pressure”和“deadline”才是答案之所在。

13题答案比较明显，而且词汇简单“family and friends”。

14题难度较大，原因是原文中信息太密集，且词组偏难。“Studying overseas can **trigger** a **personal crisis** — you may have a lot of what you might call “unfinished business” back in your own country, or you may have **interrupted personal relationships** or even sometimes have broken them off to come overseas,” 上文中加粗的文字即是答案信息，在选项中interrupted被替换为disruptions，两者都有“中断”的意思。interrupted personal relationships可以理解为出国后学生以往的人际关系被打断了，跟自己朋友、家人、同学同事的交往被中断了。上文中的斜体字“unfinished business”不是指“business problems”，而是指“没有处理的事情”。

15题中同样出现了替换，原文中“drop out of a course”被替换成“don' t complete a course”。

16题题干中的关键人名“Glenda Roberts”在原文中出现在答案之后，这可能会给考生带来一点麻烦。但原文中“local food”这个信息比较容易把握。

17、18题涉及贷款的用途，原文中的答案比较直接，考生要听出“buy books”和“furniture”，其他的选项要么没有提到，要么是错误的，如不是“no-interest loan”，而是“low-interest loan”。

19题是细节题，难度不大。

20题的答案在最后一部分，说话人在总结该服务去年取得的成绩，“in spite of staff cuts”语气明显，即尽管人手不够，但我们还是取得了这样那样的成绩。

SECTION 3

篇章结构

题　　型：笔记填空、多选题、表格填空
考查技能：听出具体信息和大意
场　　景：课外研讨场景

场景背景介绍

本节中三位学生在讨论作业情况和研究方法，类似的场景在听力第三部分很普遍。在国外的学习生活中，虽然很多事情需要自己努力完成，但团队合作同样重要。跟其他几个同学组成一个学习小组(study group)，互相帮助，取长补短，也可以实现共赢。在这样的场景中，学生们讨论的话题多集中在作业、研究方法、书目和存在的问题等方面，因此考生对这些话题的语汇要掌握。而这些话题中比较难的当属研究方法(research methods)，考生应对调查问卷(questionnaire)、采访(interview)等研究方法及其优、缺点有所了解，这样不仅有益于雅思备考，也有益于了解国外的学习生活。

本节必备词汇、词组

assignment	*n.* 作业	reckon	*v.* (英式口语)猜想，估计
task	*n.* 任务，作业	wording	*n.* 措辞
data	*n.* 数据	response	*n.* 回答
assess	*v.* 评估	reliable	*adj.* 可靠的
social science	社会科学(研究社会中的人的科学，如政治、社会学等)	drawback	*n.* 缺点
		response rate	回收率
carry out	实施	reveal	*v.* 揭示
subject	*n.* 研究对象	sample	*n.* 样本，例子
questionnaire	*n.* 调查问卷	survey	*n.* 调查
interview	*n.* 采访	tutorial	*n.* 辅导课
time-consuming	*adj.* 费时的	reading list	阅读书目

场景词汇拓展

quantitative	*adj.* 定量研究	presentation	*n.* 陈述
qualitative	*adj.* 定性研究	research methods	研究方法
rate of return	回收率	deadline	*n.* 最后期限
literature review	文献回顾	draft	*n.* 草稿
seminar	*n.* 研讨会		

文本及疑难解析

1. P138. "Rosa: Did you **get as far as** discussing which form of data collection we should go for — questionnaire or interview, isn't?"你们已经讨论了调查问卷和采访这两种数据收集方法之中我们应选择哪种这个问题了，是不是？get as far as doing something 指"已取得了…进展，已发展到…程度"。类似的例句有：They had got as far as painting the kitchen.他们已经把厨房粉刷了。

2. P138. "As long as you design the questionnaire properly in the first place, the data will be fine."只要一开始就正确的设计问卷，那么(收集的)数据不会有问题的。in the first place 意为"一开始，起初"，其他例句有：I should never have gone in the first place!我当初本就不该去！

3. P138. "Another drawback I remember it mentioned was that questionnaire data **tends** not to reveal anything unexpected, because it is limited to the questions fixed in advance by the researcher."我记得它(文章)提到的另外一个缺陷在于调查问卷不太可能揭示出乎意料的东西，因为问卷仅限于研究者事先确定好的问题。tend to do something 指"易于，经常做某事"，例句还有 People tend to need less sleep as they get older.随着年龄的增长，人们对睡眠的需求往往变少。

4. P138. "It's not **meant to be** real research, is it?"它本来就不是真正的研究，不是吗？be meant to do something 这里的意思指"用来做某事"，类似的用法如：The diagram is meant to show the different stages of the process.这个图表用来展示这个过程的不同阶段。

5. P138. "Maybe I'd better go through the article again, **just to be sure**."或许我应该再读一遍那篇文章，好弄清楚到底怎么回事。just to be sure 在口语中很常见，指"确认，弄清楚"。

6. P138. "Can we **meet up** again later this week? 要不这周晚些时候我们再碰一次？meet up 多指"为了某个目的而见面"，如：We often meet up after work and go for a drink.我们经常下班后见个面一起喝一杯。

7. P138. "— What about Friday morning?— **Suits me**." Suits me 是很常见的回答，跟"Fine with/by me"类似。

题目解析

第 21 – 24 题为完成笔记题，原文中谈话顺序很清晰，考生只要捕捉具体信息即可，本的正确发音。

第 25、26 题做题时，要抓住题干中“disadvantage”在原文中的同义词“drawback”，同时两个答案也符合学术研究中的常识，问卷调查的缺点在于回收率可能较低，且研究方式过于结构化(structured)，被调查人只能回答研究者事先准备好的问题，从而不易发现研究者没有预计到的情况。

第 27－30 题为完成表格题，答案为细节信息，难度不大。

SECTION 4

篇章结构

题　　型：选择题、笔记填空题
考查技能：听出具体信息
场　　景：关于企业犯罪的讲座

场景背景介绍

听力考试第4个section讲座的主题涵盖社会科学和自然科学的各个方面，环境、生态、考古、动物等在听力中都有所涉及。考生一方面可以通过多听多读的方法(如网上收听BBC的节目，或者收看Discovery频道)来扩大知识面和词汇量，另一方面也应熟悉学术讲座的风格和标志词(signpost words)，这些标志词可以清晰地显示出讲座者的思路，从而帮助听众跟上讲座者的节奏。这些标志词通常分为微观和宏观两类，前者更多用于细处，后者多点明讲座的脉络，听众(考生)应对它们格外敏感。(具体可见“场景词汇拓展”部分)

本节必备词汇、词组

contemporary	*adj.* 当代的	conventional	*adj.* 常规的
preoccupation	*n.* 关注之事	ignore	*v.* 忽视
unique	*adj.* 独特的	mass media	大众传媒
massive	*adj.* 巨大的	under-reported	*adj.* 报道不足的
corporate	*adj.* 企业的	in comparison with	跟…相比
illegal	*adj.* 非法的	academic circles	学术圈
in accordance with	与…一致	specialist knowledge	专业知识
quote...unquote	*v.* 用于引用语前后，表示如实引用	unaware	*adj.* 不知道的，没察觉的
commit a crime	犯罪	misfortune	*n.* 不幸
theft	*n.* 偷窃	dilute	*v.* 冲淡
embezzlement	*n.* 盗用公款	concentration	*n.* (饮料)浓度
fraud	*n.* 欺骗	carton	*n.* 硬纸盒或塑料盒
exclude	*v.* 把…排除在外	deception	*n.* 欺骗
excusable	*adj.* 可原谅的	be deprived of	…被夺取

undermine	*v.* 破坏	inquiry	*n.* 调查
illustrate	*v.* 举例说明	lay blame on	归咎于…
reference to	关于	deliberately	*adv.* 故意地
oil tanker	油轮	indifference	*n.* 漠然
crew	*n.* (船上或飞机上) 全体工作人员	innocent	*adj.* 无辜的
		loophole	*n.* 漏洞

场景词汇拓展

微观标志词

Segmentation	Temporal	Causal	Contrast	Emphasis
well	at that time	then	but	you see
oK	and	because	only	actually
now	after this	both	on the other hand	unbelievably
and	for the moment		of course	as you know
right	eventually		you can see	in fact
all right	so			naturally

宏观标志词

1. What I' m going to talk about today is something you probably know about ready.
2. We' ll see that...
3. That/this is why...
4. To begin with...
5. Another interesting development was...
6. You probably know that...
7. The surprising thing is...
8. As you may have heard...
9. This is how it came about...
10. The problem here was that...
11. The next thing was...
12. One of the problems is...
13. Here is a big problem.
14. What we' ve come to by now was that...

15. It's really very interesting that...
16. This is not the end of the story.
17. Our story doesn't finish here.
18. And that's all we'll talk about today

文本及疑难题解析

1. P139. "but **over** the past seventy years or so..." 但是在过去的约70年中…。over在此当"during"讲。

2. P139. "It's often very complex, **whereas** with conventional crime it's usually possible to follow what's going on without specialist knowledge." 它(企业犯罪)很多时候比较复杂，而对于常规犯罪而言(就不是这样)，即使没有专业知识，人们通常也可以理解其来龙去脉。whereas为转折连词，多用于正式场合。

3. P139. "As well as this, whereas conventional crime usually has a lot of **human interest**, corporate crime often has much less." 除此之外，常规犯罪通常涉及人们的生活、情感，而企业犯罪在这方面的故事要少的多。human interest 指某事由于涉及人们的生活、感情和人际关系而被人津津乐道。

4. p140. "There are two more points to do with corporate crime that **I'd like to illustrate with reference to** a specific event which occurred several years ago." 还有两点跟企业犯罪有关，我将会以几年前发生的一件具体案件为例加以说明。

5. P140. "It was an explosion **which never should have happened** and a subsequent inquiry laid the blame not on anyone who had actually been on the tanker at the time, but on the owners of the tanker." 这是一起本不该发生的爆炸，随后的调查并没有将事故原因归咎于当时实际在船上的人，而是这支船的所有者。

6. P140. "The main crime here was indifference to the human results rather than actual intention to harm anyone, but that didn't make the results any less tragic."(本案中)主要的过错是对于(可能造成的人身伤害的)结果的漠视，而不是真正要去伤害别人，但这个(区别)并没有使得悲剧性的结果有任何改变。

7. P140. "**It's not just a matter of** companies making bigger profits than they should do, **but of** events which may affect the lives of innocent people..." 这不仅仅是一个公司获得比应得的要多的利益的问题，而是一个可能会影响无辜人们生活的事情。

题目解析

31题的答案在讲座前面一部分对企业犯罪下定义时出现，文中依次出现"connected with companies"、"for the good of the company"和"for the corporate organization"，因此答案锁定在C (for companies)。

32题可以通过听出原文中"theft by employees"来答题，也可以通过对第31题的理解来排除干扰选项B和C。

33 – 38 题是讲座主题部分的笔记，结构清晰，答案依次出现。35 题的答案并没有直接给出，而是通过企业犯罪和常规犯罪的比较，说常规犯罪通常不需要专业知识，言下之意即企业犯罪需要专业知识。 此外，考生还要把握好笔记题题干中关键词和原文中实际用词的替换，如 37 题中“unimportant”在原文中的替身是“insignificant”，38 题中的“large”在原文中的对应点是“massive”。

39、40 题的答案正式讲座最后反复强调的“two points”，虽然文章难度较大，但答案被作者反复重申，如“results”、“tragic”、“serious consequences”，此外考生也可以通过排除法确定答案。A、B 显然是错的，C 在原文中被讲座人否定掉了，F 在原文后面部分没有提及。

READING

READING PASSAGE 1

篇章结构

体裁 说明文

主题 少数民族语言的危机

结构
第一段：通过那瓦霍语的困境道出少数民族语言所面临的问题
第二段：少数民族语言正面临灭顶之灾
第三段：使用者的年龄是语言灭绝真正的关键
第四段：信任危机导致语言灭绝
第五段：少数民族语言灭绝的主要原因
第六段：语言与文化的关系
第七段：预防少数民族语言灭绝的方案
第八段：解决语言灭绝问题的前景

必背词汇

第一段

Native American	印第安人；印第安人的	dying	*adj.* 垂死的；快要消失的
Navajo	那瓦霍人(散居于新墨西哥州，亚利桑那州和犹他州的北美印第安人)	middle-aged	*adj.* 中年的
		elderly	*adj.* 上了年纪的；年老的
		surprisingly	*adv.* 令人惊奇地
nation	*n.* 部落；民族	linguist	*n.* 语言学家
sprawl	*vi.* 散布；无计划地扩展	remain	*vi.* 剩余；余留

第二段

far from	远非；完全不	lost	*adj.* 失去的；消失了的
vanish	*vi.* 消失；突然不见	linguistic	*adj.* 语言上的，语言学上的
generation	*n.* 代；一代人	diversity	*n.* 多样性；差异

shrink	*v.* 缩小；减小	mass	*adj.* 大规模的；大量的；大批的
pace	*n.* 速度；速率	extinction	*n.* 灭绝；毁灭；绝种
head for	注定…要遭受	rebound	*v.* 重新跃起；回升
dominate	*v.* 支配；占优势	loss	*n.* 损失；丧失；遗失
evolutionary	*adj.* 演化的；进化论的		

第三段

isolation	*n.* 隔绝；隔离；孤立；分离	endangered	*adj.* 濒临灭绝的；有灭种危险的
breed	*v.* 产生；导致		
pepper	*v.* 使布满；使充满	relatively	*adv.* 相对地；比较而言地
necessarily	*adv.* 必定；必然地	critically	*adv.* 危急地；严重地

第四段

reject	*v.* 拒绝接受；拒绝相信	faith	*n.* 信仰；信念；忠诚
crisis	*n.* 危机	teens	*n.* 十几岁(13-19 岁)
confidence	*n.* 信任；信用；信心	induce	*v.* 引诱；劝诱
community	*n.* 社会；社区	tradition	*n.* 传统；惯例
alongside	*prep.* 在…旁边；和…在一起(相比)	voluntary	*adj.* 自动的；自主的；自愿的

第五段

kill off	消灭	globalisation	*n.* 全球化；全球主义
minority	*adj.* 少数人的；少数民族的	adapt to	适应
ban	*v.* (以官方明令)禁止；取缔	socio-economic	*adj.* 社会经济学的；涉及社会和经济因素的
discourage	*v.* 阻止；阻拦；(试图)劝阻		
promote	*v.* 促进；提升	commercial	*adj.* 商业的；贸易的
unity	*n.* 团结；联合；统一	at the least	至少；最少
reservation	*n.* 保留；保留地	data	*n.* 编辑处理有关的详细资料
effectively	*adv.* 实际上地；事实上	evolution	*n.* 演变；进化
danger list	病危病人名单	rely on	依赖；依靠
chair	*v.* 任…主席	unwritten	*adj.* 未成文的；口头的
deadly	*adj.* 致命的；极有害的；破坏性的	unrecorded	*adj.* 未记录下来的

第六段

intimately	*adv.* 密切地；亲密地	be bound up with	与…有密切关系；随…而定

preserve	v. 保护；保持；保存	perception	n. 认识；看法
shift	v. 改变；使语音改变	pattern	n. 模式；风格
deprive	v. 夺去；剥夺；使…丧失	connection	n. 联系；关系
mount	vi. 增加；增长	structure	v. 建立；组织；安排
physiological	adj. 生理学的；生理学上的		

第七段

identity	n. 同一性；相同；一致	apprentice	n. 学徒；初学者
dire	adj. 可怕的；不祥的	indigenous	adj. 当地的；本土的
foster	v. 培养；鼓励	pair up	把…配成一对
ancestral	adj. 祖传的；祖先的	weave	v. 编织
tongue	n. 语言	instruction	n. 说明；指示
bilingualism	n. 双语制；两种语言的使用	exclusively	adv. 专门地
erosion	n. 削弱；减少；损害	sufficiently	adv. 充分地；足够地
Maori	n. 毛利人；毛利语	fluent	adj. 流利的；流畅的
rekindle	v. 重新点燃；使复苏	transmit	v. 传输；传送；传播
approach	n. 方法；方式	die out	灭绝
Polynesian	adj. 波利尼西亚的；波利尼西亚人的		

第八段

preservation	n. 保存；保持	essential	adj. 必须的；基本的
revive	v. (使)苏醒；(使)复兴	mere	adj. 仅仅的；起码的
revival	n. 复兴；复活		

难句解析

1．Never before has the planet's linguistic diversity shrunk at such a pace.

参考译文：地球上语言的多样性从未以如此惊人的速度降低过。

语言点：倒装结构的使用

(1) 通常来讲句首有否定词或否定短语的时候，句子要倒装。以never/ hardly / scarcely/ little/ seldom/ not/ not until /rarely /no sooner...than/nowhere/by no means / in no case / under no circumstances 开头的句子要倒装。例如，

① No sooner had I taken a bath than the bell rang. 我刚洗澡，铃就响了。

② Never before have I heard such a story. 我从未听过这样的故事。

③ By no means did everyone learn English well enough to negotiate in it.

不可能每个人把英语都学到能用其沟通的程度。

(2) only + 状语置于句首时要倒装，例如，

Only then did she realize she was wrong. 只有在此时，她才意识到自己错了。

(3) so / neither / nor / no more 放在句首时要倒装，例如，

I can't speak French, nor can he. 我不会讲法语，他也不会。

2. It is not necessarily these small languages that are about to disappear.

参考译文： 那些行将消失的小语种并非命该如此。

结构分析： not necessarily 是“不一定”的意思。在这句话当中，it 是形式主语，真正的主语是 these small language，that 引导定语从句修饰主语。

语言点： 主语从句的用法(2)

It 做形式主语，常见的句型有：

(1) It is believed that...

say / expect / report / think / know 也可以这样使用

(2) it is + 形容词...

这些形容词可以是： easy / certain / difficult / unlikely / possible

(3) it is + 名词短语

这些名词可以是：a pity / a shame / an honour / no wonder

(4) it + 动词：seem / appear / turn out 等

3. Quite often, governments try to kill off a minority language by banning its use in public or discouraging its use in schools, all to promote national unity.

参考译文： 为了增加国家凝聚力，政府通常会通过在公共场合禁用，以及在学校中不提倡使用的方法，消灭少数民族语言。

结构分析： 这句话当中 by 引导的是方式状语，to 引导目的状语。

语言点： 不定式做状语

不定式做状语的时候要注意以下几点：

(1) 通常放在句子中间或句末

(2) 如果不定式做目的状语，可以在前面加上 in order 或 so as。例如，

I got a job on the side in order to earn money for my study.

我找到了一份兼职工作，为的是挣点学费。

(3) 还可以把 in order to 或者 to do 提到句首，提起注意。例如，

To avoid criticism, do nothing, say nothing, be nothing.

为了避免别人批评而什么也不说的人最终什么也不是。

(4) 不定式做结果状语的时候，前面可以加 only，表示引出意想不到的结果，例如，

We hurried to the railway station, only to find that the train had left.

我们匆忙赶到火车站，却发现火车早已开走了。

(5) 在 so...as to / such as to / enough...to / too...to...等词组中，不定式也表示结果，例如，

Her story is such as to arouse our sympathy. 她的故事让我们顿生同情。

在这里，such 就等于 so + 相关的形容词，所以上面这个例句就等于 her story is so sad as to arouse our sympathy.

(6) 有时候不定式也可以做原因状语。例如，

They laughed to see the funny person. = They laughed as they saw the funny person.

看到那个滑稽的人，他们笑了。

试题分析

Questions 1 —4

- 题目类型：SUMMARY
- 题目解析：

本题基本上是对整篇文章的总结，建议先做，顺便把文章浏览一遍。

题号	定位词	题解
1	6800 / variety of language / geographical	第三段第一句话 现在全世界大概有 6800 种语言，这种丰富的语言多样性主要来自于地理上的… 答案：isolation
2	government / huge decrease	第五段中部 ...the deadliest weapon is not government policy but economic pressures. ... 本题目要看清楚问的是语言消失的原因，and 表示并列，因此空中应该填与 government initiatives 对等的原因，而文中第五段前半部分提到政府政策对语言的影响，但是科学家们也指出，真正致命的原因是社会经济压力。 答案：economic globalization/globalization/socio-economic pressures 注意：不能写成 pressure
3	Increasing appreciation/ language classes/ ‘apprentice’	第七段第二句话 But a growing interest in ... 本题与其用空所在的这句话去定位，不如寻找空后面加了引号的 apprentice。第 3 空所填词一定在引号前方，再找到 language classes，然后寻找 increasing 的同义词，结果就发现了第二句当中的 growing，而根据语法，该空要填一个名词或名词词组，因此很容易就找到了 cultural

题号	定位词	题解
		identity。 答案：cultural identity
4	‘apprentice’ / teach / a	第七段 中后部 a Native American tongue... 继续用‘apprentice’做为定位词，该句话的意思是在学徒计划中，濒危语言被用来作为载体来教授人们一种…，文中的“学习”与“教授”在意思上有关联，而不定冠词 a 的要填一个专有名词。 答案是：traditional skill

Questions 5 —9

- 题目类型：配对题：人物 + 理论
- 题目解析：

先用人物定位，再通读理论，划出解题关键字，最后回文中，找出对应句子，进行改写。

题号	解题关键字	题解
5	more than one...	翻译：除非人们都去学习说不止一种语言，否则的话濒危语言是不可能得救的。 第 7 段前部，Doug Whalen 身份的后面 Most of these languages will not survive without a large bilingualism. bilingual 意思就是“能够写或说两种语言”，与 more than one language 正好对应。 答案：E
6	in itself	翻译：拯救濒危语言本身并不是令人满意的目标。 第 7 段倒数第 6 行，Mufwene 出现的地方后面。 很多时候一个人会在文中出现不止一次，而且第二次出现的时候往只说姓，或者只说名字，这就给很多考生造成困扰，因此在标人名的时候要注意，一般出现率越高的人理论越多。 But Mufwene says that preventing a language dying out is not the same as giving it new life by using it every day.通过这句话可以推测，保护语言本身并不是目标，如何让语言活起来才是真正目的。
7	think / determine	翻译：我们思考的方式也许是由我们的语言决定的。 第 6 段末句 Pagel 所说的话当中提到了说 英语的人的大脑与说法语的人大脑的不同，随后提出语言会影响我们的想法和观点。

题号	定位词	题解
8	reject / established / way of life	翻译：年轻人经常会拒绝接受社会约定俗成的生活方式。 第四段末句的意思与题目中的意思一致。
9	loss	翻译：语言的转化意味着传统文化的消失。 第6段第2句 文中的 shift 等同于题目当中的 change，而传统文化的存在正意味着人们可以采用不同的观点来看待这个世界。

Questions 10 —13

- 题目类型：TRUE/FALSE/NOT GIVEN
- 题目解析：

10. The Navajo language will die out because it currently has too few speakers

参考译文	那瓦霍语将灭绝，因为是目前的使用者太少了。
定位词	Navajo
解题关键字	because / too few
文中对应点	第三段第四句话 有 15 万人在使用那瓦霍语，证明使用者并不是很少，在接下来的一句话当中，作者又表明使语言濒临灭绝的真正原因并不是说的人少，而是说的人太老。
答案	NO

11. A large number of native speakers fails to guarantee the survival of a language

参考译文	使用者的数量多也未能保证一门语言的存活。
定位词	a large number of
解题关键字	fail to guarantee
文中对应点	第三段第四句话 根据文中给出的证据，即有 15 万人说那瓦霍语，但是这门语言仍然濒临灭绝，作者推出了题中的结论，这个结论是正确的。
答案	YES

12. National government could do more to protect endangered language.

参考译文	政府在保护濒危语言方面应该做得更多。
定位词	government
解题关键字	protect
文中对应点	文中第五段提到了政府，主要是指出政府的政策也是导致语言濒危的原因，但是此后就并未对政府的作用再多做叙述，而是转而论述社会经济压力的重要性。本题是典型的节外生枝型。
答案	NOT GIVEN

13. The loss of linguistic diversity is inevitable.

参考译文	语言多样性的消失是不可避免的。
定位词	linguistic diversity
解题关键字	inevitable
文中对应点	第七段首句 尽管语言学家已经竭尽全力，但是许多语言到了下个世纪还是会消失。这句话就表明语言多样性的消失是不可避免的。在这里，inevitable 一词尽管十分绝对，但是也不能够武断地将此题判定为 NO，因为从语言学角度来看，作者是在论述一个公理。
答案	YES

参考译文

语言的消失
——许多少数民族语言濒临灭绝

对于居住在美国西南部四州的那瓦霍人来讲，他们的语言正在遭遇灭顶之灾。大多数说那瓦霍语的人要么是中年人，要么就是垂垂老者。尽管有许多学生都在学习该门语言，可是学校却是用英文授课的。路牌、超市商品说明、甚至报纸全部是英文的。因此语言学家怀疑在百年之后还会不会有人会说这门语言也就不足为奇了。

那瓦霍语决不是惟一会有此厄运的语言。再经历两代人的时间，全球6,800种语言当中的半数就有可能从世界上彻底消失——这就相当于平均每十天就有一种语言消失。地球上语言的多样性从未以如此惊人的速度降低过。“现在，我们面临的将是两三种语言支配整个世界。”雷丁大学的进化生物学家 Marl Pagel 说，“这就是(语言的)大规模灭绝，而且我们很难知道能否从这种语言灭绝当中恢复过来。”

封闭产生了语言的多样性。结果整个世界就布满了只有几个人说的语言。只有250种语言拥有超过100万的使用者，而至少有3,000种语言使用者不足2,500人。那些行将消失的小语种并非命该如此。尽管仍有15万人在使用那瓦霍语，但这种语言还是上了濒危名单。判断一种语言是否濒危的标准不是使用者的数量，而是使用者的年龄。如果一种语言是孩子们在使用，就会相对安全些。用费尔班克斯Alassk语言中心的主任Micheal Krauss的话说就是，真正面临灭绝之灾的是那些只有老年人才懂得说的语言。

可人们为什么拒绝说他们父母的语言呢？这一切都始于一场信任危机。BATH英国濒危语言基金会成员Nicholas Ostler说：“当一个小规模社会发现自己与一个大规模，更富有的社会并肩而存的时候，其成员就会对自己的文化丧失信心。当这个社会的下一代进入青春期的时候，他们很可能不会接受(包括语言在内的)传统事物。”

这种转变往往不是自发的。为了加强国家凝聚力，政府通常会通过在公共场合禁用，以及在学校中不提倡使用的方法，消灭少数民族语言。例如，以前美国政府在印地安保留地学校推行英语授课政策，这事实上就是将那瓦霍语等少数语言推上了濒危名单。但是芝加哥大学语言学系系主任Salikoko Mufwene认为，最致命的原因并不是政府政策，而是经济的全球化。他说，“美国印地安人并没有失去对他们自己语言的信心，但是他们不得不去适应社会经济压力。如果大多数生意都是用英语来谈的，他们就不能拒绝说英语。”但是，濒危语言就真的值得去挽救吗？至少，对于语言及其进化研究来讲，(不去挽救)就会导致资料的缺失，因为该研究正是基于对现存的和过去的语言的比较而进行的。当一门既无文字记录也无录音考证的语言消失时，对于科学(研究)来讲，它也就不存在了。

语言与文化也有千丝万缕的联系，因此要想单纯保存语言而不保留文化是非常困难的。“如果一个本来说那瓦霍语的人现在要改说英语，那么他准得失去点东西。”Mufwene说道。Pagel也评价道，“而且，语言多样性的丧失也使我们无法以多种方式来看待这个世界”。越来越多的证据表明，学习一门语言可以为大脑带来生理上的变化。“比如说，你我的大脑与说法语人的大脑就十分不同，”Pagel说，这是会影响我们的思维和看法的。“我们针对不同的概念建立了不同的模式和联系，这很可能就是由我们社会的语言习惯构筑而成的。”

所以，尽管语言学家已经竭尽全力，但是许多语言到了下个世纪还是会消失。但是，一种对文化认同感越来越多的关注，也许会阻止最骇人的预言成为现实。“保持语言多样性的关键在于，让人们接受主流语言的同时，也去学习他们祖先的语言。”康那狄格州纽黑文市濒危语言基金会主席Doug Whalen说道，“如果不实行双语制度，大多数濒危语言都无法生存下去。”在新西兰，为孩子们开设的课程明显减轻了毛利语所受的损害，并且重新燃起了人们对该语言的兴趣。在夏威夷，一种相似的方式使波利尼西亚语的使用者在过去数年中增长了

8,000 人。在加利福尼亚州，“学徒”计划使得数种土著语言得以生存。“学徒”志愿者与某种印地安语的最后一些使用者中的一位组成小组，学习如编织篮子这样的传统工艺，当然交流全部都是用印地安语。通常，经过 300 个小时的训练后，他们就可以流利地说了，其流利程度足以将这种语言传给他们的子女。但是 Mufwene 指出，避免语言消失并不等同于通过每天的使用赋予其新的生命。他指出，“保存语言更像用罐子保存水果。”

然而，通过保存的确可以使一门语言起死回生。已经有例子表明，有些语言通过文字记录被保存了下来，而且还在后代中得以复兴。当然，文字记录是这其中的关键。因此，单单是这种语言复兴的可能性，就使得很多说濒危语言的人试图去创造本来并不存在的文字系统。

READING PASSAGE 2

篇章结构

体裁 议论文

主题 澳大利亚的另类疗法

结构
第一段：澳大利亚人不愿意尝试另类疗法
第二段：1990年调查：更多的人正在转向另类疗法
第三段：传统医生的转变
第四段：1993年调查：病人接受另类疗法的主要原因
第五段：病人的成分
第六段：另类疗法的前景

必背词汇

标　题

cover	*v.* 涵盖；包括	regulate	*v.* 调节；控制
acupuncture	*n.* 针灸	pathway	*n.* 神经纤维；途径
ancient	*adj.* 古代的；古老的	acceptance	*n.* 接受；接纳
healing	*adj.* 有疗效的；可愈合的	establishment	*n.* 社团；机构

第一段

conservative	*adj.* 保守的；谨慎的	orthodox	*adj.* 正统的；传统的
alternative	*adj.* 另类的；二者择其一的	prescribe	*v.* 开处方；开药
therapy	*n.* 疗法；治疗	herbal	*adj.* 草药的；草本植物的
loath	*adj.* 厌恶的；不愿意的；勉强的	account for	占…比例
pretender	*n.* 冒充者；伪装者	turnover	*n.* 营业额；成交量
come into it	成功；达到目的	pharmaceuticals	*n.* 药剂；药物；药品
hand in glove	密切地；勾结地	therapist	*n.* (特定治疗法的)治疗专家
industrialised	*adj.* 工业化的	scientifically	*adv.* 科学地；按科学方法地

第二段

disenchantment	*n.* 觉醒；清醒	*chiropractor*	*n.* 按摩师；脊椎指压治疗师
popularity	*n.* 流行；普及	*naturopath*	*n.* 自然疗法医师；理疗家
contact	*v.* 与…取得联系；接触	*osteopath*	*n.* 整骨医生

acupuncturist	*n.* 针灸医生	disillusion	*v.* 使醒悟；使清醒；使梦想破灭
herbalist	*n.* 草药医生	skeptical	*adj.* 怀疑的；好猜疑的
prior to	在…之前	empirically	*adv.* 以经验为依据地；经验主义地
consultation	*n.* 咨询；会诊		
educated	*adj.* 受过教育的；有教养的	standing	*n.* 地位；身份；级别
accepting	*adj.* 易于接受的；赞同的	erode	*v.* 毁坏；削弱；损害

第三段

resist	*v.* 抵抗；反抗	financial	*adj.* 财政的；金融的
criticize	*v.* 批评；批判	bottom line	要点；关键之处
group practice	联合医疗	practitioner	*n.* 从业者；开业者
herbalism	*n.* 草药学；草本植物学	potential	*adj.* 潜在的；可能的
incentive	*n.* 动机	clientele	*n.* 客户；委托人

第四段

attend	*v.* 参加；接受	feature	*v.* 以…为特色
practice	*n.* 常规工作；业务	exodus	*n.* 大批离去
chronic	*adj.* 慢性的；长期的	couple	*v.* 把…联系起来；并提
relief	*n.* 减轻；缓解	relevant	*adj.* 有关的；相应的
comment	*vi.* 评论；注释	inadequacy	*n.* 不足；不充分
holistic	*adj.* 整体主义的；全面的	mainstream	*adj.* 主流的
approach	*n.* 方式；方法	concur	*vi.* 同意；赞同
concerned	*adj.* 关心的；关注的	bedside manner	医生对病人的态度
impersonal	*adj.* 冷淡的；无感情的	preventative	*adj.* 预防性的

第五段

musculo-skeletal	*adj.* 肌(与)骨骼的	*candida*	*n.* 假丝酵母
complaint	*n.* 疾病	represent	*v.* 相当于；相等于
digestive	*adj.* 消化的；与消化有关的	respectively	*adv.* 分别地；各自地
emotional	*adj.* 情感的；情绪的	maintenance	*n.* 维护；保持
respiratory	*adj.* 呼吸的；与呼吸有关的		

第六段

complementary	*adj.* 互补的；补充的	seek	*v.* 追求；寻求
term	*n.* 词语；术语	conventional	*adj.* 常规的；传统的
adjunct	*n.* 附属物；辅助物		

难句解析

1. We've had a tradition of doctors being fairly powerful and I guess they are pretty loath to allow any pretenders to their position to come into it.

参考译文：我们有个传统，医生是相当权威的，我猜他们很不愿意让那些觊觎他们位置的冒牌货得逞。

结构分析：在这句话当中，being fairly powerful 是现在分词做定语来修饰 doctors。

语言点：

(1) **allow 的用法**

① allow sb. to do sth. 允许某人做某事

② allow for 考虑到；顾及到；体谅，例如，

We must allow for the possibility that the train might be late.

我们必须考虑到火车有可能晚点。

He is naughty but you have to allow for his age.

他是很淘气，但是你要考虑到他的年龄。

③ allow of 容许。例如，

Such conduct allows of no excuse. 这种行为无可辩解。

(2) to one's position 中的 position 是"地位，职位"的意思

与 position 有关的词组还有：

① be in a position to do sth. 有可能做某事。例如，

I am not in a position to answer this question. 我不能回答这个问题。

② in position 在恰当的位置

The players are in position. 球员已经各就各位。

③ out of position 在不恰当的位置。例如，

Everything is out of position. 所有的事情都一团糟。

2. The 550,000 consultations with alternative therapists reported in the 1990 survey represented about an eighth of the total number of consultations with medically qualified personnel.

参考译文：根据 1990 年调查的报道，另类疗法医生进行了 55 万次诊断，这个数字几乎占了调查中所有医疗诊断的八分之一。

结构分析：这句话的主语是 consultations, reported 是过去分词做定语，修饰 consultations。谓语是 represented，宾语是 an eighth of the total number of consultations。

语言点：过去分词做定语

过去分词做定语的时候，需要注意：过去分词的位置不同，词义也不一样，例如，

I found a concerned look in her eyes. 我发现她眼中关切的目光。

all parties concerned 相关团体

3. An increasing exodus from their clinics, coupled with this and a number of other relevant surveys carried out in Australia, all pointing to orthodox doctor' s inadequacies, have led mainstream doctors themselves to begin to admit they could learn from the personal style of alternative therapists.

参考译文：病人从诊所中大批离去，加上其他一些相关的全国性调查的结果，矛头直指正统医生的不足之处，这就使得他们开始承认应该学习一下另类疗法医师的亲切态度。

结构分析：exodus 以及 this and a number of other relevant surveys 是主语，谓语是 have led...to...，all pointing to...则是现在分词做定语，来限定主语。

试题分析

Questions 14 －15

- 题目类型：MULTIPLE CHOICE
- 题目解析：

题号	定位词	文中对应点	题解
14	Western	第一段首句	A 答案说澳大利亚医生与制药公司关系紧密，属于完全未提及型答案。B 答案认为澳大利亚医生总是和其他医师一同工作，与文中所说的事实恰好相反。 D 答案说澳大利亚医生会开出另类处方，这也是不正确的。只有 C 答案与文章叙述相符。
15	Americans	第一段倒数第二句	文中这句话说 1990 年美国人去看另类疗法医师的次数比去看传统医生的次数还多。所以答案 B 是正确的。而 A、C 和 D 答案中提到的比较关系并不存在。

Questions 16 －23

- 题目类型：TRUE/FALSE/NOT GIVEN
- 题目解析：

16. Australians have been turning to alternative therapies in increasing numbers over the

past 20 years.

译文	在过去20年当中，越来越多的澳大利亚人开始求助于另类疗法了。
定位词	20 years
解题关键字	turning to / increasing number
文中对应点	第二段首句。在过去20年中，由于人们对传统医疗不再迷信，另类疗法在澳大利亚慢慢流行起来。这句话就证明在过去20年里，比以往更多的澳大利亚人开始相信另类疗法。 turn to 求助于，例如，I don't know who to turn to. 我不知道该向谁求助。
答案	YES

17. Between 1983 and 1990 the numbers of patients visiting alternative therapists rose to include a further 8% of the population.

译文	在1983到1990年间，看另类医师的患者人数已经增长了总人口的8%。
定位词	1983 / 1990
解题关键字	a further 8%
文中对应点	第二段第二句话和第三句话。在1983年的调查中，约有1.9%的人说他们曾经看过另类疗法医师，到了1990年，这个数字上升到了总人口的2.6%。如果做减法的话，实际上人数上升了将近0.7个百分点，因此题目中所说的增加8%是错误的。
答案	NO

18. The 1990 survey related to 550,000 consultations with alternative therapists.

译文	1990年的调查涉及到了55万件另类疗法诊断。
定位词	550,000
解题关键字	relate to
文中对应点	第二段第四句话。本题关键在于理解词组relate to的意思 作为及物动词，relate有“讲述，叙述”的意思，例如， He related his experiences in Mexico. 他讲述了他在墨西哥的经历。 relate还有“证明…之间联系”的意思，例如， relate one's work to society 把工作和社会联系起来 作为不及物动词，relate通常有“关联；适用；适应；符合；认同”等意思，例如，relating to 有关；关于；涉及
答案	YES

19. In the past, Australians had a higher opinion of doctors than they do today.

译文	过去澳大利亚人对医生的评价比现在高。
定位词	doctors / 或者可以按照顺序原则从 18 题定位处向下寻找
解题关键字	had a higher opinion of ...
文中对应点	第二段末句。结果，包括医生在内的专业人士的崇高地位也就大打折扣。这句话的含义就是澳大利亚人以前对医生等专业人士有较高的评价，而现在这种观点已经遭受损害。 have a...opinion of 对…抱…态度
答案	YES

20. Some Australian doctors are retraining in alternative therapies.

译文	有些澳大利亚医生在接受另类疗法的再培训。
定位词	Australian doctors
解题关键字	retrain
文中对应点	第三段首句。take courses themselves 这个语言点就表明澳大利亚正统医生正在接受另类疗法培训，相当于以前他们接受的正统医疗培训来说，这次培训无疑是一种再培训。
答案	YES

21. Alternative therapists earn higher salaries than doctors.

译文	另类疗法医师比正统医生赚得多。
定位词	salaries
解题关键字	higher
文中对应点	第三段。并不存在的比较关系是 TRUE/FALSE/NOT GIVEN 题解题的一条黄金法则。尤其当作者将两者进行简单肤浅比较的时候，一般答案都是 NOT GIVEN。文中没有任何地方提到两种医生的薪水，证明这一点的最简单的方法就是在第三段寻找钱的符号。
答案	NOT GIVEN

22. The 1993 Sydney survey involved 289 patients who visited alternative therapists for acupuncture treatment.

译文	1993 年悉尼的调查包括了 289 名去看另类疗法医生寻求针灸治疗的患者。
定位词	1993 / 289

解题关键字	acupuncture treatment
文中对应点	第四段首句和第二句。289 名病患去看病的这 8 家诊所提供各种各样的另类疗法服务，这其中也许包括针灸疗法，但是如果说这 289 名病人都是去做针灸的，就未免有些以偏概全了。
答案	NO

23. All the patients in the 1993 Sydney survey had long-term medical complaints.

译文	1993 年悉尼调查中所有的病人都患有长期疾病。
定位	词 1993 / long-term
解题关键字	all / medical complaints
文中对应点	第四段第三句 chronic 是“长期的；慢性的”意思，complaints 在此处不是“抱怨；投诉”的意思，而是指疾病。
答案	YES

Questions 24 —26

- 题目类型：Picture Naming
- 题目解析：

解题关键：要读清题目要求，看清所填字数是不超过三个词。数字是本题目的关键，首先可以利用 musculo-skeletal 和一系列的百分数将本题定位在第五段。 然后通过对空格的 BAR 所对应的数字回文中定位，进而解题。

24. 目测该数字应该在 10% 和 15% 之间，在第五段寻找这样一个数字，结果发现 12% 所对应的是 digestive 一词，但是，很快我们会发现 Digestive 已经出现在了表格上，所以答案应该是比 12% 少一个百分点的 emotional / emotional problems。

25. 该疾病所对应的数字应该在 5% 和 10% 之间，而且应该比第 26 空更接近 10%。所以可以回第五段找两个相近并且都接近 10% 的数字，结果发现了 6% 和 5%，故此空应该填：headache。

26. 该疾病对应数字是 5%，故应该填 general ill health。

参考译文

澳大利亚的另类疗法

1994年初，澳大利亚第一批另类疗法学生在悉尼科技大学开始了他们为期四年的全职课程。除了学习其他一些疗法之外，他们的课程还包括针灸术。他们所学的理论基于中国古代对这门古老疗法的解释：那就是针灸可以调节“气”或能量在人体神经系统中的流通。这门课程足以反映另类疗法在争取医疗机构认同的斗争中所取得的成果。

由于对自然或另类疗法所采取的极端保守态度，澳大利亚在西方国家中独树一帜。悉尼大学公共健康系博士 Paul Laver 评价道：“我们有个传统，医生是相当权威的，我猜他们很不愿意让那些觊觎他们位置的冒牌货得逞。”在其他许多工业国家里，正统医生和另类医师早已亲密无间地合作多年了。在欧洲，只有正统医生才可以开草药。在德国，草药占了药品销售额的 10%。1990 年美国人去看另类疗法医师的次数比去看传统医生的次数还多，而每年，他们花在未经科学测试的疗法上的钱竟高达约 120 亿美元。

在过去 20 年中，由于人们对传统医疗不再迷信，另类疗法在澳大利亚慢慢流行起来。在 1983 年进行的全国健康调查中，有 1.9% 的人说此前两周内曾经去看过按摩师、理疗家、整骨医师、针灸医生或草药医生。到了 1990 年，这个数字已经攀升到澳大利亚人口的 2.6%。根据 Laver 博士和他的同事们刊登在 1993 年《澳大利亚公共健康期刊》上的报道：在 1990 年调查中，另类疗法医生进行了 55 万次诊断，这个数字几乎占了调查中所有医疗诊断的八分之一。“总体而言，受过良好教育又不那么轻信的民众已经对专家失望了，而且对科学和经验主义知识已经越来越怀疑了，”博士们说，“结果，包括医生在内的专业人士的崇高地位也就大打折扣。”

越来越多的澳大利亚医生，特别是那些年轻一些的医师，非但没有抵制或是批判这样一个潮流，反而开始与另类疗法医师联合开业，或是干脆自己去学习相关课程，尤其是针灸和草药医学。Laver 博士说，部分动机当然是出于经济考虑。“关键在于大多数全科医生都是商人。如果他们看到潜在的客户去别处看病，他们就想也要能提供类似的服务。”

1993 年，Laver 博士和他的同事们发表了一项调查报告，报告包括 289 名曾到 8 家另类疗法诊所寻求治疗的悉尼市民。这些诊所共有 25 名另类治疗师，提供相当广泛的另类疗法。接受调查的人都患有慢性疾病，正统疗法治疗对这些疾病的效果微乎其微。病人们评价说他们喜欢另类疗法医师所采取的全面的治疗手段，也喜欢那里友善热情、细致入微的关怀。这次调查揭示了正统医生的冷漠态度。病人从诊所中大批离去，加上其他一些相关的全国性调查的结果，矛头直指正统医生的不足之处，这就使得他们开始承认应该学习一下另类疗法医师的亲切态度。就连皇家医学院的 Patrik Stone 博士也赞同说，正统医生应该多学习另类疗法医师对待病人的态度，还有他们给病人的预防建议。

根据《澳大利亚公共健康期刊》，18% 的病人因为得了肌肉骨骼方面的疾病而去看另类医师；12% 的人则是因为消化系统疾病，这个数字只比因为感情问题而去就医的人多 1 个百分点。呼吸系统疾病患者和假丝酵母过敏者各占 7%。头疼就医者和整体感觉身体不适而就医者分别占到了 6% 和 5%，还有 4% 的人看医生只是为了保持身体健康。

这项调查表明，与另类疗法这个字眼相比，互补疗法是个更为合适的称呼。前者听起来仿佛是正统疗法的附庸，一种只有当你对传统疗法的无能为力失望后，才会去追寻的东西。

READING PASSAGE 3

篇章结构

体裁 说明文

主题 玩耍的重要性

结构
A 段：玩耍及其危险性
B 段：玩耍对动物来讲很重要
C 段：练习理论的错误
D 段：支能训练假说的不足之处
E 段：玩耍与脑子大小的关系
F 段：玩耍的时机很重要
G 段：玩耍刺激大脑发育
H 段：玩耍激活高级认知活动
I 段：如果失去玩耍，人类将会怎样

必背词汇

A 段

serious	*adj.* 严肃的；认真的	adulthood	*n.* 成人期
bushiness	*n.* 事情；事物	come along	出现；发生
engross	*v.* (使)全神关注；吸引	juvenile	*adj.* 青少年的
make-believe	*adj.* 虚幻的；假装的	*fur seal*	*n.* 海狗
cub	*n.* 幼兽；幼崽	pup	*n.* 幼崽；幼年
kitten	*n.* 小猫	spot	*v.* 发现；看到
tease	*v.* 戏弄；逗弄	predator	*n.* 捕食者；掠食者
string	*n.* 线绳；细绳	approach	*v.* 接近；逼近
carefree	*adj.* 无忧无虑的；轻松愉快的	playful	*adj.* 爱嬉戏的；顽皮的
exuberant	*adj.* 充满活力的；精力旺盛的	cavort	*vi.* 欢腾；雀跃；嬉戏

B 段

developmental	*adj.* 发育的；成长的	tail-wagging	*n.* 摇尾巴
hiccup	*n.* 打嗝；短暂的中断；间歇	indicate	*v.* 象征；表示
evolve	*vi.* 发展；进化	superficially	*adv.* 表面地；表面性地
intelligent	*adj.* 聪明的；有才智的	resemble	*v.* 相像；类似
playfulness	*n.* 玩耍；嬉戏；顽皮	in earnest	认真地
indulge	*v.* 使自己沉溺于；满足欲望	mate	*v.* 成配偶；交配
unique	*adj.* 独一无二的；独特的	socialize	*vi.* 参加社交；交往；交际

in shape	健康；处于良好状态	endurance	*n.* 忍耐度；持久力
respiratory	*adj.* 呼吸的；用作呼吸的	question	*v.* 怀疑；疑问

C 段

permanent	*adj.* 永久的；持久的	advantageous	*adj.* 有利的；有益的
point out	指出；指明	peak	*vi.* 达到顶点
result from	由于；因为	halfway	*adv.* 到一半
function	*n.* 作用；功能	suckling stage	哺乳期
optimum	*adj.* 最佳的；最适宜的		

D 段

skills-training	*n.* 技能训练	simplistic	*adj.* 过分简单化的；被过分简单化的
hypothesis	*n.* 假说；假设		
at first glance	乍看	behavioural	*adj.* 关于行为的；行为方面的；行为学的
practise	*v.* 练习；实践		
complex	*adj.* 复杂的；综合的	ecologist	*n.* 生态学家
manoeuver	*n.* 策略；花招	look at	研究；查看
inspection	*n.* 观察；视察	predatory	*adj.* 掠食的；食肉的
reveal	*v.* 展现；揭露	prowess	*n.* 杰出的才能；高超的技巧
interpretation	*n.* 解释；阐释		

E 段

positive	*adj.* 积极的；实际的	converse	*n.* 相反的事物；反面
measurement	*n.* 测量；度量	sensitive	*adj.* 敏感的；灵敏的
order	*n.* 种类；(生物)目	stimuli	*n.* (stimulus的复数)刺激；激励
given	*adj.* 指定的；特定的	mould	*v.* 使…形成；塑造

F 段

timing	*n.* 时机掌握；时间安排	window	*n.* (喻)获得信息的渠道；阶段
stage	*n.* 阶段；时期	modify	*v.* 修改；更改
clue	*n.* 线索；暗示	ease	*n.* 不费力；悠闲
plot	*v.* 图示；以图表画出	infant	*n.* 婴儿
devote	*v.* 把…专用于	absorb	*v.* 理解；掌握
course	*n.* 过程；经过	intense	*adj.* 剧烈的；强烈的
associated with	与…联系		

G 段

activate	*v*. 使开始起作用；激活	kaleidoscope	*n*. 万花筒；变化多端；千变万化
coyote	*n*. 土狼；山狗	context	*n*. 背景；环境
markedly	*adv*. 显著地；明显地	predation	*n*. 捕食；捕猎
variable	*adj*. 不定的；可变的	aggression	*n*. 进攻；攻击
unpredictable	*adj*. 不可预测的；不可预知的	reproduction	*n*. 繁殖
reason	*vi*. 推理；推测		
liken	*v*. 把…比作		

H 段

stimulation	*n*. 刺激；激励	flexibility	*n*. 弹性；适应性
suspect	*v*. 猜想；推测	improved	*adj*. 改良的；改善的
cognitive	*adj*. 认知的；感知的	potential	*n*. 潜能；潜力
enormous	*adj*. 巨大的；庞大的	back up	支持
involvement	*n*. 包含；包括；卷入；牵连	bout	*n*. 一段时间；一回合
assessment	*n*. 评估；评价	activation	*n*. 活化；激活
playmate	*n*. 玩伴	light up	点燃；激活
reciprocity	*n*. 互惠；相互依存；相关性	link-up	*n*. 连接；会合
specialised	*adj*. 专门的；专科的	enhance	*v*. 提高；提升

I 段

creativity	*n*. 创造力；创造	peer	*n*. 同龄人；同辈人
experimentation	*n*. 实验	schooling	*n*. 学校教育；学费
raise	*v*. 养育；喂养	exam-oriented	*adj*. 从…考试出发的；以考试为目标的
deny	*v*. 拒绝给予；拒绝要求	look-in	*n*. 一瞥；受到注意的份儿；成功的机会
apply	*v*. 应用；使用；适用		
interact	*v*. 互动；互相作用		

难句解析

1. Eighty per cent of deaths among juvenile fur seals occur because playing pups fail to spot predators approaching.

参考译文：百分之八十的小海狗死亡都是因为玩耍中的小海狗没能看到接近的捕食者。

语言点：fail的用法

(1) fail to do sth. 没能做某事

Doctors failed to save the girl's life.

医生没能挽救那个女孩的性命。

(2) fail 失败；使失望；失去

Millions of people have tried to quit smoking and failed miserably.

数百万人试图戒烟，但是都一败涂地。

She had to leave immediately, before her courage failed her.

她要在失去勇气之前赶紧离开。

I failed my parents by not spending more time with them.

我没有足够的时间陪父母，这让他们很失望。

(3) without fail 务必；必定

I want that work finished tomorrow, without fail. 这项工作明天务必完成。

2. Animals at play often use unique signs — tail-wagging in dogs, for example — to indicate that activity superficially resembling adult behaviour is not really in earnest.

参考译文：玩耍中的动物会用一些独特的标志——比如狗摇尾巴——来表明这种简单模仿大动物行为的举动并不是玩真的。

结构分析：这句话的主语是 animals，谓语是 use，宾语是 signs，双破折号当中的部分是插入语成分，在做题的时候可以忽略不计，to indicate 是宾语补足语，indicate 后面跟了一个宾语从句，activity 是宾语从句的主语，is 是谓语，in earnest 是表语，resembling 是现在分词做定语用来修饰 activity。

语言点：现在分词做定语

现在分词做定语的用法：

(1) 特指，名词后面现在分词做定语多数表示正在进行的动作，例如，

The girl riding the bike is my sister. 正在骑车的那个女孩是我的妹妹。

(2) 泛指，名词后面现在分词做定语多数表示一般动作，例如，

Men breaking the law will be punished. 违法的人要受到惩罚。

这里的 men 是泛指。

(3) 用作定语的现在分词一般都能被定语从句替代。

Can you see the boy playing on the ground?

Can you see the boy who is playing on the ground?

你能看到那个在操场上玩耍的男孩吗？

(4) 但是现在分词作定语只能用来叙述与谓语动作差不多同时发生的动作。

(5) 现在分词完成时 having done 一般不能作定语，但可以作状语，例如，

Having finished all his work, Jack left his workplace.

杰克做完活后，离开了工作场所。

3. I concluded it' s to do with learning, and with the importance of environmental data to the brain during development.

参考译文：我的结论是，玩耍与学习有关，也与大脑发育过程中环境资料的重要性有关。

结构分析：Conclude 引导宾语从句，宾语从句的主语是 it，指代上文提到过的玩耍，it is to do with 意思是 it has something to do with learning, 指“与…有关”。

语言点：代词指代成分的用法

阅读时候容易给大家造成困难的句子之一就是有代词指代成分的句子。比如，

Long accustomed to the assumption that each generation would be able to maintain a higher standard of living than its parents, children of the middle and working class are today facing the bleak reality that they may have to be fortunate as well as hardworking in order to do even as well as their parents did.

这句话很长，但主语却很简单，是 children, 谓语是 are facing, 宾语是 reality, that 引导了同位语从句。分析这种长难句的关键是绕过混淆成分，抓住主谓宾。

4. Bekoff likens it to a behavioural kaleidoscope, with animals at play jumping rapidly between activities.

参考译文：由于动物们在玩耍时行为总是迅速转换，Becoff 将玩耍比喻为一个行为万花筒。

语言点：

(1) liken...to...将…比喻为。例如，

① Critics have likened the new theater to a supermarket. 评论家将新的剧院比喻为超市。

② Sydney Opera House has been likened to everything from broken egg shells to sails of a sailing ship. 悉尼歌剧院被比喻为很多东西，从碎蛋壳到帆船船帆。

(2) with 可以引导伴随成分和原因状语。例如，

With all this work to do, I don' t know if I' ll have time to go out. 由于有这么多工作要做，我不知道还有没有时间出去。

He' s in bed with flu. 他感冒卧床不起了。

5. We already know that rat pups denied the chance to play grow smaller brain components and fail to develop the ability to apply social rules when they interact with their peers.

参考译文：我们已经知道，没有机会玩耍的小老鼠，大脑各部分发育得比较小，同时也不具备运用社会规则与其他小老鼠交流的能力。

结构分析：know that 后面引导宾语从句，宾语从句的主语是 rat pups, 谓语是 grow 和 fail to develop, denied the chance 是过去分词做定语来限定 rat pups。

语言点： deny 的用法

(1) 否认；否定。例如，

I' ve never denied that there is a problem between us. 我从未否认过我们之间有问题。

(2) deny sb. sth. 拒绝某人某事。例如，

She could deny her son nothing. 她无法拒绝儿子的任何请求。

(3) There' s no denying that...不可否认…，例如，

There' s no denying that this is an important event. 这不可否认是件大事。

(4) deny oneself sth.节制。例如，

He denied himself all everything. 他什么也不享受。

(5) deny oneself to...不会见；谢绝。例如，

She denied herself to all visitors. 她什么人都不见。

试题分析

Questions 27 —32

- 题目类型：LIST OF HEADINGS
- 题目解析：

题号	定位词	文中对应点	题解
27	unsusual connection	H 段末句 by allowing link-ups between...	link-up 等于 connection，后面的 play may enhance creativity 证明这种不寻常的联系是有好处的。 答案是 H
28	record/time	F 段的第二句 If you plot the amount of time...	这个 heading 的意思是由记录小动物玩耍的时间而得到的见解，关键词是时间，回到文章当中寻找对应词时，只有这个段落提到了时间。plot 一词是用图表记录的意思，在这里就等同于 record。 答案是 F
29	physical hazard	A 段中部第四行：For a start, play can even cost animals their lives.之后	问题是问哪一段包含有对玩耍带来的危险的描述。文章中只有在第一段中谈到了玩耍可能带来的危险，而且还举出了小海狗的例子来说明这种危险的存在。 答案是 A

题号	定位词	文中对应点	题解
30	mental/ exercise/ develop	H 段前三句	mental activity 是大脑活动的意思，问题问的是在玩耍过程当中，哪些大脑活动得到了练习和发展。 答案是 H
31	effects / reduction	I 段首句和二句	问题问得是哪一段包含了这样的内容：减少玩耍机会可能对儿童造成的影响。在最后一段中，作者谈到了被剥夺了玩耍机会的小老鼠大脑就发育的不好，并且用一个设问句表明了他对人类儿童的忧虑。 而且一般来讲，含有 effect 的段意都是对应文章的最后一段。 答案是 I
32	class / animals	B 段中的 Playfulness, it seems, is common only among mammals...	这一段是比较难选择的。问题中问道玩耍对于哪种动物来说很重要。Animal和class是比较难找到的定位词，只能先做掉其他题目，然后再在剩下的段落中寻找。B 段中提到了玩耍在哺乳动物中很普遍，而且在有些鸟类当中也存在，即提到了各种各样的动物。一些同学会在 E 段当中看到 fifteen orders of mammals 一词，不过仔细读下来，E 段的主要意思是在讲哺乳动物中大脑大小和玩耍之间的关系，并不是说玩耍对哪种动物重要。故答案选 B

Questions 33 —35

- 题目类型：MULTIPLE CHOICE
- 题目解析：

下列是一些看待玩耍的方式，列出作者提到的三种方式：

题号	定位词	文中对应点	题解
33	rehearsal/ adult	B 段	B 段倒数第二句：A popular explanation of play has been that it helps juvenile develop the skills they will need to hunt, mate and socialize as adults.
34	build up strength	B 段	B 段末句：Another has been that it allows young animals to get in shape for adult life...

题号	定位词	文中对应点	题解
35	organ growth	E 段	E 段首句：...reported that there is a strong positive link between brain size and playfulness...

Questions 36 —40

- 题目类型：MATCHING
- 题目解析：

LIST OF FINDINGS

A. 玩耍与大脑中的一种特殊物质有关。

B. 玩耍提供了有关周围环境的信息。

C. 进化历史的不同阶段对应着不同种类的玩耍活动。

D. 脑子小的哺乳动物玩得少一些。

E. 玩耍并不是一种为将来进行的体能训练。

F. 有些脑子比较大的鸟类也玩耍。

G. 玩耍会综合很多种行为。

H. 玩耍是一种教授生存技能的方式。

人物加理论题目的解题技巧：

- 用人名到文中定位
- 在人名周围寻找宾语从句或直接引语
- 回理论库对应

题号	定位词	文中对应点	解题关键字	题解
36	Robert Barton	E 段倒数第四行	physical surrounding	I concluded it' s to do with learning, and with the importance of environmental data to... Barton 认为玩耍与学习有关，也与大脑发育过程中环境资料的重要性有关。Environmental data 可以与 physical surroundings 对应。答案是 B
37	Marc Becoff	G 段	a wide range of	Bekoff likens it to a behavioural kaleidoscope... Becoff将玩耍比喻为一个行为万花筒，这句话也就是说在玩耍当中动物会做出各种各样

题号	定位词	文中对应点	解题关键字	题解
				的举动，正好和H选项中的a wide range of 相对应。 答案是G
38	John Byers	C段	not/ fitness	Byers points out that the benefits of increased exercise disappear rapidly after training stops, so... Byers 认为训练一结束，由增强训练所带来的好处就跟着迅速消失了，无论什么种群的动物，玩耍都倾向于在哺乳期的中期达到顶峰，然后则开始走了下坡路。这就与E答案观点一致。 答案是E
39	Sergio Pellis	E段	mammal / smaller / less	...reported that there is a strong positive link between brain size and playfulness among mammals in general. Pellis 认为哺乳动物的玩耍量与他们大脑的大小往往成正比。所以玩耍比较少的动物脑子也比较小。 答案是D
40	Stephen Siviy	H段	specific substance/ brain	Siviy studied how bouts of play affected the brain' s levels of a particular chemical associated with.. Siviy 认为玩耍能够影响大脑中一种特殊化学物质，这种物质会刺激神经细胞生长。 答案选A

参考译文

玩耍是件严肃的事

玩耍能否帮助大脑发育得更大更好？ Bryant Furlow 就此展开了调查。

A 玩耍是件严肃的事。孩子们沉溺在假想的世界中，狐狸幼崽儿嬉戏打闹，小猫玩线球，这些行为都不只是取乐而已。看上去玩耍是成人世界的辛苦工作到来之前，无忧无虑、精力充沛的消磨时光的方式，其实远非如此。首先，玩耍可能使动物们送命。比如，百分之八十的小海狗死亡都是因为玩耍中的小海狗没能看到接近的捕食者。玩耍也是相当消耗精力的。顽皮的小动物要花上百分之二三的精力来嬉戏打闹，而对于儿童而言，这个数字可以高达百分之十五。"就算只有百分之二三也是个不小的数目了。" Idaho 大学的 John Byers 说道，"你很难发现动物们如此消耗精力。" Byers 补充说。总有一定的原因使他们这么做。

B 但是，如果玩耍不像生物学家们过去认为的那样，只是发育过程中的小插曲的话，那么到底是什么促使了玩耍的发展呢？最新的观点认为玩耍可以促进大脑的发育。换句话说，玩耍使你变得聪明。尽管一些脑子比较大的鸟类也沉溺其中，但玩耍好像还是只在哺乳动物中普遍存在。玩耍中的动物会用一些独特的标志——比如狗摇尾巴——来表明这种简单模仿大动物行为的举动并不是玩真的。一种有关玩耍的普遍观点说，玩耍能帮助小动物发展成年之后捕猎、交配以及社交所需要的技能。另一个理论认为，通过增强小动物的呼吸耐力，玩耍可以帮助他们在体力上更适应成年生活。但是这两个理论近年来都遭到了置疑。

C 就拿锻炼理论来说吧。如果玩耍是为了增强肌肉，或是进行某种耐力训练，那么我们应该能够看到一些终生的效果。但是 Byers 指出，训练一结束，由增强训练所带来的好处就随之迅速消失了， 所以，任何通过小时候的玩耍增强的耐力到了成年阶段就会消失殆尽了。"如果玩耍的作用就是使身体健康的话，" Byers 说道，"那么玩耍的最佳时间就应该是对于某种小动物(身体发展)最有利的时间，但是，实际情况并非如此。" 无论什么种群的动物，玩耍都倾向于在哺乳期的中期达到顶峰，然后则开始走下坡路。

D 接着，我们又有了技能训练假说。乍看上去，玩耍的小动物好像是在练习那些成年时必须的复杂动作。但是，更为仔细的观察表明，这种解释把问题简单化了。在某项研究中，California 大学的行为生态学家 Tim Caro 观察了小猫的捕食游戏以及它们成年之后的捕猎行为。他发现，小猫玩耍的方式对成年后的捕猎技能并没有太大的影响。

E 今年早些时候，加拿大 Lethbridge 大学的 Sergio Pellis 公布说，哺乳动物的玩耍量与他们大脑的大小往往成正比。在比较了十五种哺乳动物的测量数据之后，Sergio 和他的研究小组发现，更多的玩耍会造就大一些的脑子(与身体大小比较而言)，而且这个理论反过来也成立。Durham 大学的 Robert Barton 认为，由于大一些的脑子比小一些的脑子对发育刺激更敏感，因此它们需要更多的玩耍来促进它们发育至成年期。他说："我的结论是，玩耍与学习有关，也与大脑发育过程中环境资料的重要性有关。"

F 根据 Byers 的理论，对于小动物而言，玩耍期的时机对未来的发展至关重要。如果你用图表来表明在发育期间，小动物每天用于玩耍的时间的话，就会发现一种一般与"敏感期"相关联的模式。所谓"敏感期"指的是发育过程中一个短暂的阶段，在这一阶段中，大脑会获得此前和此后都不可能获得的改变。想想孩子们在学习语言时那种婴儿们和大人们都无法做到的得心应手吧。其他学者也发现，猫、田鼠和家鼠最爱玩耍的时期恰好是这扇"机会之窗"达到峰值的时候。

G "人们没有充分注意到玩耍激活了大脑多少部件。" Colorado 大学的 Marc Bekoff 说。Becoff 研究了玩耍的小土狼，发现其中所涉及的行为显然比成年土狼的花样更多，更不可预测。他推断，这样的行为能激活大脑许多不同的部分。由于动物们在玩耍时行为总是迅速地变换，Becoff 将玩耍比喻为一个行为万花筒。"他们会做出不同环境所需要的动作——捕猎，进攻，繁殖等，而他们正在发育的大脑获得了各种各样的刺激。"

H 大脑不仅比猜想中更多地参与玩耍，而且好像还能够激活更高级的认知过程。"玩耍中有很多的认知成分。" Bekoff 指出。玩耍通常包括对玩伴的评估，互相依存的观念，以及特殊标志及规则的使用。他认为玩耍会创造一个更具行为灵活性，在今后生活中更多学习潜力的大脑。这一观点得到了 Gettysburg 学院 Stephen Siviy 研究结果的支持。Siviy 认为玩耍能够影响大脑中一种特殊化学物质的分泌，这种物质会刺激神经细胞生长。他被这种刺激可能达到的程度吓了一跳。"玩耍使一切都变得活泼起来。"通过使大脑中不常交流的部分产生联系，玩耍也许会提高创造力。

I 进一步的实验又会对如今许多社会中，孩子们被养育的方式有何影响呢？我们已经知道，没有机会玩耍的小老鼠，大脑各部分发育得比较小，同时也不具备运用社会规则与其他小老鼠交流的能力。在上学年龄越来越早，学校教育越来越应试化的今天，大家对玩耍的作用不屑一顾。谁会知道这样做会带来什么样的影响呢？

WRITING

WRITING TASK 1

考官范文

The line graph compares the typical daily demands for electricity in winter and summer in England. As can be seen, the electricity consumption in winter almost doubles that in summer at any given moment of a day. The former waves between 30,000 and 45,000 units, while the latter fluctuates between 13,000 and 20,000 units. Their development trends see more similarities than differences. From 0 to 9 o'clock, both curves move generally downward to the lowest points of more than 30,000 units and 13,000 units, and from then on, the two lines go roughly upward, respectively to the highest amount of 45,000 units at 21 o'clock and more than 20,000 units at 13 o'clock.

The pie chart reflects an average household use of electricity in England. Heating for both room and water accounts for the biggest share of more than half. The other half of electricity is almost evenly used for three sections: ovens, kettles, washing machines; lighting, TV, radio, and vacuum cleaners, food mixers, electric tools. The first section consumes a little bit higher of 17.5% while the rest two have an equal share of 15%.

From the two charts, it is clear that electricity is in higher demand in winter in England.

分析

这道图表作文题是个组合图，由曲线图和饼状图构成。写的时候，两个图分别各写一段，然后把两个图的最突出的特点总结一下，作为结尾。

曲线图部分需要描述冬季和夏季用电在一天里的变化以及两者之间的对比。文章首先进行对比，指出冬季用电基本上是夏季用电的两倍。然后用具体的数字来加以说明。接下来描写冬季和夏季用电在一天 24 小时里的变化趋势，其中重点描写用电的最高峰和最低点。

饼状图部分描述英国家庭用电的范围。首先描述比例最大的部分，然后按照大小顺序逐一描述。

文章结尾简单总结一下两个图的共同之处：图一体现的是冬季用电量超过夏季，而图二显示一半以上的电被用来给房间加热以及制造热水。所以，可以得出结论：冬季对于电的需求要比夏季大。

WRITING TASK 2

题目要求

Happiness is considered very important in life.
Why is it difficult to define?
What factors are important in achieving happiness?

题解

这道考题比较抽象。题目由三部分构成。首先是一句陈述句：幸福在我们生活中很重要。然后是两个问题：为什么很难对幸福下定义？要想获得幸福需要具备什么重要因素？

考生需要注意的是，题目中的陈述句是一个事实，不需要多费笔墨加以论证。这个事实的主要作用是为接下来的问题进行铺垫。关键是要回答问题。

范文一

It is a truism to say that happiness is very important in life. However, it is not an easy concept to define directly, even though we all know when we are happy and when we are unhappy. It has to be defined indirectly, through the things that we normally associate with happiness. These things include such things as looking forward to every day, to enjoying one's work and life in general, to sleeping well, and to laughing easily. Happiness may also be described as the absence of such negative, unwelcome things as crying, being disappointed in love, feeling under stress and, in extreme cases, clinical depression. These factors are all forms of behavior, feelings or attitudes.

Many psychologists and philosophers have paid great attention to what factors are important in achieving happiness, and have written many profound books on the subject. But it seems to me that these factors are in large measure common sense. They include such things as being brought up in a stable, loving family and learning how to enjoy work and study, as well as play. Parents, teachers and other adults also play a very important role in helping children grow up into people who relate well to others, whether strangers, acquaintances, colleagues or friends, and, most importantly, people one falls in love with. They also play a key role in helping young people develop a healthy, constructive attitude to coping with disappointment.

The truth of the above has been validated many times in my own personal life. However, I will end with mentioning something I read that might contradict much of it. Some psychologists say each individual is born with a genetically determined 'happiness level', to which, after no matter what disappointment or during what suffering, they tend to return to after a period of weeks or months.

分析

文章在第一段回答第一个问题。首先，幸福的确很重要。但是，很难直接对幸福下定义，即使我们都知道并体验过幸福和不幸福的状态。幸福只能通过间接方法，通过我们通常认为与幸福相关的一些东西来界定。比如对于每天的期盼，喜欢工作和生活，睡得香，经常笑等等。或者我们也可以认为幸福就是没有负面情绪，比如哭泣，失恋，压力重重，甚至得抑郁症等等。这些因素都是一些行为，情绪或是态度。本段通过这些例子充分说明了很难对幸福下定义的原因。

文章第二段指出，许多心理学家和哲学家对如何获得幸福非常关注，并且写了许多有关的高深书籍。但是作者觉得这些因素其实都是些常识。获得幸福需要成长在一个稳定而又充满爱心的家庭，学习如何享受工作、学习和玩耍。家长、老师和其他成年人也在小孩成长过程中扮演重要角色，帮助孩子们正确对待陌生人、同事、朋友和爱人。年轻人也从大人身上学习如何处理失望等负面情绪。本段分析了获得幸福的一些要素，也就是回答了第二个问题。

在文章结尾段，作者说自己的亲身经历充分证明了要想得到幸福所必须具备的要素。接下来，作者来了一个转折，说曾经读到过似乎和刚才的论述矛盾的一种说法。一些心理学家说每个人都天生一种特定的"幸福水平"。无论经历了什么样的失望或是磨难，人们在一段时间以后总会回到这种幸福水平上。这个结尾似乎和作者前面的论述自相矛盾，其实进一步说明了幸福作为一种状态，真的是众说纷纭，很难对此下定义，似乎也不一定非得具备什么要素。与文章开头形成前后呼应。

范文二

Happiness is very difficult to define, because it means so many different things to different people. While some people link happiness to wealth and material success, others think it lies in emotions and loving personal relationships. Yet others think that spiritual paths, rather than either the material world or relationships with people, are the only way to true happiness.

Because people interpret happiness for themselves in so many different ways, it is difficult to give any definition that is true for everyone. However, if there are different kinds of happiness for different individuals then the first step in achieving it would be to have a degree of self-knowledge. A person needs to know who he or she is before being able to know what it is that makes him or her happy.

Of course, factors such as loving relationships, good health, the skills to earn a living and a peaceful environment all contribute to our happiness too. But this does not mean that people without these conditions cannot be happy.

Overall, I think an ability to keep clear perspectives in life is a more essential factor in achieving happiness. By that I mean an ability to have a clear sense of what is important in our lives (the welfare of our families, the quality of our relationships, making other people happy, etc.) and what is not (a problem at work, getting annoyed about trivial things, etc.)

Like self-awareness, this is also very difficult to achieve, but I think these are the two factors that may be the most important for achieving happiness.

(262 words)

分析

范文共分为五段。作者在第一段回应题目中的第一个问题：为什么很难对幸福下定义？原因是不同的人对幸福有着不同的理解。接下来举例指出，有的人认为幸福与财富和物质上的成功有关，有的人则觉得幸福在于情感和相爱。而又有的人深信物质或是人与人的关系不能带来幸福，精神的追求（宗教）才是通向幸福的惟一道路。

第二段话首先用了一个承上启下的过渡句。因为人们对于幸福有着种种不同的理解，所以很难给出一个让人人满意的关于幸福的定义。在这里，这句话总结了对于第一个问题的回答。接下来，作者通过转折来引入第二个问题：然而，如果说不同的人有着不同的幸福，那么获得幸福的第一步就是首先要了解自己。人们只有了解了自己，才能知道如何让自己获得幸福。这一段指出了获得幸福的首要步骤。

第三段话作者说，当然，诸如拥有爱情，身体健康，生活无忧和环境安定都有助于我们得到幸福。但是，这并不是说没有这一切的人们就不会幸福。本段属于典型的让步段，这些外在的因素都是为了下一段的展开进行铺垫。

第四段话，作者指出，总的来说，对于生活的清晰认识在获得幸福方面更为重要。在这里 keep a clear perspective in life 显得有些抽象，所以作者运用解释说明的论证方法：所谓对于生活的清晰认识，指的是清楚地知道我们生活中什么是重要的（家庭幸福，与人和睦，关系融洽），以及什么是不重要的（工作中的问题，对小事想不开等等）。

在文章结尾，作者说，如同对于自己的了解一样，这一点（对于生活的清晰认识）也很难做到，但是正是这两点构成了获得幸福的关键。

SPEAKING

E=Examiner ***C=Candidate***

E: Good morning! My name is Steven.

C: Good morning.

E: Could you tell me your full name, please?

C: Yes, of course. My name is Cui Lingnan.

E: Do you have an English name?

C: Yes, it's Cathy.

E: Right, Cathy. Let's begin. Are you ready?

C: Sure.

E: OK. What's your major?

C: My major is English broadcasting. More specifically, learning to be an anchorperson.

E: Why you choose this major?

C: The reason is quite simple. I want to speak English not only to myself, but also to other people. There is an interview for this major, and I managed to get accepted.

E: How do you like your major?

C: Compared with a regular English major, we pay a lot of attention to language communication skills. But our foundation is a bit weaker than students who major in English language or literature. That's a weakness I'm trying to overcome.

E: Ok, let's talk about something else. What kind of food do you like most?

C: Um, nothing in particular. Ordinary Chinese food, the stuff we eat every day. I don't mind a hamburger occasionally.

E: Is there a new food you'd like to try?

C: I am a curious person, and like to try all kinds of new things. It's summer now, so I'd like to try all kinds of new soft drinks and ice-cream.

E: Do you cook?

C: Oh, now I don't. Because we don't have a kitchen in our dormitory. But at home, when my parents are out, I like to cook myself a special dinner. Like rice and eggs scrambled together, and some other things, my own creations. They can taste a bit strange sometimes, but, you know, not too bad. It's fun.

E: Do you prefer home-cooking or restaurant food?

C: I really miss my mum's cooking. Actually, both are OK. The important thing is to switch between the two, or life would be boring.

E: How about traveling. Do you like traveling?

C: Yes, I love seeing new places.

E: Why?

C: It can broaden your outlook, and the idea of a new place excites me. Plus, I think traveling can bevery relaxing, and I love long train journeys.

E: Do you prefer traveling alone or with other people?

C: I like to travel with my parents and friends. Coz you can share the beauty of the scenery and have a good chat when you feel like it, and play around together.

E: Good. Now let's move on to the second part. I'm going to give you a topic that I want you to talk about for a minute or two. You'll have one minute to prepare. Ok,here it is: Please describe an interest or hobby that you enjoy.

C: Ok.

Describe an interest or hobby that you enjoy.

You should say:

how you became interested in it

how long you have been doing it

why you enjoy it

and explain what benefits you get from this interest or hobby.

(Preparation Time)

E: Time's up. Time to start talking.

C: A favorite hobby of mine is drawing. I'm not quite sure why I like it so much. Perhaps it's simply in my blood. I believe a lot of people are like me, they just love it, for no apparent reason. I've only studied it formally for a year, because my mother thought I don't have that kind of talent, and it would be a waste of time and effort, especially considering the pressure of all the tough exams in China. But the truth is I have shown my mother I do have the talent: some logo designs which were accepted by my school, so after the college entrance examination I finally got the chance to study it in my spare time. I enjoy it so much, because you can focus on every tiny beautiful detail of the subject that you are sketching and feel its delicacy. And drawing can help you to relax, which is an important benefit in this busy world. Like, today is a sunny day, and maybe your mood is not that sunny. You can go out to sit by the water and draw. Then you'll be brightened by the sunshine. It's like you are on your own special little island, and can quiet all your emotions when you need to.

E: It's a great hobby. Do you think having a hobby is good for people's social life?

C: I think so. For example, when I first met my foreign English teacher, who is a really good artist, we got along so well, just because we share the same hobby. I mean, hobbies can shorten the distant between people, especially strangers.

E: In China, do you think people keep a good balance of their work and free time?

C: No, I don't think so. There are too many people in China, so there's a lot of competition—too much, I think, too intense. But if you want to get anywhere you have to join in and try to win. So many people spend too much time on the things they have to do and forget to enjoy the scenery by the road.

E: Any other reasons why you think people need to have an interest or hobby?

C: We are human beings, not machines. Relaxing gives you more energy for work, like recharging batteries. Having a hobby can make you relax mentally, to forget your worries for a while. And then, you know, move on.

E: Are there any negative effects of a person spending too much time on their hobby?

C: Oh, yes. Definitely. Take my father for example. He likes gardening very much and he can spend hours on that on weekends. My mum, of course, is not happy about that. She thinks that my father is so involved in his hobby that he doesn't have any time left for the family. And that IS a problem, isn't it?

E: Would you say the amount of free time has changed much in the last fifty years?

C: Yes, I think so. The amount of free time and the way we spend it have changed a lot over the last few decades. I remember when I was a child, it seemed I had plenty of free time. But the problem was that I had nothing to do in my free time. No toys, no electronics, no Internet, no Karaoke, nothing. But now it seems that I never have enough time for my studies, not to mention free time. I guess this is because we had a faster pace of life than ever before.

E: Do you think people will have more or less free time in the future? Why?

C：I'm quite optimistic about that. I would guess people will have more free time in the future. Sooner or later, people will understand that work is not the only thing that matters in life. There are other things which are equally important, like health, satisfaction, and quality of life, which are closely related to what you do in your free time.

E：Ok, thank you.

C：Thank you.

Test 3

LISTENING

SECTION 1

篇章结构

题　　型：表格填空、选择、完成句子
考查技能：时间单位换算、地名拼写、同义词等具体信息
场　　景：租房

场景背景介绍

出国读书，同学们首先要找到地方住。我们可以选择住在校园中，这样会很方便，离图书馆、教室都很近，但问题是价钱高而且课外与人们交流机会少；如果选择在当地内人家住的话，价钱一般比学校便宜还可以深入到native speaker的生活细节中去，但这样会增加一些交通费用；我们还可以选择跟几个来自不同国家的同学一起租房，好处是大家可以经常交流学习心得体会，而且可以学到不同的文化和不同的思维方式，问题是大家在一起生活难免会有一些小摩擦。出国之前大家可以到各个留学网站搜索相关评论，尤其是你的目标地或周边地区。出去之后大家也可以到学校找师兄师姐或者accommodation officer咨询有关情况。

本节必备词汇、词组

move into	搬(家)进去(与move out相对)	academic English	学术(专业)英语
homestay	*n.* (在国外的访问者)在当地居民家居住	get into sth.	进入某个领域
		sound good	听起来不错
particular	*n.* 细节，详细　*adj.* 特殊的，详细的，精确的	move out	搬出(与move in相对)，开始行动
postcode	邮政编码	accommodation	*n.* 住处，膳宿
general English	普通英语	save sb. money	给某人省钱

single person	单身(与 married person 相对)	insurance	*n.* 保险，保险单
company	*n.* 公司，陪伴	cash	*n.* 现金 *vt.* 兑现
be used to sth.	惯常，惯于	cheque (check)	*n.* 支票
swimming pool	游泳池	proportion	*n.* 比例，均衡，部分
pet	*n.* 宠物 *adj.*宠爱的，亲昵的	honour system	信用制度(出于信任而不加监督的制度，如学校的无监考考试制)
quite a bit	相当多(一般做副词修饰谓语动词)	monthly	*adj.* 每月的 *adv.* 每月一次 *n.* 月刊
deposit	*n.* 存款，押金 *v.* 存放		

场景词汇拓展

double bedroom	双人间	kitchenette	*n.* 小厨房
twin room	(旅馆)双床间	bathroom	*n.* 浴室，盥洗室
single bedroom	单人间	gas heater	烧煤气的暖气
studio apartment	*n.* 一居室的公寓	fridge	*n.* 电冰箱
library	*n.* 图书馆，藏书室，库，书房	stove	*n.* 炉
den	*n.* (舒适的)私室(作学习或办公用)，书斋	stereo system	*n.* 立体音响系统
		phone connection	(电脑)电话连线上网
living room	*n.* 客厅，起居室	entrance hall	*n.* 门廊(进门的门厅)
sitting room	*n.* 起居室		

文本及疑难解析

1. P140. “I’ll need to get some **particulars** first.” 我需要先了解一些细节。通常“particular”作形容词，但是在此是一个名词。而平常作名词的时候一般出现在“in particular”中，表示“尤其，特别”。

2. P140. “I was studying general English in Adelaide and now I’m doing Academic English, because I’m trying to get into Medicine next year.” 我在阿得来德的时候学的是普通语言，现在我学的是专业英语，因为我准备明年开始学医了。
   许多留学生在没有过语言关的情况下，出国先读语言学校，然后再读学位。有些攻读硕士学位并要换专业的学生还需要读一些桥梁课程(bridge courses)。

3. P141. “Most families do that on an honour system, but you have to wait and see.” 大多数家庭都使用信用制度来付电话费，到时候你就知道了。
   因为单独申请一个新电话号码比较麻烦，房东大多数不愿意为了给学生出租一段时间的房子另行申请。一般会和学生共用一个电话号码。付费的时候，大家靠自觉。

题目解析

1–4 题为表格填空题，总体难度不大 但是，第一题原文并没有直接给出答案，Sara 在阿得来德一年，在悉尼半年。不管是写一年还是半年都错。这里有一个简单的计算问题。第二题也有一定的难度。原文中的地名“Forest”没有给出拼写。雅思听力考试中还会出现类似的情况，比如：“South Hills”,“Spring Court”,“Fountain Road”,“Brook Street”，等等。另外还有吞音的问题，因为最后一个字母“t”不会送气。第三题的问题是词组搭配的问题。有时候，有人两个词“academic”和“English”都认识，但是放在一起就不清楚了。第四题主要是预测的问题。如果可以预测出要去听“星期几”，就可以在听的时候捕捉到信息。

5－7题为单项选择题，也比较容易。不过第五题要注意“share a room”和“twin room”的同义词关系，另外还要注意“I' ve been alone in my room at my aunt' s...”对我们的误导。第六题要注意提问 “Would you like to live with a family or...”对我们的干扰。第七题需要注意“I' m not used to a big house...”中的否定词。

8－10题是完成句子题。主要注意题目要求中的“NO MORE THAN ONE WORD”。另外还有一些细节问题，其中第八题要注意答案“deposit”的多重含义：存款，押金等等。第九题要注意“month”的派生词“monthly”。

SECTION 2

篇章结构

题　　型：单项选择、表格填空
考查技能：听出具体信息
场　　景：节目及文艺活动——介绍一个 Summer Festival 以及其中的一些表演项目

场景背景介绍

因为参与雅思出题的除了剑桥大学考试委员会之外，还有澳大利亚教育发展署(IDP)，所以雅思听力中经常会有一些内容与澳大利亚有关。本部分讲的就是澳大利亚某大学搞的一个艺术节。因为位于南半球，这里的节气和我们北半球刚好相反，所以一月份是那里的夏季。这个艺术节又刚好是在新年庆祝活动刚刚结束之后，所以原文中才会有“...recover from the first of January celebrations and they' ve put it at the end of the month.”的说法。如果不清楚这样的背景环境，许多同学会觉得很诧异。

本节必备词汇、词组

fill sb. in on sth.	在某方面给某人提供信息	green space	有草坪的绿地
in store	贮藏着，保存着，准备着	car park	停车场
timing	*n.* 适时，时间选择	stadium	*n.* 露天大型运动场
a couple of	两个，几个	in spite of	不管
allow	*vt.* 允许，承认	clown	*n.* 小丑，粗鲁愚蠢的人
recover from	*v.* 恢复，恢复知觉	acrobatic	*adj.* 杂技的，特技的
sensational	*adj.* 非常好的，耸人听闻的	purist	*n.* 纯化论者，纯粹主义者
art exhibition	艺术展览	showcase	*n.* (商店或博物馆的玻璃)陈列橱
in particular	特别，尤其	aerial display	航空展
circus	*n.* 马戏团	feature	*n.* 特征
plenty of	许多	well worth doing	值得做
distinct	*adj.* 明显的，截然不同的，独特的	puppet	*n.* 木偶
marquee	*n.* 大帐篷，华盖	routine	*n.* 例行公事，常规
canvas	*n.* 帆布　*v.* 彻底讨论探究	formation dancing	编队舞蹈
portable	*adj.* 便携式的	be taken with(by)	被征服

场景词汇拓展

convention	n. 大会，协定，习俗，惯例	sealed aquarium	密封的水箱
art and music festival	艺术音乐节	magic show	魔术表演
		hoola hoops	呼啦圈
trapeze act	空中飞人	animal training	训兽表演
grand finale	n. 终场演奏	rope walking	走钢丝

文本及疑难解析

1. P141. "...is going to **fill** us **in on** what's **in store** for us at this year's summer festival." …将告诉我们今年的"夏节"都给我们准备了些什么。本句中有两个搭配"fill sb. in on"和"in store"给考生们的理解增加了一些困难。比如："If any cracks have appeared on the tart base, fill these in with raw pastry." 如果馅饼上有裂纹的话，用一些生面糊填满。"If something is in store for you, it is going to happen sometime in the future." 如果某事已经为你准备好的话，将来总有一天会发生。

2. P141. "This is the 3rd year they've run it and the **timing**'s slightly different..." 这是他们第三年搞这种活动了，今年的时间略有不同。该句中的难点是"timing"，因为人们都知道"time"可以当名词用，但是"timing"在此是一个动名词表示"时间安排"，又比如"Mind your timing during the reading and writing test, or you'll not be able to finish the questions and the tasks." 在阅读和写作考试中要注意时间安排，否则你们既做不完阅读题也写不完作文。

3. P142. "The programme has **sensational theatre**..." 我们的节目中有很棒的表演。"sensational"是一个难点，它类似于口语中常说的"wonderful"，"theatre"是另外一个难点，他指的不是剧院，而是在剧院中的表演。

4. P142. "The purists are **suggesting** that this isn't a circus at all." 纯粹主义者认为这根本不是一个马戏团，该句难点主要是"suggesting"人们可能会想到"建议"，在此的意思是"认为"。如"I'm not suggesting that the accident was your fault." 我并不是说那事故是你的错。

5. P142. "... and there is some terrific **formation dancing**." 还有一些很棒的编队(队型)舞蹈。"formation dancing"指的是一种舞蹈形式。在表演过程中，舞蹈演员们在节奏中会变换不同的队型，如"Riverdance"——"大河之舞"。

6. P142. "I had a great time, but I did note that other older people in the audience weren't quite as **taken** with it as I was." 我很喜欢这个表演，但是我确实发现观众中的其他老人们不像我那么投入。"taken"是本句中的难点，它表示"被征服，使很投入"的意思。如："I was completely taken by the gorgeous sights of New Zealand." 我被新西兰的美景彻底征服了。

题目解析

11–14题是选择题，总体难度不是很大。11题主要考查考生理解"the end of the month"与选项C"25–31 January"之间的同义关系，同时要注意上半句"... to recover from the 1st of January celebrations..."的迷惑，因为A选项"1–13 January"中既有"1st"，也有"January"。

12 题要注意原文“looking at”与题干中“concentrate on”之间的同义关系，另外还要注意选项 A“theatre”与原文中“theatrical”之间的词干与派生词的关系。13 题相对来说在这四个题中最难，因为原文中明确提到“I' m going to tell you about 2 circus performances...”但值得庆幸的是，原文中，我们能听到转折词，“but there are plenty of others in the programme.”而且“plenty of ”也会告诉我们不止两个。14 题中要注意原文中的“rather than”，它类似于一个否定词，那么 A 和 D 两个选项就被去掉了。如果同学们能听懂“canvas”——“帆布”，也会有很大帮助，难点主要是“marquee”不是一个常用的词，有些同学可能没有听出来。

15-20 题是表格填空题，总体难度不大。15 题需要听一个并列信息，比较容易。但是 15、16 题比较近，连续两句话有两个答案，此处考查同学们边听边写的能力。同时，16 题除了答案“adult”之外，还出现了迷惑信息“children”。17 题主要考查学生的单词拼写能力，18、19 题很容易，20 题因为离前面的 19 题比较远，需要考生注意力集中。另外如果 16 题做错的话，20 题会有一定的提示作用。

SECTION 3

篇章结构

题　　型：选择题
考察技能：听出具体信息
场　　景：选课

场景背景介绍

一般从第三部分开始，就会涉及到选课，研究或写论文。本部分涉及的是“further education”——“继续教育”，即学生在离开学校之后在工作、生活中发现需要“充电”于是再次返回到学校中“继续”学习。但是因为离开学校时间太久了，有人可能已经忘记如何最有效地学习了，本部分谈论的就是这个话题。如果您是离开学校久的同学，出国后可以选择一门“如何适应学校生活、学习”之类的课程。实际上一直在学校的同学也可以选择类似课程使自己尽快适应海外的学习环境。

本节必备词汇、词组

refer to	*v.* 查阅，提到	tip	*n.* 技巧，小费
enquire about	*v.* 询问	get the most from	最大限度地利用
refresher course	*n.* 复习课程，进修课程	presentation	*n.* 介绍，陈述
build up	*v.* 树立，增进	motivational	*adj.* 动机的，有关动机的
undergraduate	*n.* (尚未取得学位的)大学生 *adj.* 大学生的	take up	*v.* 拿起，开始从事，占据
		manage to	达成，设法
postgraduate	*n.* 研究生　*adj.* 毕业后的	procrastination	*n.* 延迟，拖延
art	*n.* 艺术，文科	leisure	*n.* 空闲，闲暇
science	*n.* 科学，自然科学，理科	enrollment fee	报名费
intensive	*adj.* 精深的，透彻的	morning tea	早茶
aim at	瞄准，针对	ahead of	在…前面
wide range of approaches	多种的方法	convenor	*n.* 会议召集人
		upgrade	*n.* 升级　*vt.* 使升级，提升
strategy	*n.* 策略，军略	cope with	*v.* 处理，应付

focus on	集中	in line with	符合
stress management	压力管理	registration form	登记表
be better off	境况好		

场景词汇拓展

mandatory	*adj.* 命令的，强制的，托管的	MA	文学硕士
required	*adj.* 必需的	LLM	法学硕士
obligatory	*adj.* 义不容辞的，必须的	Mandarin	*n.* 官话，普通话
optional	*adj.* 可选择的，随意的	Cantonese	*n.* 广东人，广东话
selective	*adj.* 选择的，选择性的	Spanish	*n.* 西班牙语
elective	*adj.* 随意选择的 *n.* 选修课程	Portuguese	*n.* 葡萄牙语
course	*n.* 课程	Russian	*n.* 俄语
major	*n.* <美>主修课 *adj.* 主修的 *vi.* 主修	Arabic	*n.* 阿拉伯语
		Japanese	*n.* 日语
specialty	*n.* 专业	Korean	*n.* 韩语
MS	理学硕士		

文本及疑难解析

1. P143. "I' ve been **referred to** you because I' m enquiring about the **refresher courses** that you run." 我来找您，因为我想了解一下你们开设的进修课程。该句难点之一 "refer to"，它有许多含义：①提到，谈及 ②查阅，参考 ③关系到，涉及，应用于 ④呈交，提交，送交(to send to someone else for decision or action)。从汉语解释上，同学们会感到无所适从，但是看到第④个解释的英语解释，同学们会马上释然。由此建议同学们记单词时，去记忆其英语解释。第二个难点是一个搭配 "refresher course" —— "进修课程"。

2. P143. "I think that I really need some help **in** preparing **for** the coming semester, especially to build **up** my confidence a bit and help me study effectively." 我想我的确需要一些帮助，来准备下一个学期，尤其是帮我建立自信和有效地学习。这句话里面有三个介词，特别要注意它们分别与哪个词搭配。第一个 "in" 与 "help" 搭配，表示在哪些方面需要帮助；第二个 "for" 与 "preparing" 搭配，表示准备的目的或目标；第三个 "up" 与 "build" 搭配，表示建立起自信。

3. P143. "It' s aimed at students like you who are uncertain about what to expect at college, and looks at a fairly wide range of approaches to university learning, to motivate you to begin your study and build on your own learning strategies." 这门课(为了成功而学习)一直都是为(针对)像你这样对大学生活没有明确期待的学生准备的；这门课的目标是为你们提供各方面的学习方法，以激发你们开始研究并明确自己的学习策略。首先这句话很长(42 个单词)，考生们有可能听到后面忘了前边在说什么，实际上只要抓住该句的主句结构即可。"It' s aimed at...and look at...to motivate...and build on..." 也就是说前两个动作是谓语动词，后两个是目的状语。

4. P143. “The process of learning and exploring a subject can lead to a whole new way of looking at the world, and the study skills and techniques that you build up can be applied in all sorts of different ways.”学习和探究一门课程的过程可能会导致你对世界有全新的观察视角，而且你在研究中使用的技巧可以运用到不同的领域。这句话有39个单词，也很长，同样是一个并列句“...can lead to..., ...can be applied...”。在了解该句话的意思和结构的基础上，考生同时也可以明白一个道理：我们出国学习不仅是在学知识，更重要的是，我们要去学方法，尤其是思维方式。将来，你的优势不是知识而是贯通中西思维方式，无往而不胜的思维方式。

题目解析

先看21－25题。这五个题除了23与24题距离很近，难度较大外，其他三题不是太难。21题要注意A选项“people going back to college”与原文“returning to study”的同义关系。22题要注意用题干回原文定位“on the 1st and 2nd of February”。23题要注意C选项“clarity”与原文“write more clearly”中的“clearly”都是“clear”的派生词，24题也同样是analyse的两个形式，即“analytically”与“analysing”的关系。25题则要注意B选项“encourage interest in learning”与原文“feel positive and enthusiastic about their study”之间的相互解释或近义关系。

26－30题的难度与21－25题接近，但是29与30题之间的时间跨度很短，可能会让考生有跟不上的感觉。26题原文中有一个提示词“key”而且提到了“time management”和A选项中的“time”完全吻合难度不大。27题主要是听原文“ahead of”与C选项中“in advance”之间的同义关系。28题需要考生理解原文中“consecutive”——连续、不间断的含义，才能正确选到B选项。但是许多考生可能会不太清楚“consecutive”与“continuous”之间的差异，前者不会间断，如“The Chicago Bulls won 3 consecutive NBA Champions, with the brilliant performances of Michael Jordan.”因为迈克尔·乔丹的出色表现，芝加哥公牛队连续三次获得NBA总冠军。而后者可以间断，如“It rained continuously for 3 weeks.”雨断断续续下了三个星期。29题只需回原文定位“stress management”即可，30题要注意原文“basics”与B选项“at the beginning”的同义关系。

SECTION 4

篇章结构

题　　型：填空与表格填空，单项和多项选择
考查技能：听出具体信息和大意
场　　景：报告——关于学生会活支中心选址问题

场景背景介绍

除了上课之外，留学生将会有一些业余时间，尤其是本科生会把时间花在学生活动中心里。那里有各种各样的设施如本节介绍的各种体育项目，如健身、桌球、壁球、羽毛球等。但更重要的是“Student Counselling Centre”可以为学生们解决各种各样的实际问题，包括衣食住行还有打工许可等等。这里会给你提供各种服务和建议，包括经济方面和法律方面的，各种保险，等等。你只需要交纳一定数额的会费便可享受到“Student Union”的各项服务，而本节讲述的是关于“Student Union”的选址和其他设施问题的调查报告。

本节必备词汇、词组

grateful	*adj.* 感激的，感谢的	consensus	*n.* 一致同意，共识
Student Union	学生会	crucial	*adj.* 至关紧要的
feasible	*adj.* 可行的，切实可行的	outskirts	*n.* 边界，(尤指)市郊
ultimate beneficiary	最终受益者	hall of residence	学校公寓
facility	*n.* 设施，工具	cite	*vt.* 引用，引证，提名表扬
arrive at	到达，达到	lecture rooms	报告厅
options	*n.* 选项，选择权	access	*n.* 通路，访问 *vt.* 存取，接近
submit	*v.* 提交，递交		
questionnaire	*n.* 调查表，问卷	living quarters	住宅，住舱
approximately	*adv.* 近似地，大约	premises	*n.* 房屋或其他建筑物
collate	*v.* 比较，校对	table games	桌上游戏(桥牌，桌球等)
draw up	*v.* 草拟	gym	*n.* (gymnasium)体育体育馆，体操
key point	关键点		
in broad terms	宽泛的说	travel agency	旅行社

insurance center	保险中心	largish	*adj.* 相当大的
Student Counselling Centre	学生咨询中心	elitist	*n.* 优秀人材，杰出者 *adj.* 优秀人材的，杰出者的
refectory	*n.* (修道院，学院等处的)食堂，餐厅	surveillance	*n.* 监视，监督
		security personnel	安全(部门)人员

场景词汇拓展

charity	*n.* 慈善，施舍，慈善团体	immigration	*n.* 外来的移民，移居入境
newsagent	*n.* 报纸或定期刊物之经销商	grants	*vt.* 同意，准予，承认(某事为真)
supermarket	*n.* 超级市场		
mall	*n.* 购物商场，商业街，林阴路	medical & legal problems	医疗和法律问题
cheap tickets	折价车票		
catering services	饮食服务	badminton	*n.* 羽毛球
diner	*n.* 用餐者，餐厅	basketball	*n.* 篮球，篮球运动
dinning hall	餐厅	squash	*n.* 壁球
canteen	*n.* 小卖部，食具箱，饭盒，(军用)水壶	volleyball	*n.* 排球
		cricket	*n.* 蟋蟀，板球
cafeteria	*n.* 自助餐厅	rugby	*n.* 英式橄榄球

文本及疑难解析

1. P144. "We **appreciate** that some of our ideas may not be feasible in the circumstances, but we feel that it is important that the ultimate **beneficiaries** of the facilities should have some **say** in its design." 我们知道有些想法可能不太可行，但我们认为有一点很重要，这些设施的最终受益者对设计应该有一定的发言权。该句是一个有35个单词的并列复合句，前后两个部分又都是复合句，但是难点在于其中的几个单词。"appreciate" 在人们眼中或心目中是欣赏、感激的意思，在此表示"明白，知道"；"beneficiaries" 指受益者，其词根为benefit；最后一个词是 "say" 在这里不是动词而是名词表示"说法、看法、想法"。

2. P144. "Finally the SU committee **collated** the results and drew up a report." 最后，学生会整理好了调查结果，并写出一个调查报告，这个句子的难点是动词 "collate"，它最根本的意思是"校对、核对"，还可以指"授予牧师有俸禄或薪水的职位"，但在此引用的意思是"检查或整理"。比如，"collate the pages of the new edition of the dictionary."(检查)整理这本词典新版的印张，(包括错帖、漏帖检查)。

3. P144. "So, **in broad terms** the **consensus** was as follows." 宽泛地说，大家的意见如下。该句的难点有两个 "in broad terms" 和 "consensus"。"in...terms" =…地说，所以 "in broad terms" = 宽泛地讲，一般作插入语。比如："The students, in broad terms, are all rather diligent." 总的来说，学生们都

很努力。(意思是说大部分都很勤奋，但有个别人不太勤奋。)"consensus" 是指大多数人的意见或舆论。比如："The consensus was to abandon the project." 大多数人的意思是放弃该项计划。

4. P145. "Essentially the jury **is out** on that." 评委会(委员会)成员基本上认为这个建议是不值得考虑的。"be out" 在此是 "不可能的，不能接受的，不值得考虑" 的意思，这与它的本意大相径庭。比如："These last two proposals seem definitely out." 最后的这两项提议看来肯定是行不通了。

题目解析

31–32 题类似于句子填空题，其中 31 题主要是 "questionnaire" 的拼写问题，可能有些同学不太熟悉后半部分，32 题主要是要注意题目要求 "No More Than Two Words AND/OR A Number"。我们听到的是 "approximately two thousand" 是三个单词，但是我们可以把后半部分用阿拉伯数字来写，在此建议所有数字都写成阿拉伯数字，既省时间，又不容易犯错误，而且更重要的是只算一个词。

33–37 题是表格填空题。33 题比较容易，34 题的答案 "halls of residence" 被提到了两遍是重复信息，而且还有解释 "living quarters"。主要注意 33 与 34 题距离较近。35 题很容易，但同时注意 36 题同样与之很近，不过 36 题很容易用题干中的词组 "close to" 定位，而且原文没有任何变化。37 题要注意重新组织语言，否则会超出题目要求的 "三个以内的词。" 其他词都可以省略，但是答案中的主词 "facilities" 必须保留。

38–40 题是选择题，尤其是 38 和 40 题是多选题，难度较大。而且，38 题要注意 "gym" 与 "fitness centre" 之间的同义关系。39 题也很难，许多考生会选 A 选项，因为很容易听到 "waste of funds" 但是从常识角度来讲，"no students could use it" 是不可能的，太绝对了。40 题主要是词汇问题 "surveillance" 的意思是 "监视、看守、监督、监管"。

READING

READING PASSAGE 1

篇章结构

题型 说明文

主题 贷款计划对流浪儿童的重要性

结构
第一部分：国际流浪儿童组织简介
第二部分：国际流浪儿童组织相关背景知识
第三部分：国际流浪儿童组织的援助计划
- 速递服务
- 擦鞋合作社
- 青年创业计划

第四部分：国际流浪儿童组织的经验教训
第五部分：结论

必背词汇

标　题

micro-enterprise	*n.* 微型企业；小企业
credit	*n.* 贷款
street	*n.* 贫困的环境；贫困的区域
youth	*n.* 青年；少年
do without	没有…也行；没有…而设法对付过去
bun	*n.* 小圆面包
decent	*adj.* 得体的；大方的；体面的
second-hand	*adj.* 二手的；旧的
confident	*adj.* 信的；有信心的
expand	*v.* 扩大；扩展
cash management	现金管理
reinvestment	*n.* 再投资

第一段

small-scale	*adj.* 小规模的；小型的
business training	商业训练
relatively	*adv.* 相对地；比较地
direct	*v.* 指引；引导
circumstance	*n.* 环境；条件
partner	*n.* 合伙人；股东
lesson	*n.* 教训；经验

第二段

typically	*adv.* 典型地；具有代表性地	crime	*n.* 犯罪；犯罪行为
end up	结束；告终	abuse	*n.* 滥用；虐待
due to	由于；因为	unskilled	*adj.* 简单劳动的；无需技能的
combination	*n.* 联合；合并；综合	labour-intensive	*adj.* 劳动力密集的
dearth	*n.* 缺乏；不足	shine	*v.* 擦亮
adequately	*adv.* 充分地；充足地	informal	*adj.* 非正式的；不正规的
fund	*v.* 资助；为…提供资金	trading	*n.* 交易；贸易
breakdown	*n.* 破裂；分离	take pride in	以…为傲
violence	*n.* 暴力；暴虐	entrepreneurship	*n.* 企业家身份
attractive	*adj.* 有吸引力的；有魅力的	independence	*n.* 独立；自主
adventurous	*adj.* 充满危险的；有危险的	paid	*adj.* 受雇佣的；领薪水的
play	*n.* 赌博；游戏；比赛	flexible	*adj.* 灵活的；可变通的
exposed	*adj.* 暴露的；无遮掩的	participate	*v.* 参与；参加
exploitative	*adj.* 剥削的；榨取的	domestic	*adj.* 家庭的
urban	*adj.* 城市的；市内的		

第三段

work with	与…合作	collective	*n.* 合作社；集体企业
innovative	*adj.* 创新的；革新的	*Dominican Republic*	多米尼加共和国：西印度群岛上位于伊斯帕尼奥拉岛东部的一个国家
courier	*n.* 信使；信差	purchase	*v.* 购买；收购
Sudan	*n.* 苏丹：非洲东北部一国家，位于埃及南部	equipment	*n.* 装备；器材
participant	*n.* 参加者；参与人	facility	*n.* 工具；设备
supply	*v.* 提供；供给	initiative	*n.* 主动行动；倡议
deliver	*v.* 递送	*Zambia*	*n.* 赞比亚：非洲中南部一国家
parcel	*n.* 包裹；小包	joint	*adj.* 联合的；合办的
gradually	*adv.* 逐渐地；渐渐地	access	*n.* 享用权；享用机会
take up	开始从事；资助；赞助		
Bangalore	班加罗尔：印度中南部马德拉斯以西一城市		

第四段

emerge	*vi.* 显现；形成	ideally	*adv.* 理想地；完美地
entrepreneur	*n.* 企业家	relationship	*n.* 关系；关联

build	*v.* 营造；修建；构筑	guardian	*n.* 监护人
establish	*v.* 建立；建造	home visit	家访
involvement	*n.* 卷入；牵连；参与	situation	*n.* 情况；状况
essential	*adj.* 基本的；必须的	fixed assets	固定资产
relevant	*adj.* 相关的；有关的	kit	*n.* 工具箱；成套的工具
abide by	坚持；遵守	stall	*n.* 货摊
enforce	*v.* 执行；加强	consideration	*n.* 考虑；体谅
critical	*adj.* 重要的；关键的	charge	*v.* 收费
loan	*n.* 贷款	interest	*n.* 利息
tremendous	*adj.* 巨大的；极大的	modest	*adj.* 适度的；不太多的
involve	*v.* 包括；包含	bank rate	银行利率

第五段

impoverished	*adj.* 贫困的；赤贫的	effective	*adj.* 有效的；实际的
seek	*v.* 寻找；探求	means	*n.* 方法；手段
fulfill	*v.* 履行；实现	extend	*v.* 扩充；延伸
provision	*n.* 提供；供应	in association with	与…联合
entrepreneurial	*adj.* 企业家的	productive	*adj.* 多产的；富有成效的
ambition	*n.* 雄心；野心		

难句解析

1. Although small-scale business training and credit programs have become more common throughout the world, relatively, little attention had been paid to the need to direct such opportunities to young people.

参考译文：尽管在世界范围内，小规模的商业培训及贷款计划已经越来越普遍，然而相对而言，很少有人注意到年轻人也需要获得这样的机会。

语言点：direct 的用法

关于 direct 作为动词的用法:

(1) direct sb. to sth.

A nurse directed us down the hallway to I.C.U. 一位护士引导我们穿过走廊来到特护病房。

(2) direct sb. to do sth.

The judge directed the jury to find her not guilty. 法官引导陪审团判她无罪。

(3) direct that

He directed that his body should be buried in his hometown. 他要求死后被埋在家乡。

2. Typically, children do not end up on the streets due to a single cause, but to a combination of factors: dearth of adequately funded schools, the demand for income at home, family breakdown and violence.

参考译文： 通常来讲，儿童流离失所并非由某个原因造成，而是若干因素综合所致：比如缺乏拥有足够资金的学校，家里等着用钱，父母离异以及家庭暴力等。

语言点：

(1) Not...but...的用法

不是…而是…。例如，

It's not your fault but mine. 这不是你的错而是我的错。

注意要区分 not only...but (also)...不仅…而且…强调的是两个相关事实，尤其是第二个事实。当 not only 位于句首的时候，要求倒装。例如，

Not only did they win, but they also changed the nature of their team.

他们不仅赢得了比赛，而且还改变了球队的性质。

(2) end up 的用法

end up doing sth. 以…告终；结果却是…。例如，

Most dieters end up putting on more weight. 大多数减肥者最终却增重了。

3. However, it is also a place where some children are exposed, with little or no protection, to exploitative employment, urban crime, and abuse.

参考译文： 然而，由于缺乏或根本没有保护，有些孩子在那里遭到剥削，遭遇暴力事件甚至虐待。

语言点： expose 的用法

expose sb./ sth. to sth. 使…暴露在；使遭受；使曝光。例如，

① The report revealed that workers had been exposed to high levels of radiation.

报告揭露工人们暴露在高度辐射之下。

② expose one's skin to the sun 使皮肤遭日晒

③ We must realize the danger of exposing children to the violence and sex on TV.

我们必须认识到儿童接触电视上的暴力和色情内容的危害。

试题分析

Questions1－4

- 题目类型：MULTIPLE CHOICE
- 题目解析：

题号	定位词	文中对应点	题解
1	box / beginning	标题下方的方框中	题目是问文章开头的方框当中的引言是什么意思。A答案：exemplify 例证；举…例子；B答案是解释国际流浪儿童组织建立的原因；C答案：outline 描述，描画轮廓；D答案中highlight是指突出、强调。
2	purpose / S.K.I	Introduction 部分第二段首句	to support the economic lives of street children...等同于D答案，而其他三个选项基本未提到。
3	reason / end up	Background 部分的第一段首句	...the demand for income at home...等同于 poverty，而D答案crime并不是儿童流浪的原因，而是其可能产生的后果。
4	independent	Background 部分的第二段	A，B，D三个答案都比较极端，只有C符合本文的主题。

Questions 5－8

- 题目类型：TABLE COMPLETION
- 题目解析：

题号	定位词	文中对应点	题解
5	country / courier service	Street Business Partnership 部分第一点	Sudan / India
6	courier service	Partnership 部分第一点	bicycles
7	Dominican Republic	Street Business Partnership 部分第二点	Shoe Shine Collective
8	Zambia	Street Business Partnership 部分第三点	life skills

Questions 9 —12

- 题目类型：YES/NO/NOT GIVEN
- 题目解析：

9. Any street children can set up their own small business if given enough money.

参考译文	只要被给予足够的金钱，任何流浪儿童都可以开创自己的事业。
定位词	set up / money
解题关键字	Any
文中对应点	Lessons learned 部分第一点 Being an entrepreneur is not for everyone, for every street child.
答案	NO

10. In some cases, the families of street children may need financial support from S.K.I.

参考译文	有些情况下，流浪儿童的家人也需要从 S.K.I 寻求帮助。
定位词	families / S.K.I.
解题关键字	families
文中对应点	Lessons learned 部分第四点 这一点当中虽然提到了流浪儿童的家人，但是并没有说明他们是否要从 S.K.I. 那里得到帮助，属于纯粹未提及型的 NG。
答案	NOT GIVEN

11. Only one fixed loan should be given to each child.

参考译文	每个孩子只被提供了一笔固定的贷款。
定位词	loan
解题关键字	Only one
文中对应点	Lessons learned 部分第五点 ● 题目当中如果含有 ONLY / ONE 这样的词，往往选 NO。 ● 从文中我们也可以看出孩子们不只可以申请一笔贷款。
答案	NO

12. The children have to pay back slightly more money than they borrowed.

参考译文	孩子们归还的钱数要比他们借的多那么一点点。
定位词	pay back
解题关键字	more

文中对应点	Lessons learned 部分第六点 All S.K.I. programs have charged interest on the loans. 所有的计划都要收取利息，即为要多还一点钱。
答案	YES

Questions 13

- 题目类型：MULTIPLE CHOICE
- 题目解析：

题号	定位词	答案位置	题目解析
13	conclude	Conclusion 部分	However, we believe that credit must be extended in association with other types of support...

参考译文

流浪儿童的小型企业贷款

“我来自一个贫困的大家庭。我们已经很多年没吃过早餐了。自从加入了国际流浪儿童组织，早饭我们就吃得起糖和面包了。我还给自己买了体面的二手服装和二手鞋子。”

DOREEN SOKO

“我们有经商的经验。现在我非常有信心扩大我的生意。我学过现金管理以及节省开支的方法，所以现在存了些钱进行再投资。生意已经成了我生活的一部分。还有，以前我们素不相识——现在，我们已经交到了很多新朋友。”

FAN KAOMA

赞比亚青年创业计划的参与人

简介

尽管在世界范围内，小型企业培训及贷款计划已经越来越普遍，然而相对而言，很少有人注意到年轻人也需要获得这样的机会。更少的人会去留意那些无家可归或家境贫困的孩子。

在过去的九年里，国际流浪儿童组织已经与非洲、拉丁美洲以及印度的伙伴组织进行合作，来改善流浪儿童的经济状况。此文的目的主要是为了和大家分享一下他们所总结的经验教训。

背景

通常来讲，儿童流离失所并非由某个原因造成，而是若干因素综合所致：比如缺乏拥有足够资金的学校，家里等着用钱，父母离异以及家庭暴力等。对于孩子来讲，街道可能是个令人着迷的地方，充满了冒险游戏和赚钱机会。然而，由于缺乏或根本没有保护，有些孩子在那里遭到剥削，遭遇暴力事件甚至虐待。

在街头工作的孩子们通常都是从事一些无需技术但工作时间超长的劳动力密集型工作，比如擦鞋、搬运货物、门童或洗车，以及不正规交易。有些孩子甚至通过乞讨或干盗窃等非法勾当来赚钱。同时，也有些流浪儿童以能够养活自己和家人而自豪，而且他们很喜欢所做的工作。许多孩子会选择做生意是因为那可以使他们相对独立一些，而且做生意也比做其他许多有偿工作要少受一些压榨；生意的灵活性还使他们有时间去参与其他活动，比如上学或是做家务。

流浪儿童就业互助计划

国际流浪儿童组织与拉丁美洲、非洲及印度的伙伴组织合作，开发了让流浪儿童赚钱的新机会。

- 国际流浪儿童组织速递服务首先在苏丹展开。这项计划为参与者提供自行车用以递送包裹或信件，买自行车的钱会从参与者的工资中一点一点扣除。在印度的班加罗尔，一项类似的计划也已经展开。
- 在多米尼加共和国，一项与基督教女青年会合作，名为擦鞋合作社的计划也已经成功展开。这项计划借钱给参与者购买擦鞋箱，还给他们提供一个安全的地方来放置擦鞋工具，同时还提供了供他们存钱的设备。
- 赞比亚的青年创业计划是与红十字协会以及基督教女青年会合办的项目。通过商务培训、生存技能训练以及提供贷款机会等方式，该项目的参与者得以开办自己的小生意。

经验教训

在国际流浪儿童组织的计划实施过程中，出现了下列教训：

- 不是每个人都是做生意的料，流浪儿童也一样。理想状态下，孩子们至少应该参与计划六个月以上，这样双方之间可以建立起信任关系。
- 参与者的投入对于建立相关计划十分重要。如果孩子们在制定规程过程中起到关键作用，他们就更可能去遵守并执行这些规定。
- 关键是所有的贷款都要与培训计划联系起来，培训计划应该包括基本商业技能及生存技能的开发。

- 如果条件允许的话，容许家长或监护人参与计划是十分有好处的。家访使工作人员有机会知晓孩子们的住址，并且可以更好地了解每个人所处的环境。
- 开始的时候应该给孩子们提供一些小额贷款，以便他们购买如自行车、擦鞋设备以及市场摊位的原材料等固定资产。当从业者有了经验之后，就可以考虑扩大生意规模，并且考虑提高贷款金额。国际流浪儿童组织计划中的贷款额度通常在30到100美元不等。
- 国际流浪儿童组织所有的计划都会对贷款收取利息。这样做的主要目的是使贷款人习惯为借来的钱支付利息。通常来讲，这种利息都很低(一般低于银行利率)。

结论

我们需要认识到，为贫困的年轻人提供贷款以满足他们的经济需求是十分重要的。通过提供小额贷款，实现年轻人的经商梦，是帮助他们改变人生的有效途径。然而，我们认为贷款必须与其他形式的援助一起开展，才能帮助年轻人在生意兴隆的同时，发展出其他关键的生存技巧。

相关背景

* Street Kids International 国际流浪儿童组织

Street Kids International, an international charity based in Canada, strives to be the lead organization in developing, disseminating and advocating the practical solutions needed to give street kids around the world the choices, skills, and opportunities to make a better life for themselves. Street Kids International builds its programs and public education efforts around a philosophy of empowering and supporting street youth.

* Y. W. C. A 基督教女青年会

The YWCA is the oldest and largest multicultural women's organization in the world.

Across the globe, the YWCA have more than 25 million members in 122 countries, including 2 million members in 300 local associations in the United States.

Their mission is to eliminate racism and empower women, provide safe places for women and girls, build strong women leaders, and advocate for women's rights and civil rights in Congress.

READING PASSAGE 2

篇章结构

题型 说明文

主题 火山爆发的威力

结构 A 段：火山爆发对地球的影响
B 段：火山爆发的原因
C 段：火山爆发的种类
D 段：火山爆发的不可预测性

必背词汇

标 题

earth-shattering	*a.* 惊天动地的	headline	*n.* 大字标题；(*pl.*)新闻提要
erupt	*vi.* (火山等)迸发，爆发		

A 段

ultimate	*a.* 最后的，最终的；根本的，基本的	surge	*n.* 汹涌，澎湃；激增 *vi.* 汹涌，涌动
earth-moving	*a.* 移山倒海的	lava	*n.* 熔岩
machinery	*n.* (总称)机械，机器；机构	volcanism	*n.* 火山活动；火山作用
blow the top	*v.* 生气，怒不可遏；此处指火山爆发	volcanic	*a.* 火山的
scatter	*v.* 驱散；散开，撒开	shape	*n.* 形状；情况 *vt.* 使成形，塑造；实现
fine	*a.* 美好的；纤细的	rift	*n.* 裂缝，隙缝 *v.* 使断裂；使裂开
ash	*n.* 灰，灰末	mountain chain	山脉
practically	*ad.* 几乎，简直；实际上	construct	*v.* 建设，建造；创立
hurl	*v.* 猛投，猛掷	topography	*n.* 地形学，地形
fragment	*n.* 碎屑，片断	ocean floor	海底基岩
stratosphere	*n.* 同温层；平流层	basement	*n.* 地下室，建筑物的底部
bang	*vi.* 猛敲，猛撞 *vt.* 发出砰的响声	basalt	*n.* 玄武岩
mushroom	*n.* 蘑菇	stable	*a.* 稳定的，牢固的 *n.* 马厩；培训基地
molten	*a.* 熔化的，炽热的，铸造的		

atmosphere	*n.* 大气层；气氛，环境
ice-cap	*n.* 冰帽
active	*a.* 有活力的，积极的，主动的
cubic	*a.* 立体的，立方的；三次的
continental	*a.* 大陆的，大陆性的；欧洲大陆的
crust	*n.* 地壳
crater	*n.* 火山口，弹坑
vapour	*n.* 蒸气，雾气
nitrogen	*n.* 氮
carbon dioxide	*n.* 二氧化碳
sulphur dioxide	*n.* 二氧化硫
methane	*n.* 甲烷，沼气
ammonia	*n.* 氨
hydrogen	*n.* 氢
multiply	*v.* 使增加；使繁殖；乘 *vi.*增加，繁殖
mass	*n.* 大量；(*pl.*)群众 *a.* 群众的；大规模的

B 段

geologist	*n.* 地质学家
core	*n.* 果心；核心，要点
surround	*v.* 包围，环绕
semi-molten	*a.* 半熔化的
mantle	*n.* 地幔
brittle	*a.* 脆的；易损坏的
outer	*a.* 外部的，外层的
soft-boiled	*a.* 半熟的
runny	*a.* 松软的，水分过多的
yolk	*n.* 蛋黄，卵黄
firm	*a.* 结实的；坚定的 *n.* 商行，公司
squishy	*a.* 粘糊糊的
shell	*n.* 外壳，甲；炮弹
crack	*n.* 破裂声；裂缝 *vi.* 发出爆裂声 *vt.* 使破裂
bubble out	噗噗地涌出
set	*v.* 放；调整 *vi.* (日、月等)落下；凝结
archipelago	*n.* 群岛
Hawaiian Islands	夏威夷群岛
overlie	*v.* 躺在…上面
treacle	*n.* 糖浆；蜜糖
convection	*n.* 传送；对流
current	*a.* 现时的；通用的 *n.* (水、气、电)流；趋势
fracture	*n.* 破裂；裂痕 *vi.* 破裂
bump	*n.* 碰撞，颠簸；肿块 *v.* 碰撞，颠簸
grind	*v.* 磨，碾碎
overlap	*n.* 重迭 *v.* (与…)重叠
centimeter	*n.* 公分，厘米
zone	*n.* 地区，地带，区域
collision	*n.* 碰撞，冲突

C 段

weakness	*n.* 缺点，弱点
hot spot	热点；灾难多发区
swiftly	*ad.* 迅速地，敏捷地
vast	*a.* 辽阔的；巨大的
magma	*n.* 岩浆，糊剂，糊
inch	*n.* 英寸；少许，一点儿 *v.* 慢慢地移动
granite	*a.* 花岗岩，花岗石

extrusion	*n.* 挤出，推出，赶出
dyke	*n.* 堤坝
squeeze	*v.* 挤压，压榨
toothpaste	*n.* 牙膏
Ireland	*n.* 爱尔兰岛；爱尔兰(共和国)
Wales	*n.* 威尔士
Karoo	*n.* 非洲南部的干旱高原
South Africa	南非
horizontally	*ad.* 水平地
sheet	*n.* 张，片，页
Deccan plateau	德干高原
slurp	*n.* 啧啧吃的声音　*v.* 啜食
trap	*v.* 使陷于困境
glow	*vi.* 发白热光
froth	*n.* 泡，泡沫，琐物
lip	*n.* 边缘
Jupiter	*n.* 木星
Uranus	*n.* 天王星
volcanologist	*n.* 火山学家
Blast	*v.* 炸毁，摧毁　*n.* 爆炸，爆破
pumice	*n.* 轻石，浮石
crystalline	*a.* 水晶的，晶体状的
Giant's Causeway	巨人堤道
mid-ocean	*n.* 海中央
apart	*ad.* 相距，相隔；分，离开；除去
Philippines	*n.* 菲律宾共和国，菲律宾群岛
rough	*a.* 表面粗糙的；粗野的；大致的　*ad.* 粗暴地
tectonic	*a.* 筑造的，建筑的，构造的
dramatic	*a.* 戏剧的；引人注目的，给人留下深刻印象的
Manila	*n.* 马尼拉
Rockies	*n. pl.* 落基山脉
Mexico	*n.* 墨西哥
world-shaking	*a.* 惊天动地的
Krakatoa	*n.* 喀拉喀托火山(印度尼西亚一火山岛)
Sudan Straits	*n.* 苏丹海峡

D 段

predictable	*a.* 可预言的，可预想的
geological	*a.* 地质学的，地质的
quiet period	火山的休眠期
cap	*n.* 帽子，盖子 *vt.* 盖住；胜过，优于
cone	*n.* 圆锥体，球果
slop	*v.* 溢出；溅出
rim	*n.* (圆形物的)边缘
plug	*n.* 塞子，插头　*v.* 堵，塞住
block	*n.* 大块(石料等)；街区；阻塞物　*vt.* 阻拦
irresistible	*a.* 无法抗拒的，令人着迷的
remove	*n.* 消除，去掉；搬走，运走；搬迁
fierce	*a.* 巨大的，强烈的
cancel	*v.* 取消，作废；删去，划掉
starve	*v.* 使饿死，使挨饿
fail	*vi.* 失败；衰退　*vt.* 使失望；使不及格
frost	*n.* 冰冻，严寒；霜，结霜 *v.* (使)结霜，下霜
potentially	*ad.* 潜在地

难句解析

1. It helps to think of a soft-boiled egg with a runny yolk, a firm but squishy white and a hard shell.

参考译文：想像一个半熟的鸡蛋会有些帮助，流淌的蛋黄，坚实但又黏稠的蛋清，还有一层坚硬的蛋壳。

结构分析：

在这里 it 是形式主语，真正的主语是 to think of ...。

语言点：

(1) help 的用法

help 在这里做帮忙、有帮助讲。

关于 help，还有下列搭配值得记忆：

a. cannot help but + 动词原形　不得不；不会不；必须。例如，

I can't help but admire her courage. 我不得不佩服她的勇气。

b. help out 救出；摆脱困难。例如，

Highways help out with the transportation problems. 高速公路有助于解决交通问题。

c. help over 帮助克服。例如，

He helps me over my difficulties. 他帮助我渡过难关。

d. God helps who helps himself. 自助者天助。

e. It can't be helped.　实在没有办法了。

f. helping hand 援助；支持

(2) think of 的意思

a. 思考；考虑

What are you thinking of ? 你在想什么?

b. 想起；记得

Will you think of me after I left? 我走了你会想我吗?

c. 想一想；想像

Just think of the price of that car! 你想想那辆车有多贵!

d. 有…的想法；认为可能

He would never think of giving up the project. 他决不会放弃那个计划的。

e. 对…有特殊看法

What do you think of John? 你认为约翰这人怎么样?

2. These fracture zones, where the collisions occur, are where earthquakes happen. And, very often, volcanoes.

参考译文：这些破碎的地方正是碰撞发生的地方，也是地震发生之处，通常也是火山出现的地方。

结构分析：

第一个 where 引导了非限制性定语从句，修饰主语 these fracture zones，are 是系动词，where earthquakes happen 是表语从句。

And, very often, volcanoes.是一个省略句型。就等同于 And volcanoes often emerge at these fracture zone.

3. The gases trapped inside the boiling rock expand suddenly, the lava glow with heat , it begins to froth, and it explodes with tremendous force.

参考译文：沸腾的岩石中所包含的气体突然膨胀，熔岩因为受热而闪闪发光，岩浆开始冒泡，接着以巨大的力量爆发。

结构分析：

第一个分句的主语是 the gases，trapped inside the boiling rock 是过去分词作定语修饰主语。两个 it 指代的是上句话提到的 magma。

试题分析

Questions 14—17

- 题目类型：LIST OF HEADINGS
- 题目解析：

题号	段落主题句	题解
14	A 部分：第一段首句 Volcanoes are the ultimate earth-moving machinery. 第二段： Eruptions have rifted continents...a basement of volcanic basalt. 第三段开头： Volcanoes have not only made the continents, they are also thought to have made the world's first stable atmosphere and ...	A 部分说明了火山活动的作用，正好和 iii 选项中的火山与地球的特征吻合，因此答案为 iii。

题号	段落主题句	题解
15	B 部分： 第一段：整个段落描述了火山爆发的起因。 第二段最后： These fracture zones, where the collisions occur, are where earthquakes happen. And, very often, volcanoes.	通过扫描这两个段落，发现其中主要将地球比喻成一个鸡蛋，并且由此说明了火山爆发的原因。因此答案应该是 i。
16	第二段：Sometimes, it is slow... 第三段：Sometimes the magma moves very swiftly indeed. 第四段：The biggest eruptions are deep on the mid-ocean floor.	此部分出现了大量的火山名字，由此我们可以预测该段落讲的是火山喷发的不同类型。因此答案是 iv。
17	第一段：But volcanoes are not very predict-able.	vi 答案是说火山爆发的不可预测性。

Questions 18—21

- 题目类型：SHORT ANSWER QUESTIONS
- 题目解析：

题号	定位词	文中对应点
18	sections of the earth's crust / volcanic activity	C 部分的第四段 ...and you can see the rough outlines of what are called tectonic plates — the plates which make up the earth's crust and mantle.
19	molten rock from the mantle	C 部分第二段： Sometimes it is slow: vast bubbles of magma — molten rock from the mantle — ...
20	zone/ the Pacific Ocean	C 部分第四段： The most dramatic of these is the Pacific "ring of fire"...
21	Mount Pinatubo / inactive	D 部分第一段： In the case of Mount Pinatubo, this took 600 years.

Questions 22－26

- 题目类型：SUMMARY
- 题目解析：

题号	定位词	题解
22	produce / atmosphere	A 部分的第三段： Volcanoes have not only made the continents, they are also thought to have made the world's first stable atmosphere and provided all the water for the oceans, rivers and ice-caps. 火山不仅制造出陆地，也为地球提供了大气，为海洋、河川和冰帽提供了水。 答案：water
23	There are different types of eruptions. / Sometimes / moves slowly	首先可以根据之前做过的 LIST OF HEADINGS 题判定，C 部分讲到了不同类型的火山爆发。然后寻找 slowly 这个词。定位点在 C 部分的第二段：Sometimes it is slow: vast bubbles of magma — molten rock from the mantle — inch towards the surface. inch 在这里是指"慢慢移动，渐进"。 答案：magma / lava
24	quickly / horizontally Northern Ireland / Wales / South Africa	C 部分第二段： Sometimes — as in Northern Ireland, Wales and the Karoo in South Africa — the magma rose faster, and then flowed out horizontally on to the surface in vast thick sheets. In the Deccan Plateau in western India, ... 此处要求填一个地名 答案：west India
25	third / lava / very quickly / violently	C 部分第三段： Sometimes the magma moves very swiftly indeed. It does not have time to cool as it surges upwards. The gases trapped inside the boiling rock expand suddenly, the lava glows with heat, it begins to froth, and it exploded with tremendous force. 这个空要求填一个动词，而且要注意时态。 答案：explodes
26	magma / emitted	C 部分第三段 Sometimes the magma moves very swiftly indeed. It does not have time to cool as it surges upwards. The gases trapped inside the boiling rock expand suddenly, ... emit 发射；发出 答案：gases

参考译文

火山——惊天动地大消息

1991年6月9日，Pinatubo火山突然爆发，结果，有关过去和现在火山爆发威力的文章再度登上了报纸的头版。

A 火山就是终极“移山倒海”的机器。一次猛烈的喷发可以把一座山的山头轰掉几千米，将细灰几乎洒遍全世界，把岩石碎片抛进平流层，遮蔽整个大洲的天空。

然而，这种典型的喷发——锥形山体，轰隆巨响，蘑菇云升起，熔岩喷涌——只是长篇故事中的一小章。火山作用，这个由火山活动而来的名词，的确塑造了我们的世界。火山喷发撕裂大陆，举起山脉，构筑岛屿，最终造就了整个世界地形。五大洋的海底基岩就是火山喷发形成的玄武岩。

火山不仅造就了大陆，也许还造就了地球上第一个稳定的大气层，并且为大洋、河流以及冰川提供了水资源。现在全球有600多座活火山。这些火山每年都要为地球增加两、三立方公里的岩石。想像一下，过去3,500年中这600多座火山一直在喷发，这些岩石就足够解释地壳是如何形成的了。

从火山口喷发出来的主要是气体。其中有90%是来自地心深处的水蒸气：火山一连喷发了3,500年，这就足够解释大洋中的水是从哪里来的了。其余气体有氮气、二氧化碳、二氧化硫、甲烷、氨气以及氢气。同样经过了3,500年的积累，这些气体的量就足以解释大气层之“大”了。我们能活着，正是因为火山提供了我们需要的土壤、空气和水。

B 地质学家认为地球有一个熔化的核心，周围是半熔化的地幔，外边是一层脆脆的外皮。想像一个半熟的鸡蛋会有些帮助——流淌的蛋黄，坚实但又黏稠的蛋清，还有一层坚硬的蛋壳。在煮的时候，蛋壳只要有一点点开裂，蛋清就会噗噗地冒出来，在裂缝周围形成一座小小的山脉——就像夏威夷群岛那样的火山群岛。只是地球大得多，里面的地幔也烫得多。

尽管在上层压力下地幔是固态的，但是它们仍然可以像蜜糖一样“流淌”。这种流动据信是以对流形式进行的，力量足以使地壳这“蛋壳”破裂成板块，并且使这些板块互相碰撞摩擦，甚至使它们以一年数厘米的速度互相重叠。这些破碎的地方正是碰撞发生的地方，也是地震发生之处，通常也是火山出现的地方。

C 这些区域正是脆质带，也就是地震多发区。每次喷发都不尽相同，但是简而言之，在脆弱的地方，地幔深处的岩石被加热到 1,350 摄氏度，并开始膨胀上升。当地幔变化的时候，压力就会减小，因此地幔就开始膨胀并变成液体，然后迅速上涨。

有时候喷发很慢：岩浆——地幔中熔化的岩石——的巨大气泡慢慢接近地表，慢慢变冷，最后作为花岗岩突起显露出来。(在斯凯岛和大玄武岩山，熔岩堤坝像牙膏一样挤出来，延伸成为英格兰北部哈德良长城的一部分。)有时候——比如在北爱尔兰，威尔士以及南非的干旱台地卡鲁——岩浆上升得很快，然后以大厚块的形式水平地涌上地面。在印度西部的德干高原，经过超过 50 万年咕嘟咕嘟的火山喷发，积累了超过 200 万立方公里的熔岩，其中有些厚达 2,400 米。

有时候岩浆移动得十分迅速。在向上喷涌的过程中没有时间冷却。沸腾的岩石中所包含的气体突然膨胀，熔岩因为受热而闪闪发光，岩浆开始冒泡，接着以巨大的力量爆发。然后，下面稍微凉一点的熔岩开始漫出火山口。这种情形曾经发生在火星上，也曾经发生在月球上，甚至在木星和天王星的卫星上也曾经出现过。通过研究这些证据，火山学家们得以了解过去大喷发的威力。轻石是不是很轻并且充满孔洞？其喷发的力量是巨大的。岩石是否很重，是否像北爱尔兰巨人堤一样，有着巨大的结晶玄武岩形状？那就是一场缓慢、温和的喷发。

最剧烈的喷发发生在大洋中间深深的海底，新的熔岩将大陆撕开，每年将大西洋加宽五厘米。观察一下火山、地震和像菲律宾和日本这样的群岛，你就会看到被称为地壳板块的大致轮廓——地壳板块组成了地球的地壳和地幔。这其中最明显的例子就是太平洋上的“火环”，那里曾经发生过最剧烈的喷发——马尼拉附近的 Pinatubo 喷发，洛基山脉中的圣海伦山喷发，还有十年前的墨西哥 El Chichón 山喷发，更不用提 1883 年苏丹海峡喀拉喀托山震惊世界的喷发。

D 然而火山喷发并不总是能被预测，那是因为地质时间与人类时间不同。在休眠期，火山用熔岩将自己盖起来，用溢出火山口的熔岩形成坚硬的锥型体；随后熔岩慢慢冷却成为又大又硬，稳固的岩颈，岩颈会阻止进一步的喷发，直到压力大到无法抵挡为止。拿 Pinatubo 山为例，这个过程花了 600 年。

然而，有时候，只有一个小小的征兆，火山就喷发了。1902 年 5 月 8 日早上 7 点 49 分，Martinique 的 Pelée 山爆发了。28,000 人的城镇，只有两人幸存。在 1815 年，一次突然喷发炸掉了印度尼西亚的 Tambora 山 1,280 米的山顶。那次喷发如此剧烈，以至于喷进平流层的火山灰遮蔽了天空，使得欧洲和美洲直接进入秋季。六月下雪，八月上霜，粮食因此而歉收，上千人忍饥挨饿。火山，尤其是那些安静的火山，是潜在的世界新闻。

相关背景

*Mount Pinatubo

Pinatubo, Mount, active volcano in the Philippines, in the central part of the island of Luzon, at the juncture of Tarlac, Zambales, and Pampanga provinces. Mount Pinatubo is almost 90 km north of Manila and about 24 km east of Angeles, where the United States Air Force Base known as the Clark Air Base was located. Until 1991, Mount Pinatubo was classified as inactive because it had been dormant for at least 600 years. In June and July of that year, the volcano erupted several times, throwing millions of tons of ash and other volcanic material over 15,000m (almost 50,000 ft) high into the atmosphere. Much of this volcanic material spread around the world in the upper atmosphere. Locally, the ash reached a depth of more than 3 m (10 ft). Heavy tropical rains turned the ash to mud and triggered massive mudslides. By late August 1991 it was estimated that 550 people had died because of the eruption and its aftermath. In addition, more than 650,000 people had lost their livelihood, and 100,000 hectares (almost 250,000 acres) of agricultural land had been devastated. The ash covered nearby Clark Air Base and sped up the U.S. pullout from Clark, which was until 1991 one of the largest U.S. Air Force bases outside of the United States. Mount Pinatubo erupted again in August 1992, causing more destruction. Mount Pinatubo is 1,780 m (5,840 ft) high.

*Great Whin Sill

One of the most notable occurences of whinstone in the British Isles is the Great Whin Sill, which runs through Northumberland, just south of Scotland. At places it is over 200 feet thick, and where it protrudes above the surface it can be quite a formidable structure. Part of Hadrian's Wall runs atop the Great Whin Sill.

*Giant's Causeway

Giant's Causeway, rocky promontory on the northern coast of Northern Ireland. It consists of thousands of polygonal columns of basalt, ranging to more than 6 m (20 ft) in height. It is thought by geologists to have formed when an ancient lava flow cooled and solidified. Its name is derived from a local legend that the formation was built by giants as part of a roadway to Scotland.

READING PASSAGE 3

篇章结构

题型 说明文

主题 如何获得语言资料

结构 A 段：获得语言资料的方法
B 段：语言学家作为资料提供者的好处和坏处
C 段：影响语言研究的因素
D 段：录音方式的好处和坏处
E 段：录像方式的好处和局限性
F 段：如何用结构化会议的方式取得语言资料
G 段：建立语料库对语言研究的意义

必背词汇

第一段

procedure	n. 程序，手续；过程，步骤	investigation	n. 研究，调查了解
available	a. (用于物)可利用的；可见到的	casual	a. 偶然的；临时的，非正式的；草率的
obtain	v. 获得，得到		
intensive	a. 集中的，强化的，精细的，深入的	introspection	n. 内省，反省
		mother tongue	n. 母语，本国语
field	n. 领域	carry out	v. 完成，实现，贯彻，执行

第二段

source	n. 根源，来源，出处	usage	n. 用法，使用；惯用法，习语
informant	n. (为语言学调查)提供数据的讲本地话的人；资料提供人	judge	v. 判断；裁决；审判
		ambiguity	n. 模棱两可；歧义
native speaker	n. 说本族语的人	acceptability	n. 可接受，承认，合意
utterance	n. 语句	property	n. 特性
translation	n. 翻译；译文，译本	intuition	n. 直觉
comment	n. 评论，意见	convenience	n. 方便，便利
correctness	n. 正确性	approach	n. 接近，方法
judgement	n. 判决，审判；判断力；判断，看法	norm	n. 标准，规范；平均数
		generative	a. 生成的

linguistics	*n.* 语言学	enquiry	*n.* 询问
uncertain	*a.* 不肯定的；靠不住的	non-linguist	*n.* 非语言学家
objective	*n.* 目标，宗旨　*a.* 客观的；外界的，真实的	unavoidable	*a.* 不可避免的
		work on	继续工作，设法说服，影响
recourse	*n.* 依靠；依赖；求助	child speech	儿童语言

第三段

factor	*n.* 因素	characteristics	*n.* 特性
describe	*v.* 描绘，描写；形容，把…说成	social setting	社会环境
interact	*vi.* 相互作用，互相影响	formality	*n.* 礼节，程序，拘谨，正式手续
sample	*n.* 样品，样本	quality	*n.* 质量；品质，特性
aspect	*n.* (问题等的)方面；样子，面貌	scrupulous	*adj.* 谨慎小心的、细心的
identity	*n.* 身份，本体；同一性质，相同处	sampling theory	抽样法理论，抽查法理论
		employ	*v.* 使用；雇用
influence	*n.* 影响；权势；感应 *vt.* 影响，感化，左右	investigative	*a.* 研究的，调查的，好研究的
		technique	*n.* 技巧，手艺；技能，技术

第四段

tape-record	*v.* 用录音带录音	be aware of	知道
accurate	*a.* 准确的，精确的，正确无误的	ethical	*a.* 伦理的，道德的；合乎道德的
repeatedly	*a.* 反复地，再三地	objection	*n.* 反对，异议
naturalistic	*a.* 自然的，自然主义的，博物学的	anticipate	*vt.* 预料，预期
		alternatively	*adv.* 交互地；交替地
abnormally	*adv.* 反常地，不规则地	attempt	*n.* 企图，试图　*vt.* 尝试，试图
sound quality	音质	microphone	*n.* 麦克风，扩音器
devise	*v.* 设计，发明	stimulate	*v.* 刺激，使兴奋；鼓励，鼓舞
minimize	*v.* 将减到最少，使降到最低	style	*n.* 风格，文体；时尚，流行式样；种类，类型
paradox	*n.* 矛盾；似矛盾而正确的说法		
behave	*vi.* 举动，表现；运转 *vt.* 使运转正常	locality	*n.* 位置，地点，发生地

第五段

audio	*a.* 音频(的)，音响(的)；声音(的)	ambiguous	*a.* 模棱两可的
unclear	*a.* 不易了解的，不清楚的，含混的	supplemented	*a.* 补充的
		non-verbal	*a.* 非用言语的；非语言性的

participant	*n.* 参加者，参与者	video	*n.* 电视，录像 *a.* 电视的，录像的
context	*n.* 上下文；(事情等的)前后关系，情况	transcription	*n.* 抄写；注音
facial	*a.* 脸部的，脸上的	benefit	*vi.* 受益于
expression	*n.* 表达，表示，表现，措辞，词句；表情	additional	*a.* 附加的，另外的
alter	*v.* 改变；更改	commentary	*n.* 评论，评注；实况广播报导，现场口头评述
limitation	*n.* 限制，局限性	observer	*n.* 观察者，观察员；评述者

第六段

structured	*a.* 有明显结构的	restricted	*a.* 受限制的，有限的
session	*n.* 会议；一次开会(或开庭)；一段时间	feature	*n.* 特征，特色；五官之一；(报纸的)特写
systematically	*adv.* 系统地，有秩序地	pronunciation	*n.* 发音，发音方法
bilingual	*a.* (能说)两种语言的	elicit	*v.* 引出 探出
interpreter	*n.* 译员，口译人员	elicitation	*n.* 引出，诱出，抽出
cover	*v.* 覆盖；涉及	substitution	*n.* 替换
work-sheet	*n.* 工作表	stimulus	*n.* 刺激物
questionnaire	*n.* 调查表		

第七段

representative	*n.* 代表 *a.* 代表性的；代理的	selective	*a.* 有选择性的
compile	*v.* 编辑，汇编	collection	*n.* 收集，搜集，采集，收藏品
corpus	*n.* 素材；语料		
unbiased	*a.* 没有偏见的	hypothesis	*n.* 假设
statement	*n.* 陈述，声明；财务报表，申报单	principle	*n.* 原则，原理；道义，信念
		by contrast with	和…形成对照；和…比起来
frequency	*n.* 频率；屡次，频繁	inevitably	*ad.* 不可避免地
accessible	*a.* 可得到的，易接近的；可进入的	coverage	*n.* 涵盖面；覆盖面
		derive	*vi.* 起源
variable	*a.* 可变的，易变的 *n.* 变量	introspection	*n.* 内省，反省
extract	*v.* 取出，拔出；提取，榨 *n.* 摘录；提炼物	experimentation	*n.* 实验，试验

试题分析

Questions 27—31

- 题目类型：LIST OF HEADINGS
- 题目解析：

题号	定位词	题解
27	recording	D段首句 Today, researchers often tape-record informants. 题目问：哪一段讲到了录音对人们谈话方式的影响。
28	body language	E段 Where possible, therefore, the recording has to be supplemented by the observer's written comments on the non-verbal behaviour of the participants, ... 题目问：哪一段讲到了记录人们肢体语言的重要性。
29	social situation	C段 Age, sex, social background and other aspects of identity are important, as these factors are known to influence the kind of language used. 题目问：哪段提到了语言受到社会背景的影响。
30	self-conscious	D段 Some recordings are made without speakers being aware of the fact — a procedure that obtains very natural data, ... 题目问：哪一段提到了如何帮助资料提供者变得自然一点。 self-conscious的意思是"不自然的，扭捏的，难为情的"。
31	specific data various methods	F段 A large number of points can be covered in a short time, using interview work-sheets and questionnaires. There are also several direct methods of ... 题目问：哪段提到了产生详细信息的不同方式。

Questions 32—36

- 题目类型：TABLE COMPLETION

● 题目解析：

本题考查的是各种获得语言资料方式的好处和坏处，可以根据已经给出的信息来推测空格处所填的东西。

题号	定位词	文中对应点
	convenient / not objective enough	B 段 But a linguist's personal judgements are often uncertain, or disagree with the judgements of other linguists, at which point recourse is needed to more objective methods of enquiry, using non-linguists as informants. 答案：linguists / linguists act as
33	non-linguist	B 段： ...at which point recourse is needed to more objective methods of enquiry, using non-linguists as informants. The latter procedure is unavoidable when working on foreign languages, or child speech. 答案：foreign languages
34	recording / sound	D 段： But obtaining naturalistic, good-quality data is never easy. People talk abnormally when they know they are being recorded, and sound quality can be poor. 答案：quality
35	video / speaker	E 段： A facial expression, for example, can dramatically alter the meaning of what is said. 答案：facial expression
36	video / miss certain things	E 段： Video recording avoid these problems to a large extent, but even they have limitations (the camera cannot be everywhere), and transcriptions always benefit from any additional commentary provided by an observer. 答案：camera / video camera / recording

Questions 37－40

● 题目类型：SUMMARY

● 题目解析：

注意这道题目的要求，当中指明了在 G 段寻找答案。细读题目要求是节省做题时间的最好方式。

题号	定位词	题解
37	comment	G 段：A corpus enables the linguists to make unbiased statements about frequency of usage, ...
38	while / focus on	Some corpora attempt to cover the language as a whole, taking extracts from many kinds of text; others are extremely selective, providing a collection of material that deals only with a particular linguistic feature.
39	length of time	The size of the corpus depends on practical factors, such as the time available to collect, process and store the data.
40	those who speak	An important principle is that all corpora, whatever their size, are inevitably limited in their coverage, and always need to be supplemented by data derived from the intuitions of native speakers of the language, through either introspection or experimentation.

难句解析

1. But a linguist's personal judgements are often uncertain, or disagree with the judgements of other linguists, at which point recourse is needed to more objective methods of enquiry, using non-linguists as informants.

参考译文：然而，一名语言学家的个人判断通常要么是不确定的，要么就与其他语言学家的意见相左，此时就需要求助于更为客观的提问方式，让语言学家本人以外的人来充当资料提供者。

语言点：

(1) 由 which 引导的非限制性定语从句

a. which 可以用来引导非限制性定语从句，在从句中做主语或者宾语等。先行词可以是单个名词，主句的一部分，或是指前面整个句子。例如，

① He likes swimming, which is a good exercise. 他喜欢游泳，这是个很好的锻炼方式。

② She tore up the photos, which upset me. 她把照片撕了。这让我不快。

用在非限制性定语从句中的 which 就相当于 and this 或 and that 或者 and it.

b. 除了做主语和宾语之外，which 还可以作限定词与名词相连，此时 which 作定语。例如，

① He may hate this, in which case we ought to wait for him.

他可能会有怨恨，这样的话我们还是该等他。

② He lost temper, at which point I decided to go home.

他发脾气了，这样我就决定回家去了。

③ The tiger is at large, which circumstances is very serious.
老虎外逃了，这种状况很严重。
此时的 which 被称为关系形容词，只能用在定语从句中。

(2) point 的用法：

a. at the point of 正在…的时候；就要…的时候

b. come to the point 谈到正题

c. have one's points 有独到之处

d. up to a point 在一定程度上；有一点

e. what's the point? 那又有什么关系？

2. Video recording avoid these problems to a large extent, but even they have limitations (the camera cannot be everywhere), and transcriptions always benefit from any additional commentary provided by an observer.

参考译文：录像方式在很大程度上可以避免这样的问题，但是就算是这个方式也存在局限性(摄像机不可能安得到处都是)，而且文字誊本总是要得益于观察者另外提供的注解。

语言点：benefit 的用法：

(1) benefit 作名词时的意思

a. 益处；好处。例如，

① She is beautiful without benefit of make-ups. 她不化妆也很漂亮。

② The changes are to our benefit. 这些变化对我们有利。

b. 义演；义卖。例如，

a benefit concert 慈善音乐会

(2) benefit 做不及物动词时有“得益；得到好处”的意思。例如，

① People who stole did not benefit from the ill-gotten gains.
窃贼们并未从不义之财中得到好处。

② Many thousands have benefited from the new treatment. 数千人从新疗法中获益。

(3) 有关 benefit 的词组还有：

a. for the benefit of 为了某人的利益；给某人看

b. benefit society 互济会

3. An important principle is that all corpora, whatever their size, are inevitably limited in their coverage, and always need to be supplemented by data derived from the intuitions of native speakers of the language, through either introspection or experimentation.

参考译文：一个重要的原则是，无论大小，所有的语料库在覆盖面上都不可避免地存在局限性，因此，它们就总是需要通过内省或实验的方式，被源自母语者的直觉的资料补充。

结构分析:

principle 是主语，is 是系动词，that 引导表语从句，whatever their size 是插入语。表语从句的主语是 all corpra；谓语是 are limited，need to be supplemented；derived 是过去分词作定语来修饰 data；through 引导的是状语。

语言点：表语从句

(1) 连词 that, whether 可以引导表语从句。例如，

The point is whether you' d like to go with us. 问题是你愿不愿意跟我们一起去。

(2) 可以引导表语从句的关系代词和关系副词有：what, who, which, where, when, why。例如，

① My question is where you have been. 我的问题是你去了哪里。

② That was when I was nine years old. 那是我九岁的时候。

(3) 含有表语从句的句子有时可以倒装成含有主语从句的句子，进而变成 it 作形式主语的句子。例如，

The most important thing is whether they can come here early.

Whether they can come here early is the most important thing.

It is the most important thing whether they can come here early.

最重要的是他能不能早早赶到这里。

参考译文

获得语言资料

A 我们有很多种可以用来获得语言资料的方式。这些方法既可以是精心准备，深入细致的国外实地调查，也可以是在自家摇椅上进行的，对母语的一次不经意的反思。

B 无论用何种方式，总有人要充当语言资料的来源——这个人就叫做资料提供者。资料提供者(理想状态下)应该是以该语言为母语的人，他可以提供做分析之用的语句，还可以给出有关该语言的其他信息(如翻译，正误评判，用法判断等)。在研究本国语言时，语言学家本人往往充当资料提供者一角，比照他们的直觉，来对语句的歧义现象、可接受度及其他特性加以评判。这种方法因其便利性而被广泛使用，而且还被看作是生成式语言研究方式的规范。然而，一名语言学家的个人判断通常要么是不确定的，要么就与其他语言学家的意见相左，此时就需要求助于更为客观的提问方式，让语言学家本人以外的人来充当资料提供者。

C 在研究外语及儿童语言的时候，第二种方式是不可避免的。

在选择资料提供人的时候要考虑多种因素——你面对的是单个说话人(当语言从未被描述过的时候出现的通常状况)，还是两个人互动；是小组还是大规模的样本。年龄、性别、社会背景以及身份的其他方面都很重要，因为据信这些因素会影响使用语言的类别。对话的话题和社交场合的特征(比如正式程度)也极其相关；同样，资料提供者的个人资质(比如语言流畅度和连贯性)也十分重要。对于较大规模的研究来说，要对所采用的抽样方式一丝不苟，而且无论在什么情况下，都要决定采用最好的调查技术。

D 如今，语言研究者通常都会为资料提供人录音。这就使语言学家针对这些语言的某些论断变得可以接受检查，并且还能提供一种使这些观点更为精确的方式(反复听“难”懂的语言)。但是想要获得自然的、高质量的资料可没那么容易。当得知被录音的时候，人们说话的方式就不同了，而且音质可以很差。因此，一系列的录音方式就被设计出来以便尽可能地解除研究者的矛盾(如何能够观察人们的行为方式又不让他们知道正在被观察)。有时候，说话人是在毫不知情的情况下被录音的——这一方式可以获得极自然的材料，但是道德方面的反对意见也是预料之中的事。另外，也可以尝试让说话人忘记录音这回事，比如把录音机藏起来，或是使用无线麦克风。还有一种管用的方式，就是提出一个说话人能够迅速融入的话题，从而激发一种自然的语言风格(比如询问年长的资料提供者：在他们的家乡，时代是如何变迁的)。

E 然而，磁带录音的方式并不能够解决语言学家面临的所有问题。讲话通常又不清楚，又有歧义。因此，如果可能的话，要对参与者的非语言行为以及整体语境做出书面评述，作为对录音的补充。例如，一个面部表情就可以彻底改变一句话的意思。在很大情况下，可以用录像方式避免这样的问题，但是就算是这个方式也存在局限性(摄像机不可能安得到处都是)，而且文字誊本总是要得益于观察者另外提供的注解。

F 语言学家还需要大量使用结构化会议，当中他们系统地要求资料提供者说出有关某种动作、物体及行为的语句。如果资料提供者是说双语的，或者通过翻译的帮助，我们就有可能用到翻译技巧(比如你们怎么说桌子这个词)。通过使用面试表格和调查问卷，我们能够在很短的时间里覆盖大量的知识点。通常，研究者只想获得有关某个语言变项的信息，在这种情况下，就必须使用一套严格设置好的问题：比如说，发音上的某个特殊规则，可以用要求资料提供者读出一组严格设定的单词的方法引出来。我们还有几种直接的诱导方式，比如让资料提供人填写替换表中的空格(比如：我____看到一辆汽车)，或者给他们做改错练习(“能不能说我能不看到？”)。

G 为了语言分析而被编纂起来的语言代表

样本被叫做语料库。语料库使得语言学家能够对一种用法的频率加以客观陈述，而且还可以为其他的研究者所用。语料库的范围和规模是各不相同的。有些语料库试图将语言作为一个整体来研究，从不同类型的文章中节选材料；其他的则十分挑剔，只提供针对某个特殊语言现象的一组材料。语料库的大小是由实践因素决定的，比如说可以用来搜集、处理、存储资料的时间：要想为几分钟的演讲做一个精确的原文，可能要花上数小时的时间。有时候，一个小资料样本就足以证明一种语言学假说。相反地，重大研究项目的语料库加起来足有上百万字。一个重要的原则是，无论大小，所有的语料库在覆盖面上都不可避免地存在局限性，因此，它们总是需要通过内省或实验的方式，被源自母语者直觉的资料补充。

WRITING

WRITING TASK 1

考官范文

The chart gives information about post-school qualifications in terms of the different levels of further education reached by men and women in Australia in 1999.

We can see immediately that there were substantial differences in the proportion of men and women at different levels. The biggest gender difference is at the lowest post-school level, where 90% of those who held a skilled vocational diploma were men, compared with only 10% of women. By contrast, more women held undergraduate diplomas (70%) and marginally more women reached degree level (55%).

At the higher level of education, men with postgraduate diplomas clearly outnumbered their female counterparts (70% and 30%, respectively), and also constituted 60% of Master's graduates.

Thus we can see that more men than women hold qualifications at the lower and higher levels of education, while more women reach undergraduate diploma level than men. The gender difference is smallest at the level of Bachelor's degree, however.

分析

本题是一幅柱状图。横坐标为百分比，纵坐标为不同层次的中学后资历（职业技术文凭、本科文凭、学士学位、研究生文凭和硕士学位）。另外，每种资历男子和女子分别各为一根柱。

文章开头对于题目进行了改写，提供了时间、地点和研究对象等重要基本信息。

第二段话开头指出本柱状图最重要特征：男女在获得不同资历的比例上存在巨大差距。然后按照获得资历的从低到高的顺序进行描写。先写最低级别的，指出在这个级别上男女差异最大，分别为90%和10%。然后指出，在接下来的本科文凭和学士学位上，女子比男子的比例要高。

第三段指出在较高程度的教育上，无论是研究生文凭还是硕士学位方面，男子明显多于女子，用数字进行了说明。

文章结尾段进行总结，指出在较低和较高程度教育方面，男子比例较大，而在获得本科文凭方面女子超过男子。在获得学士学位方面，男女差异最小。

WRITING TASK 2

题目要求

Creative artists should always be given the freedom to express their own ideas (in words, pictures, music or film) in whichever way they wish. There should be no government restrictions on what they do.

To what extent do you agree or disagree with this opinion?

题解

创造性艺术家应该拥有以自己想要的任何方式(通过文字、图画、音乐或影像)来表达思想的自由。对此政府不应该加以任何限制。你在何等程度上同意或是不同意这个观点?

本题为典型的论点题，要求考生针对题目中的论点进行支持或是驳斥。考生在审题时需要仔细分析题目中包含的两组对比关系：个人（艺术家）与政府，创造与限制。个人与政府既有内在矛盾，又有共同利益。创造与限制虽然似乎水火不容，却可以分别进行分类。

范文一

On the specific issue of creative freedom versus government restrictions, I am full of the opinion that the latter should give place to the former.

Creation is the soul of art. And creation can only be nurtured in an environment of freedom. Human history has shown that the flourishing eras of artistic works were always those accompanied by great freedom, no matter whether ideologically or politically. These artistic creations enriched people's spiritual life of the time, left the generations to have a valuable legacy, and overall make a good part of human civilization for ever. Without them, human civilization might take on another look undesirable to us all.

Nearly any restriction is bound to impede artistic expression. Of all, the most destructive force is from the government with the strong power behind it. Improper government restrictions kill artistic creation. Without artistic creation, people's spiritual life will be in stagnation. And this will further affect people's physical life directly or indirectly. Ultimately, the whole society is seen in an appalling state. Those dark ages in human history generally fell into this formula.

Therefore, for more colorful life of human beings, artistic creations should be encouraged in freedom. It is the responsibility of the government to help foster such an art-friendly atmosphere, rather than exert restrictions.

分析

文章首段开门见山，作者指出在创造性自由和政府限制这对矛盾上，坚决支持自由，反对限制。

第二段论证为什么要保护创作自由。首先，创作是艺术的灵魂。而创作只有在自由的氛围下才可能实现。人类历史表明，艺术作品兴盛的时代总是拥有充分自由的时代，无论是意识形态方面还是政治方面。这些艺术创作丰富了当时人们的精神生活，为后代留下了宝贵遗产，也构成人类文明的重要组成部分。没有这些艺术作品，人类文明可能会呈现出我们不愿意看到的景象。

第三段论证为什么反对限制。几乎任何限制都必然会阻碍艺术表达。而限制中最具破坏性的就是具有强大力量的政府影响。政府的不当限制会毁了艺术创造。而没有艺术创造，人们的精神生活就会停滞不前。物质生活也会受到影响。最终全社会都会变得可怕。人类历史上的黑暗时期经常都是这样。

文章的主体段落分别从正反两反面论证了为什么坚决支持创作自由，反对政府限制。在此之后，文章结尾进行了总结。为了追求更加丰富多彩的生活，艺术创造自由应该得到鼓励，而政府的职责应该是扶助这样一种氛围，而不是去强加限制。

范文二

To a very large extent, I believe that the work of creative artists should not be restricted by any government.

Of course, we have to admit that there are some forms of restriction that should be imposed on artists. History and modern day experience make it very clear that people can be influenced in unhealthy ways by what they read, see and hear. By unhealthy, I mean things that promote such things as racial prejudice, sexual inequality, selfishness, violence, cruelty to people or other animals, and environmental destruction. One thinks, for example, of Nazi propaganda that contributed so efficiently to the slaughter of millions of Jews, gypsies and other minorities, of the violence in films and computer games that some psychologists believe can encourage anti-social and violent behavior in children, and of pornographic movies that can foster exploitative attitudes to women and children.

Although I believe certain restrictions should be applied to the work of creative artists, I hold that artistic freedom is so important that governments should not interfere directly. It is self-evident that the more life means to us, then the richer life becomes for us. To a large extent, the work of creative artists helps us to see ourselves, other people and the world around us in different ways. When we see these things in different ways, we often learn to appreciate them more, which in turn means they mean more to us and thus enrich and add to the quality of our lives. In addition, creativity in others can stimulate our own creativity, the use of which psychologists and my own experience tell me satisfies a real human need and helps us to be more fully human.

Thus, I shall argue that government should not stifle original ideas by severe restrictions but allow sufficient freedom as long as creative artists do not work against basic human value.

分析

文章开头明确提出观点：创造性艺术家的创造自由不应该受到任何政府的限制。

第二段话进行让步，分析并论证在某些情形下进行某种形式限制的必要性。本段主要通过举例进行论证。首先提出观点，人们可能会受到看到或听到的东西的不健康影响。所谓不健康，指的是宣传推动种族歧视，性别歧视，过度自私，暴力，残忍地对待人或动物以及大肆破坏环境等等。比如，纳粹通过各种艺术手段宣传，最终导致屠杀犹太人、吉普赛人和其他少数民族，电影和电子游戏暴力助长儿童的反社会和暴力行为，色情影片推动对于妇女和儿童的剥削与压迫。在这些方面加以限制自然是非常合理的。

第三段进行作者主要立场的论证。虽然对于创造性艺术家的工作可能需要加以某种形式的限制，但是艺术自由非常重要，政府最好不要随便干预。首先，不言自明的是，我们越能理解生活的意义就越能体会生活的丰富多彩。在很大程度上，创造性艺术家的作品帮助我们以新的方式看待我们自己，其他人，以及我们周围的世界。当我们用不同方式来看待这些的时候，我们经常能够有更深的体会，我们的生活质量也从而得到丰富和提高。除此之外，他人的创造性可以激发我们自己的创造性。而正是创造性的使用使得我们的需求更加得到满足，更加具有人类的特征。

最后简单总结一下。总之，政府不应该通过严格的限制扼杀原创性而是应该给予创造性艺术家充分的创造自由，只要艺术家们不违背人类的基本价值观念。

SPEAKING

E=Examiner ***C=Candidate***

E: Good morning.

C: Good morning.

E: My name is Andrew. Would you tell me your full name, please?

C: It' s Zhang Ting. You can call me Angela.

E: OK. Thank you, Angela. Now let' s talk about what you do. Do you work, or are you a student?

C: I' m a college student at Beijing Foreign Studies University. My major is English.

E: Why did you choose English?

C: Well, actually, my parents chose it. They said people who are fluent in English will never have a problem finding a good job.

E: Did you agree at the time?

C: Kind of, I suppose. But I really wanted to study music, mainly piano.

E: How do you feel about it now?

C: I can see their point now, and I' m very excited at the idea of going to England for my MA. But I really miss playing the piano. There' s no free lunch, I guess.

E: Sure. Now let' s talk about your hometown. What' s the most interesting thing to do in your hometown?

C: Tianjin is quite a fun place, but for me the most exciting thing to do there is to try the different restaurants. The food is great, very inexpensive.

E: Is there anything you don' t like about your hometown?

C: Well, Tianjin is a lovely city, but it' s not very clean. It' s polluted because of the many industries and factories, and all the cars and trucks, of course. Air pollution is a big problem.

E: How do you normally get around Tianjin?

C: By bike, usually, coz Tianjin is quite flat, or I take a bus. Taxis are too expensive to use every day.

E: What about long distance travel?

E: How do you normally get around Tianjin?

C: By bike, usually, coz Tianjin is quite flat, or I take a bus. Taxis are too expensive to use every day.

E: What about long distance travel?

C: I like traveling by train. It' s convenient and it' s cheap. I enjoy simply gazing out of the window and watching the changing scenery.

E: Going back to Tianjin. What do you think the government should do to improve transportation in your hometown?

C: Well, there' s a lot that the government could do. For one thing, it could build more roads, because we have more and more cars on the road; for another, it should develop the underground system, coz for me it' s the best mode of transportation for commuters. You know, it' s fast, cheap, regular, and environment-friendly.

Describe a river, lake or sea which you like.

You should say:

what the river, lake or sea is called

where it is

what the land near it is like

And explain why you like the river, lake or sea.

E: Thank you. Now I' m going to give you a topic. I' d like you to talk about it for two minutes. Before you talk, you have one minute to think about what you' re going to say. You can take some notes. Here is you topic.

E: All right, remember you have two minutes. I'll tell you when time is up. You can speak now.

C: Well, let me tell you a bit about the Sea River. It' s very famous among the locals, and flows right through Tianjin. It is called Sea River because it is larger than an ordinary river, like the sea is. The Sea River to the locals is like the Yellow River to the Chinese people. It is of great importance to the city, and is a major reason underlying the development of the city. The whole city grew around the river. In the past, there were many villages along its banks and the people there mainly relied on fishing and boat building. I can imagine how simple and uncomplicated their lives were. But nowadays things have changed greatly. The villages are gone, and hundreds of skyscrapers and other buildings have taken their place. And the Sea River got severely polluted. Before, parks and gardens alongside the river now, so the Sea River is taking on a new face, and it's much prettier.

E: What do people enjoy doing when they go to rivers, lakes or the sea? Why do you think these activities are popular?

C: I think people who visit rivers, lakes or the sea and who do not have easy access to these water areas, first, they enjoy the sightseeing, although lots of people who live near to water also enjoy strolling along the beach or river bank, or just sitting and relaxing looking at the water. And of course there are more energetic things that a lot of people enjoy, like scuba diving and surfing. In winter, people enjoy skating on frozen rivers or lakes.

It seems to me that water functions as a cleanser, so the air there is fresh and clean, which we seldom have in big cities. And gazing at a river or other area of water also cleanses people's minds, I mean it helps you to relax and forget your worries. Besides relaxation, water-based activities can also bring us excitement. Take surfing, for example, people who go surfing — I've seen movies of people surfing those huge waves in Hawaii—they love the thrill of danger. When they find themselves still alive afterwards, they must feel terrific, with a great sense of achievement.

E: I guess so. Have you ever been surfing?

C: Only a couple of times, when I was in Hainan last year. But the waves were only a meter high, not like those monsters in Hawaii. Not very dangerous, but it was great fun. I'd love to try some bigger waves.

E: Do you think you'll have a chance when you're in England?

C: I hope so. I saw a movie — I think it was shot on the southwest coast of England — about surfers. There was a really dangerous place to go surfing, but that was what the characters in the film loved. I think I'd look for some place a bit safer.

E: Same here. Apart from relaxation and excitement, can you think of any other benefits people get from activities they enjoy in water?

C: Well, there's the sense of achievement I mentioned just now. And of course, swimming and surfing are great exercise. Those old people who go swimming all year round always seem to look much younger than they are.

E: Do you go swimming very often?

C: Actually, I go almost every day. The university pool opens at six thirty every morning, and I find an early morning swim is a great way to start the day. Sometimes I go later, around ten at night — it seems to help me sleep.

E: Do you prefer swimming in a swimming pool or swimming in the sea, or in a lake?

C: Oh, I much prefer the sea, but not when it's too cold. In Tianjin, I often go to the beach for a swim. But that's impossible when I'm at university, so I have no choice but to use the pool.

E: What about the canals?

C: No way! They always look so green and dirty. I can't imagine how people can swim in them.

E: Can you think of any advantages or disadvantages of going to the sea or to a swimming pool?

C: Well, the first thing is that many people don't have easy access to the sea, so they have no choice but to go to a swimming pool, or a lake or river if there's one not too far away. So that's a big advantage of swimming pools — they can be built almost anywhere. And you can swim all year round in most of them: you don't have to worry about the weather. But sometimes they get too crowded, which is a disadvantage if you want to swim lengths. Our university pool has lanes for serious swimmers, which people can't use for just splashing around in. Disadvantages of the sea? Let me think. Yes, there's the question of safety. Swimming pools employ people to make sure no one drowns. A lot of popular beaches have lifeguards, which makes things safer, but there's still a much greater chance of getting into trouble in the sea than in a swimming pool. Swimming pools don't have strong currents that can pull you out to sea, or jelly fish or sharks. But I still prefer swimming in the sea to in a swimming pool.

E: Why do you think this is?

C: I love the space. I feel so wonderful just swimming and swimming, without having to turn around every 50 meters. And some swimming pools can be a bit dirty, where it's easy to get an ear infection. On the other hand, a lot of beaches around China are much polluted, and much unhealthier than a well managed swimming pool. And swimming pools don't have — what's it called?— red tides. But I don't know if it's dangerous to swim in a red tide.

E: Can't be good for you, I suppose. OK, let's change the subject. You said the Sea River is a major reason that Tianjin developed. I guess you mean its use for transportation. Compared with other forms of transport, can you think of any advantages and disadvantages of water transport?

C: Well, water transport is greatly influenced by the weather, especially by strong winds. But then again, so is air transport. Also it is much slower than road, rail or air transport, so it is not good for things that go bad quickly and have to be moved a long distance. Water transport is much cheaper than air transport; I'm not sure how it compares with the railway for the same distance. And of course it' s the only way to transport bulk things like coal and grain, or cars, between continents.

E: How important is it for a town or city to be located near a river or the sea?

C: In the past, towns or cities located near a river or the sea, I mean with a natural harbor, developed faster and earlier than other places. A major reason is the convenience of transportation. Look at those cities along the east coast of China. They are much richer and more developed than the cities in the middle and west of China, and of course are closer to international markets, so they were where traders from other countries as far away as Africa came. And before the railways were developed, ships were the only way to move large quantities of goods. So towns or cities near a river or the sea became important ports. Actually, I' ve forgotten about the Silk Road, which for centuries was obviously the only way to transport, mostly luxury goods like silk and spices, between landlocked areas of China and Central Asia, even Europe. What do they call camels? "Ships of the desert", that' s it. But they have mostly been replaced by rail and road transportation.

E: You spoke earlier about water pollution. Do you think there are any problems with shipping in this regard?

C: Well, I don't know a lot about it, but I have read, and seen a few things on TV, that some irresponsible ship captains just throw their waste oil and other rubbish straight into the sea. I guess they don't want to pay for it to be treated properly when they get to port. But with satellites and other things it's getting easier to spot ships doing this, and probably, at least I hope, the captains and crews are becoming more aware of environ mental protection. I know many countries have really heavy fines for ships that pollute in their territorial waters.

E: You're right. I'm from the US, and the owners of ships that break environmental laws can be in big trouble. Anyway, that's enough. We can finish the interview now. Any thing else you' d like to say?

C: Only to thank you for being such a kind interviewer. I was very nervous when I came in, but soon relaxed when you were so nice.

E: Thank you. And, good luck in the future.

C: Thank you. Goodbye.

E: Goodbye.

Test 4

LISTENING

SECTION 1

篇章结构

题　　型：笔记填空
考查技能：听出具体信息
场　　景：日常生活——准备一个告别晚会

场景背景介绍

在学习和工作过程中，有些同学或同事可能会因为种种原因离开学校或单位，比如转学、退休等。一般为了欢送要走的同学 / 同事，其他人会为他们举办一个告别晚会。本文中所涉及的就是这样的话题。一般首先要确定时间，在什么时候举行，什么时候发送邀请，都要邀请哪些人。然后要确定地点和晚会中所要进行的各种表演项目以及晚会所需要的各种物品。当然，最重要的是要给离开的同学 / 同事送什么样的礼物。

本节必备词汇 、词组

farewell	*n.* 辞别	handy	*adj.* 手边的，便利的
double the work	事倍功半	have a little think	曾经想过
take notes	作笔记	a set of	一套
near the time	时间紧迫	social fund	社会基金
dinning room	餐厅	tape deck	录放音座，磁带卡座，大型录音机
ought to	应该		
office staff	办公室全体职员	later on	稍后
faculty head	系主任	set up	设立
draw the line	划一界线，划定最后界限	student leader	学生干部

场景词汇拓展

finish at	几点结束	instant coffee	速溶咖啡
begin at	几点开始	real coffee	煮咖啡
due to	因为	espresso coffee	浓咖啡
starting off	开始	hot dish	热菜
further information	补充信息	have to dash	马上要走了
look forward to	期望，期待，盼望	meet up	偶遇
common room	公共休息室	sort out	挑选，解决
by the way	在途中，顺便	at the moment	此刻
flatmate	租同一套公寓的人		

文本及疑难解析

1. P145. “We don’t want to leave it so late that it’s double the work.”我们不想拖的太晚，那样会事倍功半。该句主要注意“it’s double”的用法。

2. P145. “I think a hotel will probably **work out** rather expensive.”我觉得去旅馆太贵了。“work out”的本意为“可以解决，设计出，做出，计算出，消耗完，挤(出去)M，冲(出去)”，但是在这里没有什么具体含义。

3. P146. “And then we **ought to** be thinking about invitation.”下一步我们该考虑邀请谁。 “ought to ”后面可以跟动词原形，而此处原文中使用“be thinking”使句子更生动。比如：“we ought to be playing bridge now.”现在我们该打桥牌了。

4. P146. “No， better **draw the line**， I don’t think it’s necessary.”不，我反对，我认为这没有必要。“draw the line”这个词组有两个意思，第一个表示划界线、区别，比如：“Some times it’s difficult to draw the line between backbiting and malicious gossip.”有时候很难区别背后的闲言碎语和恶意中伤。第二个意思：限制、反对，比如“Her father draws the line at her coming in after midnight.”她父亲不准她半夜以后进门。第二个意思适用于本文。

题目解析

1–10题都是笔记填空题，难度普遍不大。第一题主要考查词汇“venue”的含义“地点”。如果不认识这个单词肯定会影响作题，因为不知道去听什么。第二题比较容易定位，用“Director”和“all the teachers”两面夹击就可以抓住答案。不过第三题距离较近，有些难度。第四题，原文中有三个日期，最后一个日期“Tenth”才是答案。第五题用“during”可以直接定位答案。第五题要小心后边“$90”的迷惑。第七题主要注意写答案时不要超过题目要求。8、9题难度不大，第十题与第九题距离很近，但是后面有重复信息，降低了难度。

SECTION 2

篇章结构

题　　型：选择表格填空
考查技能：听出具体信息
场　　景：旅游信息—自动电话咨询

场景背景介绍

自动电话咨询服务是我们生活中密不可分的一部分，我们在申请护照过程中向大使电话咨询时，听到的是自动电话咨询系统。当我们向海外大学电话咨询时，往往也会听到自动电话咨询系统。如果出国之后想咨询有关银行服务，向电影院咨询票务、向旅游公司咨询旅游业务一般也会听到自动电话咨询系统的回答。有些系统会在最后加上人工服务，但许多根本没有人工服务项目。

本节必备词汇、词组

deal with	处理，涉及	in detail	详细地
appropriate	*adj.* 适当的	guarantee	*n.* 保证 *vt.* 保证，担保
latest price list	最新的价格表	cater for	供应伙食，迎合
complaint	*n.* 诉苦，投诉	pride	*n.* 自豪 *vt.* 使自豪，使自夸
discerning traveller	精明的(有分辨力的)旅行者	communal tables	公共餐桌
Western Europe	西欧	on top of	在…之上，另外
watch out	密切注视，当心，提防	plus	*prep.* 加上 *adj.* 正的，加的

场景词汇扩充

flight reservation	预定机票	intersection	*n.* [数]交集，十字路口，交叉点
hotel reservation	预定旅馆	don't litter	不要乱丢垃圾
visa	*n.* 签证 *vt.* 签证	no parking	禁止停车
flight ticket	飞机票	speed limit	速度限制
one-way ticket	单程票	toll	*n.* 通行税(费)，费
round-trip ticket	往返票,双程票	tipping	*adj.* 倾翻的，倾卸的 *n.* 倾卸台

lobby	*n.* 大厅，休息室	voucher	*n.* <美>优惠购货券
front desk	前台		

文本及疑难解析

1. P147. “We have been offering a wide variety of walking holidays to suit all tastes for just 3 years, **but already** we have won two awards for excellence in this field.” 我们为您提供各种各种各样的步行假日安排，满足各种日常的需要，已经在这个领域内两次获得优秀奖。首先要注意在英语中“虽然”和“但是”不会同时出现，这与汉语有明显差异。另外要注意“already”的用法。正常语序为“we have already won...”。原文是为了强调，所以将“already”提前。比如“I already have told you how to deal with your mistakes.”我早就已经告诉你怎样去处理你的错误了。

2. P148. “We also pride ourselves on our **friendly** service, particularly important for the increasing numbers of people who choose to holiday alone. Unlike...” 我们还为我们提供的友好服务而骄傲。最近，选择单独度假的人越来越多，我们的服务尤其对这些人很重要，不像…” 该句的难点在于对“friendly”的理解，虽然字面意思可以理解为“友好的”，但实际上针对的是后面一句“Unlike almost all travel operators who happily charge large supplements for single rooms, we guarantee that no single client will pay more.” 不像其他的(大部分)几乎所有的旅游经纪人都会愿意对单人间多收费，我们不会让任何一位单独客户多交费。

3. P148. “...after dinner at **communal** table designed to make all our guests feel part of a family atmosphere...” 为了让大家感觉到家庭气氛，我们设计了集体餐桌。“communal”最基本的意思是“公有的”，在此引申为“集体公用的，共同的”。比如：a ~ shower 公共浴室，cook a ~ pot 烧一大锅饭，a ~ decision 共同决定。

4. P148. “**On top of that**, we are able to include free maps...for you to better enjoy the walking and even plan in advance, if you wish.”
除此之外，我们还给您提供免费的地图，这样您可以更好地享受徒步旅行，如果您愿意的话，您甚至于可以提前做出计划。首先要注意“on top of”的用法，从字面意思上看相当于“在…顶上”，但实际上的意思是“除此之外，还有…”相当于“besides”的用法。
比如，“On top of the entrance fee, you have to pay to each special service”除了门票费用外，您还需要对各项服务付费。“on top of”还有一个意思，“紧挨着，紧邻”，比如，“On top of the bank, there’s a post office.”银行旁边有一个邮局。

题目解析

11－15题为单项选择题，难度不太大。11题只需要用“cost”定位便可。12题有一定的迷惑性，因为我们能听到“western Europe”，“throughout the whole”以及“outside this area”。其中“throughout the whole”修饰“western Europe”，而“outside this area”是将来的事情，所以A为正确选项。但是因为A选项中有一个“绝对词”“only”，所以很多同学会望而生畏。13题只需听到“catering for”即可作对该题，另外“all”与A选项中的“a range of”也很匹配。14题用“holiday alone”定位可以听到答案，不过要注意听到的否定词“No”否定的是“More”，所以应该选A——表示与其他客户一样多。15题的迷惑性在于“every night”(C选项)，但原文中说的是“Nearly every night”，我们就不能选C了。

16－20题是表格填空题，其中读完题之后，同学们就会意识到16和19题缺数字，18题缺“maps”的并列信息，都不算太难，17与20题用“from”和“of”两个介词去定位也不算难。特别需要注意的是19题和20题距离较近，有一定难度。

SECTION 3

篇章结构

题　　型：表格填空、配对
考查信息：听出具体信息
场　　景：研究——讨论5个实验

场景背景介绍

雅思听力考试的第三部分除了讨论与专业、课程有关的话题外就是课上或课外研究场景，其中最难的当属特殊领域中的特殊研究，虽然本文中涉及的五个实验都不是很难，但第一个题关于气垫船的工作原理，第二个是关于测量单位，第三个是饱和溶液中析出晶体，第四个是研究光的构成原理，最后一个是做一个录音机。五个实验涉及不同的五个范畴而且有一些专业术语如：“hovercraft, copper sulphate, amplifier”等。以后遇到这种问题，大家千万不要灰心，只要认真读题，定位需要的信息就可以了。

本节必备词汇、词组

get hold of	抓住，得到	equipment	*n.* 装备，设备
hovercraft	*n.* 气垫船，水翼船	hand drill	手钻
balloon	*n.* 气球	bolt	*n.* 门闩，螺钉
engine	*n.* 发动机，机车，火车头	amplifier	*n.* 扩音器，放大器
		go through	经历，经受
cushion of air	气垫	turn sb. off	使某人远离
paperclips	*n.* 纸夹子	for good	永久地，一劳永逸地
units of measurement	度量衡单位	fortnight	*n.* 两星期
rock salt	岩盐，石盐	decent result	像样的结果
copper sulphate	硫酸铜	write up	详细描写
dissolve	*v.* 溶解，解散	babyish	*adj.* 幼稚的,稚气的
crystal	*n.* 水晶，结晶	cut out	切掉
segment	*n.* 段　*v.* 分割	start off	出发，开始
merge	*v.*合并	end up	竖着，结束，死，结果
ordinary light	自然光	store sth. for later	留到以后

场景词汇拓展

gadget	*n.* 小器具，小玩意	lime	*n.* 酸橙，石灰
installment	*n.* 部分	slurry	*n.* 泥浆，浆
saturate	*v.* 使饱和，浸透，使充满	reflection	*n.* 反射，沉思
unsaturated	*adj.* 没有饱和的，不饱和的	prism	*n.* 棱镜，棱柱
solution	*n.* 解答，溶解	lightening	*n.* 闪电，发光
sulphur	*n.* 硫磺	silicon	*n.* 硅，硅元素
oxide	*n.* 氧化物	semiconductor	*n.* [物] 半导体
carbon dioxide	*n.* 二氧化碳	magnet	*n.* 磁体，磁铁

文本及疑难解析

1. P148. "**what's this** I hear about a **big assignment** we've got to do?" 意为"到底怎么回事，我听说留了很多作业要做是吗？""what's this"不是问"这是什么"，而是相当于汉语中的"怎么了？""怎么回事？""big assignment"不是指"大"而是指"多"。在听磁带的过程中，大家会听到许多认识但是不确切——不能马上找到汉语对事物的词，这时不要强求，否则就会陷入"边听边翻译"的恶习中去。

2. P148. "we've got to find two science experiments **to do** with a group of eight-year-old children at the local primary school." 意为"我们得做(找)两个科学实验，而且要和当地小学的8岁的孩子们一起做。"这句话中"to do"后边有两个介词词组，第一个做状语，修饰"to do"，第二个做定语修饰"children"。介词的用法灵活多变，是考生听力中的障碍，大家一定要多注意介词，尤其是和动词及形容词的搭配。

3. P149. "**Mind** you, you only need 20 balloons and a table — you don't need any special engines or anything like that." 意为"注意，(我们)只需要20个气球和一张桌子，不需要任何发动机或其他类似的东西。"Mind"当动词时有许多含义。比如，"Mind(记住)my words"；"Mind (务必)you go"；"Mind (照料)a flock of sheep"；"Mind(服从)your father"；"Don't mind(介意)his bluntness"等等。

4. P149. "Well, just **put down** the rock salt then, um, **apart from that** you only need a **jar** of water." 意为"好的，就记下石盐，嗯，除此之外只需要一广口瓶水"。首先是"put down"，在这里它不是"放下"而是"写下来"的意思。"apart from that"类似于"besides"或者是"on top of that"。这里的"you"不是确指"你"而是泛指，甚至可以指"我们"。最后就是"jar"的意思，同学们都知道它是"坛子"的意思，但是我们不可能在实验室里摆很多泡菜坛子吧，它应该是广口瓶的意思。

5. P150. "No, I don't like **the sound of** that one at all." 意为"我一点也不喜欢这个实验"。在这里"the sound of"并不是指这个实验发出的声音，可以指"听起来，听上去"或者"这个实验的含义"或译成"这个实验可能会导致什么"。"sound" 可以当动词表示"发声"，当形容词表示"健康的、扎实的、彻底的"等等。

6. p150. “We won’t get a very good mark if the children don’t actually enjoy the experiments, and I suppose we could **turn** them **off** science for good.” 意为“如果孩子们不喜欢这些实验，我们不会得到好分数，而且我想这会让他们从此之后不再喜欢科学”。这句话中“turn”和“off”不是固定搭配，应该是“turn sb. off sth.”——“使某人远离或讨厌…”。“for good”不是“为了好”而且“永久地”的意思。“for good”也经常被说成“for good and all”，如：“We thought she’d come for a visit, but it seem she’s staying for good.”意为“本来我们以为她是来作客的，但看来她是永远不会走了”。

7. P150. “...we had to wait **up to** a fortnight before we saw any half way decent result.”意为“我们不得不等上两星期，即便是这样也看不到什么像样的结果”。“up to”表示“长达”。“decent”在此表示“过得去的，尚可以的，像样的。”比如，“He got quite a decent meal in a restaurant.”——他在一家餐馆里吃了一顿像样的饭。

题目解析

21－26题是表格填空题，难度不大。同学们只需要抓住纵轴——五个实验和横轴：需要的仪器和实验的目的。21题是与“table”并列的“20 balloons”，不难。22题要用题干中的“Need”定位原文中的“importance”才能听到答案“units of measurement.”23和24题比较容易，因为两个题虽然离得比较近，但是都是重复信息。25和26题也可以直接用题干中的词去定位答案。

27－30题是配对题，这几个起主要考查同学们听同义词、近义词的能力，其中27题是“risky”与选项H“dangerous”是同义词，28题是“it needs to be something a bit more active and interesting than that”与选项B“boring”是反义关系；29题需要听懂“fortnight”——两个星期与选项E“too long”之间的同义关系；30题最难需要听懂“too ambitions”与选项C“too difficult”之间的近义关系。

SECTION 4

篇章结构

题　　型：笔记填空，单选和多项选择
考查技能：听出具体信息
场　　景：讲座——澳大利亚的鲨鱼与捕鲨网

场景背景介绍

大约在一千万年以前，澳洲大陆从南极洲陆块分裂而出，与外界隔绝。岛上特殊的生态，像是一个独立的动物实验室，保留了许多珍奇独特的动物品种，比如：牛犬蚁、琴鸟、袋鼠、恐怖的蜥蜴、塔斯马尼亚怪兽和鸭嘴兽等等，它们有着各自奇特的造型和与众不同的生活习性。虽然本文讲述的是大家熟悉的鲨鱼，但是关于捕鲨网的来历以及用途，很多同学也并不是很清楚。

本节必备词汇、词组：

reputation	*n.* 名誉，名声	Tahiti	塔希提岛(位于南太平洋，法属波利西亚的经济活动中心)
hunt one' s pray	打猎，猎取食物(猎物)		
dangerous creature	危险的生物		
essentially	*adv.* 本质上，本来	barb	*n.* 鱼钩
breed	*v.* (使)繁殖 *n.* 品种，种	maximum temperature	最高温度
acute	*adj.* 敏锐的，[医]急性的，剧烈	big seas	汹涌的大海
		sandpaper	*n.* 沙纸
sense of smell	嗅觉	rolling waves	浪涛汹涌
skeleton	*n.* (动物之)骨架，骨骼	underneath	*adv.* 在下面 *prep.* 在…的下面
cartilage	*n.* [解剖]软骨		
meshing	*n.* 网孔	strong currents	巨浪
pliable	*adj.* 易曲折的，柔软的	fin	*n.* 鳍，鱼翅
be crowded with	充满，满是	less effective	不太有效
scale	*n.* 刻度,鱼鳞	scavenge	*v.* 打扫，以(腐肉)为食

场景词汇拓展

vole	*n.* 野鼠类	badger	*n.* 獾
bison	*n.* 美洲或欧洲的野牛	ferret	*n.* 白鼬，雪貂
buffalo	*n.* (印度、非洲等的)水牛，美洲野牛	squirrel	*n.* 松鼠　*v.* 贮藏
		bear	*n.* 熊
wolf	*n.* 狼，残忍贪婪之人，极度的穷困 *vt.* 狼吞虎咽，大吃 *vi.* 猎狼	fox	*n.* 狐狸
		lark	*n.* 云雀
beaver	*n.* 海狸(毛皮)	raven	*n.* 大乌鸦，掠夺 *v.* 掠夺，狼吞虎咽
elephant	*n.* 象，一种纸张的尺寸		
hare	*n.* 野兔	cuckoo	*n.* 杜鹃鸟，布谷鸟
otter	*n.* 水獭，水獭皮	swan	*n.* 天鹅，杰出的诗人、歌手，天鹅座
marmot	*n.* 旱獭，土拨鼠		

文本及疑难解析

1. P151.　“sharks **vary in** weight with size and breed...”鲨鱼的体重因大小或种类不同而不同。本句中有两个介词“in, with”。前者是大家很容易理解，而且也会用，是与动词“vary”的搭配。但是后者对大多数同学来说是只可理解不会使用。比如，“Most Chinese students pronounce English quite differently from native speakers with stresses and tone.”——许多中国学生与母语是英语的人发音大相径庭，主要是重音和语调(两个方面)。

2. P151.“...this means that the net **on New South Wales beaches** are set on one day, and then lifted and taken on to sea **on the next day**.”意为“也就是说，前一天人们把网安在新南威尔士的海滨，然后收起来第二天再放回到海里去。”同学们对“beach”的理解一般是“沙滩”，但在这里指的是“海滨”。第二个难点就是“on New South Wales”引起的歧义，它会导致有些人想到第二天要把网要放到“Sydney”或“Melbourne”。最后要注意“on the next day”修饰的只有“take out to sea”而对“lifted”没有任何影响。

3. P151.　“The New Zealand authorities also looked at it, but considered meshing uneconomical — as did Tahiti in Pacific.”意为“新西兰政府看过防鲨网，但是认为不够经济，太平洋里的塔希堤地区也这样认为。该句的难点在后半句，“as did Tahiti in Pacific”。这是一个倒装句，意思相当于“Tahiti in Pacific also thought meshing uneconomical.”。

4. P151.　“**It’s** not that they think sharks are afraid of nets, or because **they** eat holes in them, because neither of these is true.”意为“并不是人们认为鲨鱼怕这些网子，或者是鲨鱼在网上咬洞，因为这两者都不是真的。”该句的难点在于句中的五个代词，第一个代词“it”指上一句“有些人认为用捕鲨网捕捉鲨鱼不是最好的方法。”第二个代词“they”指上一句中的“some people”。第三个代词“they”指的是“sharks”。第四个代词them 指“nets”。第五个代词“these”指该句的前两部分。

题目解析

31 – 34 题为笔记填空题，难度都不大。31 题用最高级“heaviest”可以定位到答案“795 kg”。32 题是并列信息与“fins”并列的是“tail”但是要注意题干中的“aids”与原文中的“helps”的同义关系。33 题用食物“food”和海洋“ocean”可以定位到答案“floor”，前边还提过“bottom”，如果没有听到，写“bed”——“海床”也可以得分。34 题是重复信息，“eyesight”有一定的迷惑性。

35 – 38 题材是单项选择，很容易，只不过 35 题要注意 A 选项中的“along”与原文中 parallel 的同义关系；36 题要注意 B 和 C 选项是迷惑项，但原文中都出现了，只不过被否定了，按顺序原则也该选 A。37 题要注意 C 是迷惑项；38 题要注意 11 月到 2 月在南半球是夏天，而且 warmest 也可以帮助我们确定 B 选项。

39 – 40 题是多选题。因为原文中出现了“especially”，而且 B、E 两个选项在原文中几乎没有任何变化，所以难度不大。

READING

READING PASSAGE 1

篇章结构

体裁 说明文

主题 影响运动员表现的主要因素

结构

第一段：20世纪运动员成绩的提高

第二段：基因在提高运动成绩中的角色

第三段：训练的作用

第四段：增强式训练模式

第五段：营养在提高运动成绩中的角色

第六段：集中训练的作用

第七段：生物力学

第八段：运动员自身创新的重要性

第九段：未来前景

必背词汇

athletic	*adj.* 运动的	appreciably	*adv.* 略微，有一点
federation	*n.* 同盟，联盟	tempt	*v.* 诱惑，引诱，吸引
steady	*adj.* 稳固的，稳定的	individual	*n.* 个人，个体；*adj.* 单独的，个人的
massive	*adj.* 厚重的，结实的		
release	*n.* &*v.* 释放，让渡	emeritus	*adj.* 名誉退休的，退休的
sprint	*n.* 短跑	duplicate	*v.* 复写，复制，使加倍
endurance	*n.* 持久(力)，耐久(性)	plyometrics	*n.* 增强式训练
dramatic	*adj.* 戏剧性的，生动的	interval	*n.* 间隔，距离
marathon	*n.* 马拉松赛跑	nutrition	*n.* 营养，营养学
genetics	*n.* 遗传学	adequately	*adv.* 充分地
athlete	*n.* 运动员	coach	*n.* 教练
adage	*n.* 格言，谚语	deficiency	*n.* 缺乏，不足
gene pool	基因库	mineral	*n.* 矿物质

assert	*v.* 断言，声称	sawdust	*n.* 木屑
methodology	*n.* 方法学，方法论	pit	*n.* 深坑，深渊
biomechanics	*n.* 生物力学	foam	*n.* 泡沫
joint	*n.* 关节	psychologist	*n.* 心理学者
unorthodox	*adj.* 非正统的，异端的	mundane	*adj.* 世界的，世俗的，平凡的
simulation	*n.* 仿真，假装，模拟	variable	*n.* 可变物，变量
innovation	*n.* 改革，创新	foreseeable	*adj.* 可预知的，能预测的
cushion	*n.* 垫子，软垫	fundamental	*adj.* 基础的，基本的

难句解析

1. Whereas most exercises are designed to build up strength or endurance plyometrics focuses on increasing power —— the rate at which an athlete can expend energy.

参考译文：虽然绝大多数的训练用来提高力量或者持久性，增强式训练则注重增强爆发力——即运动员使用能量的速度。

语言点：which 紧跟介词时的用法

在从句中作宾语或介词宾语时，which和that常可省略。但在紧跟介词时，只能用which，不能用that，而且不能省略。例如，

① Read the passage to which I referred in my talk. 读一读我在讲话中提到的那段文字。

② The situation in which he found himself was very difficult. 他发现自己的处境非常困难。

在口语中，如果介词和它的宾语分开，也可以省略。例: The situation (that/which) he found himself in was very difficult.

2. 'If we applied the Russian training model to some of the outstanding runners we have in this country,' Yessis asserts, 'they would be breaking records left and right.'

参考译文：Yessis断言："如果对我们国内的一些杰出赛跑运动员采取俄罗斯的训练模式，他们将会经常破记录。"

语言点：表示现在或将来情况的虚拟条件句

这类句子或表示与事实相反的情况或实现可能性不大的情况。例如，

① If I had a map I would lend it to you. 如果我有地图我就借给你。(但我没有)

② If you left your bicycle outside, someone would steal it.
如果你把自行车放在外边，有人会偷的。(当然你不会这样做)

③ If I lived near my office, I' d walk to work. 如果我住在办公室附近，我就会步行上班。

④ If I were you, I' d plant some trees round the house. 如果我是你，我会在房子周围种上树。

3. That understanding took the later analysis of biomechanics specialists, who put their minds to comprehending something that was too complex and unorthodox ever to have been invented through their own mathematical simulations.

参考译文：这些专家绞尽脑汁去理解这种过于复杂和非传统的方法，而这一方法在他们自己的数学模拟中都没有出现过。

语言点：put/set/turn one' s mind to sth. 的用法

常用词组 put/set/turn one' s mind to sth. 的意思为"专心于某事物"。例如，

You could be a very good writer if you set your mind to it. 如果专心写作，你能够成为一名非常优秀的作家。

试题分析

Questions 1 —6

- 题型: TURE / FALSE / NOT GIVEN
- 题目解析

题号	定位词	文中对应点	题解
1	record, 1900	第 1 段第一句	题目：现代官方运动员记录始于大约 1900 年。 原文：自从 20 世纪早期国际田联开始记录成绩以来，运动员奔跑的速度，跳的高度，投掷重物的距离稳步提高。因此答案为 TRUE。
2	before the twentieth century		题目：20 世纪之前，运动员的成绩几乎没有什么提高。
3	burst of nergy	第 1 段第 2 句及第 3 句	题目：运动员的成绩提高幅度最大的项目是需要爆发力强的项目。 原文：在那些被称为力量项目，需要能量的相对短

题号	定位词	文中对应点	题解
			暂，爆发性释放，比如 100 米跑和跳远，时间和距离都提高了 10% – 20%。在持久项目中，运动成绩提高得更多。很明显爆发性项目不是运动员的成绩提高幅度最大的项目，因此答案为 FALSE。
4	genetics	第 3 段第 1 句及第 2 句	题目：基因在运动员的表现上起的作用。 原文：识别基因优秀的个体只是第一步。加州大学 Fullerton分校的运动科学系的退休教授Michael Yessis认为基因在运动员的表现上只起三分之一的作用。
5	parents of top athletes		题目：顶尖运动员的父母自己通常也是成功的运动员。 原文没有提到题目中的内容，因此答案为 NOT GIVEN。
6	gifted athletes, younger age	第 2 段第 3 句	题目：运动不断提升的国际重要性意味着有天分的运动员有可能被发现的更早。 原文：在过去的一个世纪里，人类基因库的成分并没有显著地变化，只是全世界有越来越多的人参与了这项运动，诱惑运动员提高成绩的物质奖励也越来越多，因此现在比以往更有可能尽早发现那些独具运动员基因的个体。 因此答案为 TRUE。

Questions 7 —10

- 题型：TURE / FALSE / NOT GIVEN
- 题目解析

题号	定位词	文中对应点	题解
7	American runners	第 3 段第 4 句及第 4 段第一句	根据大写字母 American runners 定位到原文第 3 段第 4 句，原文的表述是：US runners, despite their impressive achievements, are ‘running on their genetics’. 因此答案为 genetics。
8	former Soviet Union	第 3 段最后 1 句	此题较难。根据大写字母 former Soviet Union 定位到原文第 3 段最后 1 句，原文的表述是前苏联率先应用

题号	定位词	答案位置	题解
			plyometrics 来训练运动员，结合第 4 段首句：plyometrics focuses on increasing power，因此答案为 power。
9	inadequate diet	第 5 段最后 1 句	根据 inadequate diet 定位到原文第 5 段最后 1 句，该段主要讲营养方面对于运动员得到影响。最后一句明确指出，...deficiency in trace mineral can lead to injuries, 因此答案为 injuries。
10	key, setting	第 6 段第 1 句 new records	此题较难，根据题目顺序在原文第 6 段中找到答案及第 2 句，即打破记录的关键因素为 training。

Questions 11 －13

- 题型：TURE / FALSE / NOT GIVEN
- 题目解析

题号	定位词	文中对应点	题解
11	Biomechanics films	第 7 段第 2 句至第 4 句	此题根据专有名词 Biomechanics films 定位到原文第 7 段第 2 句，原文的表述是：生物力学将一个在运动中的运动员拍下来，然后将她的表现资料数字化，在三维空间上记录下每一个关节和肢体的运动。通过在三维空间采用牛顿定律，“我们可以得出结论：这个运动员的奔跑速度不够快，在起跑的过程中并没有强有力地使用胳膊”，Dapena 说道。Dapena 用这些方法帮助跳高运动员。因此答案为 A。
12	Biomechanics specialists，选项中共有的 Fosbury flop	第 8 段第 2 句至第 4 句	此题根据 4 个选项中共有的大写字母 Fosbury flop 迅速定位到原文第 8 段第 2 句至第 4 句，原文的表述是：…生物力学专家后来对他的方法进行了分析，并理解了这一方法。答案为 D。
13	John S. Raglin	最后 1 段第 2 句及第 3 句	此题根据人名定位到原文最后 1 段第 2 句及第 3 句，原文的表述是：印第安纳大学的运动心理学家 John S. Raglin 说：“核心表现不是更高，更快，更强这一简单或者平凡的事。有很多的变数进入这一方程式，我们对很多案例的理解都是最基本(fundamental)的。我们还有很长的路要走。”因此答案为 B。

参考译文

多高？多快？
——人类的运动极限没有尽头

自从20世纪早期国际田联开始记录成绩以来，运动员奔跑的速度，跳的高度，投掷重物的距离都在稳步提高。在那些需要爆发力的项目，比如100米跑和跳远项目中，时间和距离都提高了10% - 20%。在耐力项目中，运动成绩提高得更多。1908年的奥运会上，美国队的约翰 · 海因跑出了2小时55分18秒的马拉松成绩。在1999年，摩洛哥的选手海耶斯以2小时05分42秒的成绩创造了新的世界记录，几乎提高了30%。

没有任何一个人的理论可以解释成绩的提高，但是最重要的因素是基因。印第安纳大学的运动科学家Jesus Dapena援引一常用谚语说“运动员必须小心选择自己的父母。”在过去的一个世纪里，人类基因库的成分并没有显著地变化，只是全世界有越来越多的人参与了这项运动，诱惑运动员提高成绩的物质奖励也越来越多，因此现在比以往更有可能尽早发现那些独具运动员基因的个体。Dapena问道：“在20世纪20年代，能找到像短跑运动员迈克 · 杰克逊一样的人吗？我敢肯定是能的，只是人们从未意识到他身上具有的才能。”

识别基因优秀的个体只是第一步。加州大学Fullerton分校的运动科学系的退休教授Michael Yessis认为基因在运动员的表现上只起三分之一的作用。但是，辅以正确的训练，我们可以做得更好。他认为美国的赛跑选手尽管已取得了众多骄人成绩，但他们是“靠他们的基因在跑”。通过使用更多的科学训练方法，“他们将跑得更快”。这些方法包括力量训练。这些训练再现运动员在比赛中的动作，并应用了前苏联首先使用的一种训练技巧——增强式训练模式。

虽然绝大多数的训练用来提高力量或者持久性，增强式训练注重提高力——即运动员使用能量的速度。Yessis解释到，在一个短跑运动员跑步时，她的脚和地面接触少于1/10秒，在这1/10秒中，一半的时间用于着地，另一半的时间用于蹬地。增强式训练能帮助运动员最好地利用这一短暂的间隙。

营养是另一个没有得到运动教练足够重视的方面。Yessis坚称，即使吃了补品，很多运动员也没有得到最好的营养。每一项活动都有自己的营养需求。到目前为止，几乎没有教练懂得微量矿物质的缺乏是怎样使运动员受伤的。

在打破记录方面，集中训练也起了作用。Yessis断言：“如果对我们国内的一些杰出赛跑运动员采取俄罗斯的训练模式，他们将会经常破记录。”但是，他没有预测能在多大程度上破记录。“实际上极限在什么地方是很难说的，但是只要我们的训练不断增强，就会有提高，哪怕只有1/100秒。”

最重要的新方法之一就是生物力学，研究运动中身体的学科。生物力学将一个在运动中的运动员拍下来，然后将她的表现资料数字化，在三维空间上记录下每一个关节和肢体的运动。通过在三维空间采用牛顿定律，“我们可以得出结论：这个运动员的奔跑速度不够快，在起跑的过程中并没有强有力地使用胳膊，”Dapena说道。Dapena用这些方法帮助跳高运动员。然而，到目前为止，生物力学对运动员的进步起到的作用不大。

革命性的观点同样还来自运动员自己。比如，在1968年墨西哥城的奥运会上，一个相对来说不是很出名的运动员迪克·F，使用了一个向后跳跃的方法获得了金牌，他的这个方法和当时已有的跳高方法完全不同，马上被命名为F式落法(既背越式)。他本人并不知道他正在做什么。生物力学专家后来对他的方法进行了分析，并理解了这一方法。这些专家绞尽脑汁去理解这种过于复杂和非传统的方法，而这一方法在他们自己的数学模拟中都没有出现过。F式落法还需要另一个条件来提高运动员的成绩：运动装备上的革新。在迪克·F例子中，这一元素正是运动员着陆的垫子。传统意义上，跳高运动员都会着陆在填满木屑的深坑里。但是到了迪克·F的年代，填满木屑的深坑被软泡沫垫子代替了，而这种垫子是这种跳法再理想不过的装备了。

终于，大多数研究人员被运动员的充沛的体力和人类身体的力量所折服了。“一旦你开始研究运动，你就会发现这是一个令人懊恼的复杂的问题。”印第安纳大学的运动心理学家John S. Raglin说：“不是简简单单的更高，更快，更强就可以提高核心成绩的。有很多的变量要引入这一方程式，我们对很多情况的理解都是最基本的。我们还有很长的路要走。”在可预见的将来，记录将被打破。

READING PASSAGE 2

篇章结构

体裁 说明文

主题 考古学介绍

结构

第一段：考古学是什么	第二段：考古学的本质
第三段：考古学、人类学和历史学相联系	第四段：人类学介绍
第五段：体质人类学的联系	第六段：考古学和文化人类学的联系
第七段：考古学家的任务	第八段：考古学和历史学的联系
第九段：历史的分类	第十段：考古学、科学及历史学的比较

必背词汇

archaeology	*n.* 考古学	anthropologist	*n.* 人类学家
treasure	*n.* 财富，财产	restricted	*adj.* 受限制的，有限的
analyst	*n.* 分析家，分解者	distinguish	*v.* 区别，辨别
excavation	*n.* 挖掘，发掘	biological	*adj.* 生物学的
painstaking	*adj.* 辛苦的，艰苦的	branch	*n.* 分枝，分店
conservation	*n.* 保存，保持，守恒	ethnography	*n.* 人种志，民族志
heritage	*n.* 遗产，继承权，传统	contemporary	*adj.* 当代的，同时代的
loot	*v.* 掠夺，抢劫，劫掠	artefact	*n.* 人工品
detective	*adj.* 侦探的	interpret	*v.* 解释，说明，口译
vehicle	*n.* 车辆，载体	dwelling	*n.* 住处
portrayal	*n.* 描画，描写	distinction	*n.* 区别，差别
capture	*v.* 俘获，抓住，夺取	pre-history	*n.* 史前
discipline	*n.* 纪律，学科	convenient	*adj.* 便利的，方便的
anthropology	*n.* 人类学	formulate	*v.* 用公式表示，阐明
humanity	*n.* 人性，人类	coherent	*adj.* 一致的，连贯的
characteristic	*n.* 特性，特征		

试题分析

Questions 14 —19

- 题型：TURE / FALSE / NOT GIVEN
- 题目解析

题号	定位词	文中对应点	题解
14	creativity, investigative work	第1段第1句	题目：考古学既包括创新也包括认真的分析调查工作。 原文：考古学部分是对过去财富的发现，部分是科学分析的严谨工作，部分是创造性想像的练习。因此答案为TURE。
15	ancient languages		题目：考古学家必须能够翻译古代语言文本。 原文没有提及题目的内容，因此答案为NOT GIVEN。
16	movies	第2段最后一句	题目：电影为考古学家的工作提供了真实的画面。 原文的表述是：相反，这些描述(指上句所说的电影)和现实差距甚远(far from reality such portrayals are)，因此很明显答案应为FALSE。
17	anthropolo-gist	第4段第1句至第3句	题目：人类学家从不止一个角度来定义文化。 原文：最广义的人类学是研究人类的科学，包括我们作为动物的身体特征以及被我们称为文化的人类特有的非生物特征。在这种意义上的文化包括了人类学家爱德华·泰勒在1871年总结的“作为社会成员的个体所习得的包括知识、信仰、艺术、道德、习俗以及其他一切能力和习惯。”而当人类学家谈到某个特定社会的文化时，这个文化就是狭义的概念，指这个社会的独特的非生物特征，这一特征使该社会区别于其他社会。很明显，人类学家至少是从两个角度即广义和狭义来定义文化，因此该题答案为TRUE。
18	anthropology		题目：考古学比人类学要求更加苛刻。 原文当中没有提到题目中的内容，因此答案为NOT GIVEN。
19	Europe, 3,000 BC	第8段最后一句	题目：欧洲的历史自公元前3000年就有记录了。 原文中的表述是：传统的历史始于公元前3000左右西亚的文字记载，而世界的其他大多数地区的历史要比这晚很多。因此答案为FALSE。

Questions 20 — 21

- 题型：多选题
- 题目解析

该题的要求是从 A — E 五个选项中选出文中提到的两个关于人类学的陈述。这道题有些难度，根据文章结构分别在第 4 段最后 1 句及第 5 段首句找到答案即选项 D 和 E。

Questions 22 — 23

- 题型：多选题
- 题目解析

该题的要求是从 A — E 五个选项中选出文中提到的两个考古学家的任务。根据文章结构可以在原文第 7 段当中找到答案，分别为选项 C 及选项 D。

Questions 24 — 27

- 题型：Summary
- 题目解析

题目要求中明确说明此 summary 选自原文最后两段，因此定位起来比较容易。

题号	文中对应点	题解
24	原文倒数第 2 段最后 1 句	和 written records 形成对应的只有原文倒数第 2 段最后一句中的 oral histories 词组。
25，26	原文最后 1 段第 1 句	作者用来描述考古学的两个角度均出现在原文最后 1 段第 1 句，即 humanistic study 和 historical discipline。
27	原文最后 1 段倒数第 2 句	原文最后 1 段倒数第 2 句很明显的告诉我们，被作者用来和考古学家进行比较的只有一种人即科学家。因此答案为 scientist。

参考译文

考古学的本质和目的

考古学部分是对过去财富的发现，部分是科学分析的严谨工作，部分是创造性想像的练习。同时也是在阳光下辛苦地在中东挖掘，在雪中的阿拉斯加和因纽特人一起工作，研究罗马大不列颠的下水道。但是它也是辛苦解释工作，以使我们理解在人类历史中这些东西代表了什么。它保持了世界文化遗产，使之免受掠夺和疏忽的伤害。

考古学既是一个在田野的体力活动，也是在书房或实验室的智力追求。这正是它的巨大吸引力的一部分。这种充满了危险和侦探性质的工作的混合体是小说作家和电影导演的完美载体，从阿加莎·克里斯蒂的《东方快车谋杀案》到斯蒂芬·斯皮尔伯格的《夺宝奇兵》。虽然这些描述和现实差距甚远，但是它们抓住了最本质的事实：考古学是一个令人激动的探询，一个对关于我们自身和过去知识的探询。

但是考古学是怎样和诸如人类学和历史学这样的学科相联系呢，这些学科也同样研究人类历史？考古学本身是一门科学吗？考古学家在今天世界中的责任是什么？

最广义的人类学是研究人类的科学，包括我们作为动物的身体特征以及被我们称为文化的人类特有的非生物特征。在这种意义上的文化包括了人类学家爱德华·泰勒在1871年总结的“作为社会成员的个体所习得的包括知识、信仰、艺术、道德、习俗以及其他一切能力和习惯。”而当人类学家谈到某个特定社会的文化时，这个文化就是狭义的概念，指这个社会的独特的非生物特征，这一特征使该社会区别于其他社会。人类学是一个非常宽泛的学科，通常分为三个更小的学科：体质人类学、文化人类学和考古学。

体质人类学或者生物人类学，正如其名字一样，关注于人类生物或体质特征的研究以及这些特征是怎样发展的。文化人类学或者社会人类学分析人类文化和社会。它的两个分支是人种志(对单个活文化的第一手研究)和民族学(从人种出发，比较各不同文化，得出关于人类社会的通用法则)。

考古学是“文化人类学的过去时”。文化人类学家经常把他们的结论建立在目前社区的生活经历上，然而考古学家主要通过残存的物质研究过去社会——建筑、工具和其他人工制品，这些构成了过去社会留下来的物质文化。

然而，今天的考古学家最重要的任务之一就是知道如何解读从前的物质文化。那些罐子是怎么用的？为什么有些住所是圆形的，而有些是方形的？在这里，考古学和人种学的方法重合了。几十年来，考古学家延伸出了种族文化考古学，和人种学者一样，他们住在当代的社区中，但是他们带着特定的目的，就是要了解社会是如何使用物质文化的，比如人们是怎样制造工具和武器，人们为什么要在现在的地方建立住所，等等。而且，考古学在保护遗址方面起了积极的作用。传统研究构成了一个不断发展的领域，在这个领域里，人们认识到世界的文化遗产是一个正在减少的资源，这一资源对不同的人们有着不同的意义。

如果考古学只研究过去，那么它有什么是区别于历史学的呢？就最广义的意义而言，考古学是人类学的一个方面，同时也是历史学的一部分，在这里的历史是指3百万年前人类产生以来的所有人类历史。实际上，在那段漫长的岁月里，超过99%的时间，考古学这一研究过去的物质文化的学科是惟一有意义的信息资源。传统的历史始于公元前3000左右西亚的文字记载，而世界的其他大多数地区的历史要比这晚很多。

人们一般是这样把人类的历史一分为二的：史前(即文字记录出现以前的时期)和狭义的历史即有文字见证的这段历史。对于研究所有文化和所有时期的考古学而言，不管有没有文字，历史和史前的区别只是承认文字重要性的传统分界线，绝不会减少包含在口述史中有用信息的重要性。

由于考古学的目的是理解人类，所以它是一个人文主义的学科。而且，由于考古学研究的是人类的过去，所以它是一个有关历史的学科，但是它在根本上区别于文字历史的研究。考古学家发现的物质不会直接告诉我们去思考什么。历史记载是一种声明，意见及评判。在另一方面，考古学家发现的物体本身并未直接告诉我们什么。从这个角度来说，考古学家的实践更像科学家的实践。科学家收集数据，进行实验，提出假设，用更多的数据验证假设，然后得出结论，设计模型，而这一模型看起来最适合总结在数据中观察到的模式。而考古学家需要描画出关于过去的一幅图画，正如科学家需要建立一个关于自然世界的连贯的思维框架。

READING PASSAGE 3

篇章结构

体裁 说明文

主题 医疗资源的稀缺问题

结构 第一段：发达国家共同面对的问题　第二段：可持续的经济发展
第三段：医疗和人权之间的联系　第四段：政府在医疗中的角色
第五段：医疗资源近期的发展情况

必背词汇

allocate	*v.* 分派，分配	realization	*n.* 实现
apportion	*v.* 分配	awareness	*n.* 知道，晓得
distribute	*v.* 分发，分配	contrary	*adj.* 相反的，逆的
proportion	*n.* 比例，均衡	institution	*n.* 公共机构，协会，制度
treatment	*n.* 待遇，对待，处理	autonomous	*adj.* 自治的
priority	*n.* 优先，优先权	personal	*adj.* 私人的，个人的
consideration	*n.* 体谅，考虑	liberty	*n.* 自由，特权
onwards	*adv.* 向前地，在先地	deprive	*v.* 剥夺，使丧失
outlook	*n.* 景色，展望，前景	confusion	*n.* 混乱，混淆
finitude	*n.* 界限，限制	autonomy	*n.* 自治
clientele	*n.* 诉讼委托人，客户	resistance	*n.* 反抗，抵抗
resource	*n.* 资源，财力	obligation	*n.* 义务，职责，债务
provision	*n.* 供应，规定	public good	公共产品
fossil	*adj.* 化石的，陈腐的，守旧的	declaration	*n.* 宣布，宣言，声明
capacity	*n.* 容量，才能	demographic	*adj.* 人口统计学的
severe	*adj.* 严厉的，严格的，	consumer	*n.* 消费者
obvious	*adj.* 明显的，显而易见的	predict	*v.* 预测
incredible	*adj.* 难以置信的	consequence	*n.* 结果
assume	*v.* 假定，设想	match	*v.* 相配，相称
invisible	*adj.* 看不见的，无形的		

难句解析

1. Thus, in the 1950s and 1960s, there emerged awareness in Western societies that resources for the provision of fossil fuel energy were finite and exhaustible and that the capacity of nature or the environment to sustain economic development and population was also finite.

参考译文：在 20 世纪 50 年代和 60 年代，西方社会意识到：化石燃料能源的供应资源是有限的，并能被耗尽，自然界或环境维持经济发展和人口增长的能力也是有限的。

语言点：there 引导的特殊句型

there 引导的是一种特殊的句子，there 放在句首好似主语，但真正的主语在后面，表示"有…"之意。there 后常跟 be 动词，构成英文中最常见的句型之一，此外 there 后也可跟其别的动词(通常为不及物动词)。例如，

① There remained just 20 dollars. 只剩 20 美元了。

② There came about a war between the two countries. 两国之间爆发了一场战争。

③ There followed a flood of indignation in the newspapers. 随后报纸发出一片愤怒的声音。

2. People are not in a position to exercise personal liberty and to be self determining if they are poverty sicken, or deprived of basic education, or do not live within a context of law and order.

参考译文：如果为贫穷而苦恼，或者被剥夺了基础教育，或者没有生活在法律法规的框架下，那么人们就不能拥有个人自由，自主行事。

语言点：in a position to 的用法

In a position to 是英文中的常见词组，意思是"能够做某事或准备做某事"。例如，

① I' m not in a good position to answer your questions. 我不能回答你的问题。

② I' m in a position to accept your price. 我准备(能够)接受你的报价。

试题分析

Questions 28 －31

- 题型：List of Headings
- 题目解析

题号	段落主题句	题解
28	Every health system in an economically developed society is faced with the need to decide what proportion of the community's ...	原文第1段第2句的表述是：在经济发达的社会(economically developed society)，每一个卫生系统都需要做出决定(正式或非正式)：在卫生保健方面投入资源应占社会全部资源的多大比例？这些资源应该如何分配？什么样的疾病和残疾以及什么形式的治疗应该享有优先权？社会中的哪部分成员应该在卫生需求方面给予特别关照？什么形式的治疗是最节省成本的？由此可见原文首段均在围绕发达国家共同面对的问题进行阐述，所以答案为选项 iv。
29	However，at exactly the same time as this new realisation of the finite character of health-care resources was sinking in, an awareness of a contrary kind was developing in western societies：that people have a basic right to health-care as a necessary condition of a proper human life.	首句的主要意思是：然而，就在这种认为卫生资源是有限的新思想销声匿迹的同时，一种相反的思想在西方社会发展起来了。这种思想认为享受卫生保健是人们的一项基本权利(basic right)，而这种权利是人们正常生活的必要条件。直到该段末句，都在阐述医疗和人权的关系问题，因此答案为选项 i。
30	It is also accepted that this right generates an obligation or duty for the state to ensure that adequate heath-care resources are provided out of the public purse.	该段第二句的表述是：还有一个观点也是被普遍接受的：这种权利使得国家(state)有义务有责任确保从公共预算中划拨足够的资金提供卫生服务。该段由此直到末句都在阐述国家在保障医疗服务中的应承担的义务及扮演的角色，因此答案为选项 iii。

题号	段落主题句	题解
31	The second set of more specific changes that have led to the present concern about the distribution of heath-care resources stem from the dramatic rise in heath costs in most OECD countries...	该段第二句的表述为：大多数经合发展组织的国家的卫生费用急剧增加，这再一次引发了一系列改变(changes)，使人们开始关注医疗卫生资源的分配问题。下面内容均是针对该句所举的具体例子及这一系列改变带来的结果或影响，因此答案为选项 v。

Questions 32-35

- 题型：Matching
- 题目解析

此题由于选项均为时间，因此用选项在原文中定位比较简单。

题号	文中对应点	题解
32	B 段第 2 句至第 4 句	题目：人们意识到医疗资源是有限的。 原文：在 20 世纪 50 年代和 60 年代，西方社会出现了一种意识：化石燃料能源的供应资源是有限的，并能被耗尽，自然界或环境维持经济发展和人口增长的能力也是有限的。换句话说，我们开始意识到一个显而易见的事实，就是增长是有限制的。 因此答案为 B。
33	E 段第 2 句	题目：医疗保健费用的急剧上涨。 原文：大规模的人口数量及社会的变化导致大多数经济合作发展组织的国家的卫生费用急剧增加，这再一次引发了一系列改变，使人们开始关注医疗卫生资源的分配问题。结合例子当中的时间，得出答案及选项 B。
34	B 段最后一句	题目：一种观点：经济的增长能够产生所有人们所需的医疗资源。 原文：回溯起来，有一个观点现在看来不可思议：在 1939 年到 1945 年的世界大战结束后的几年内，很多国家建立了国民卫生体系，人们认为这样的国民卫生体系至少在理论上能够满足任何人群的所有基卫础生需求，经济增长中“看不见的手”将提供一切所需。因此答案为 A。

题号	文中对应点	题解
35	D段第2句及第3句	题目：接受国家在提供医疗保障中的角色。 原文：还有一个观点也是被普遍接受的：这种权利使得国家有义务有责任确保从公共预算中划拨足够的资金提供卫生服务。 国家本身没有义务去建立卫生健康体系，但是有义务去保证这样一个体系的存在。 结合该段首句中的时间 1970s，答案为选项B。

Questions 36 －40

- 题型：YES /NO / NOT GIVEN
- 题目解析

题号	定位词	文中对应点	题解
36	Personal liberty	C 段最后两句	题目：人们从来都没有将个人的自由和独立与医疗直接联系起来。 原文：如果为贫穷而苦恼，或者被剥夺了基础教育，或者没有生活在法律法规的框架下，那么人们就不能拥有个人自由，自主行事。同样，基础卫生保健也是人实现自由的一个条件。很明显个人自由和医疗保健是密切相关的，因此答案为NO。
37	right, limits	C 段第 1 句	题目：几乎在人们认识到医疗资源是有限的同时，医疗保健开始被看作是人们的一项权利。 原文：然而，就在人们开始了解到医疗资源是有限的同时，一种相反的思想在西方社会发展起来了。这种思想认为享受卫生保健是人们的一项基本权利，而这种权利是人们正常生活的必要条件。原文和题目的表述一致，因此答案为 YES。
38	OECD countries	E 段第 2 句	题目：近年来，OECD 国家人口数量的改变对医疗费用产生了影响。 原文：大规模的人口数量及社会的变化导致大多数经济合作发展组织的国家的卫生费用急剧增加，这再一次引发了一系列改变，使人们开始关注医疗卫生资源的分配问题。答案为 YES。

题号	定位词	文中对应点	题解
39	OECD government	E段	题目：OECD 国家的政府一直低估了医疗供应的需求程度。 根据大写字母OECD定位到原文E段，该段没有提到题目中的内容，因此答案为NOT GIVEN。
40	Economically developed countries, elderly	E段	题目：在大多数经济发达国家，老年人将不得不为他们的未来医疗做一些特殊的准备。 原文没有提到题目中的内容，因此答案为NOT GIVEN。

参考译文

稀缺资源的问题

A

卫生保健资源应该如何分配或指定以保证它们能以最公平、最有效的方式分布，这个问题已经不算新了。在经济发达的社会，每一个卫生系统都需要做出决定(正式或非正式)：在卫生保健方面投入资源应占社会全部资源的多大比例？这些资源应该如何分配？什么样的疾病和残疾以及什么形式的治疗应该享有优先权？社会中的哪部分成员应该在卫生需求方面给予特别关照？什么形式的治疗是最节省成本的？

B

新近的发展是，自20世纪50年代以来，人们看待资源有限性及卫生资源有限性的态度都有了总体的改变，另外关于使用卫生资源的用户和社区所需做出的开支方面也有了具体的变化。在20世纪50年代和60年代，西方社会意识到：化石燃料能源的供应资源是有限的，并能被耗尽，自然界或环境维持经济发展和人口增长的能力也是有限的。换句话说，我们开始意识到一个显而易见的事实，就是增长是有限制的。卫生保健资源同样也会有一些限制的新观念就是这个显而易见的事实的一部分。回溯起来，有一个观点现在看来不可思议：在1939年到1945年的世界大战结束后的几年内，很多国家建立了国民卫生体系，人们认为这样的国民卫生体系至少在理论上能够满足任何人群的所有基础卫生需求，经济增长中“看不见的手”将提供一切所需。

C

然而，就在这种认为卫生资源是有限的新思想销声匿迹的同时，一种相反的思想在西方社会发展起来了。这种思想认为享受卫生保健是人们的一项基本权利，而这种权利是人们正常生活的必要条件。像教育、政治程序、法律程序、机构、公共秩序、沟通、交通和金钱供给一样，卫生保健被看作是人们行使作为自治人类的权利的必需的一项基本社会的设施。如果为贫穷而苦恼，或者被剥夺了基础教育，或者没有生活在法律法规的框架下，那么人们就不能拥有个人自由，自主行事。同样，基础卫生保健也是人实现自由的一个条件。

D

虽然权利这个词有时在语言上会混淆，但是到20世纪70年代晚期，大多数社会都承认人们有享受卫生保健的权利(虽然在美国，人们享有卫生保健的正式权利这一观点受到了相当大的抵触)。还有一个观点也是被普遍接受的：这种权利使得国家有义务有责任确保从公共预算中划拨足够的资金提供卫生服务。国家本身没有义务去建立卫生健康体系，但是有义务去保证这样一个体系的存在。换句话说，基础卫生保健是一种公共产品，而不是需要花钱去购买的私人产品。世界卫生组织在1976年的宣言中写道："享受可能达到的最高标准的健康是每一个人的基本权利，不因种族、宗教、政治信仰、经济或社会情境而异。"正如刚才所提到的，在一个自由的社会，基础卫生是行使个人自治的一个必不可少的条件。

E

当卫生保健资源不能满足需求的这一现象比较明显的时候，人们要求国家满足他们享有卫生保健的这一基本权利。大规模的人口数量及社会的变化导致大多数经济合作发展组织的国家的卫生费用急剧增加，这再一次引发了一系列改变，使人们开始关注医疗卫生资源的分配问题。例如，老年人现在是最主要的(相对来说也是最昂贵的)卫生健康资源消费者。在欧共体总体中，健康资源的消费从1960年占GDP的3.8%到1980年的7%，而且这一增长趋势将会持续。(在美国，目前的数字是占GDP的12%，澳大利亚是7.8%)。

结果，在20世纪80年代在各国卫生部长、经济学家和政治家身中都出现了一股极度的悲观情绪(和以往人们的悲观推测类似，比如关于能源需求和燃料问题，或是人口增长问题)在这样的论调中，他们认为资源是稳定的或是减少的，而医疗费用却是不断上涨的。

WRITING

WRITING TASK 1

范文

The line chart compares the visits to and from the UK from 1979 to 1999. Visits both to and from the UK have been in constant increase, while visits abroad by UK residents always surpassed that to the UK by overseas residents. From 1979 to 1985, both figures rose from 12 to 20 million and from 10 to 12 million respectively. Since then, both moved substantially upward with the overseas visits by UK residents increasing by a larger scale.

As is shown in the bar chart, among the five most popular countries visited by the UK residents, the country with the largest number of British tourists was France (around 11 million), followed by Spain (around 9.5 million). USA, Greece and Turkey lagged far behind, with tourists amounting to 3.5 million, 2.5 million and 2 million respectively.

In general, the figure of visits to and from the UK was on the rise, with UK residents abroad outnumbering overseas visitors in the UK and the most popular destination country for UK residents were France and Spain.

分析

本题由曲线图和柱状图构成。曲线图体现进出英国人数随时间变化的变化，而柱状图则反映英国游客出游目的地的比较。

第一段描写曲线图，首先进行比较，指出无论是英国出游人数还是外国赴英国旅游人数都在增加，而前者多于后者。然后描写各自变化，以数字来支持。

第二段描写柱状图。按照人数的多少分别一描写英国游客最喜欢去的五个旅游目的地。

最后一段总结两个图的各自最明显趋势：出游人数的增加和旅游人数最多的两个目的国。

WRITING TASK 2

题目要求

In many countries schools have severe problems with student behaviour.

What do you think are the causes of this?

What solutions can you suggest?

题解

在许多国家的学校存在着严重的学生行为问题。分析这个问题的原因并提出相应解决方法。

这道题属于问题题型。考生应该提出问题，然后分析问题的原因，最后提出解决问题的建议。

本题的难点之一在于对于题目中"severe problems with student behaviour"（学生行为不端）这个短语的理解。难点之二在与题目中明确指出"in many countries"（在许多国家），考生就应该在论证时不能光把论证局限在中国的现状上，虽然中国的例子可以作为论证的依据。

在分析原因和提出建议的时候应该不要只围绕学校展开。问题出现在学校，但是根源可能在别的地方。要解决学校出现的学生行为不端问题，不仅仅是学校出力就够了的。

范文一

When we think of severe problems with student behavior, most people think first of violence, like the tragic shootings in recent years at various schools, mostly in the United States. Furthermore, violence is not the only serious behavioral problem in schools. Lack of interest in learning, vandalism and stealing are perhaps the other major problems, but these problems are related to each other. For example, a lack of interest in learning can lead to frustration and boredom, which in turn can lead to antisocial behavior.

There are many factors related to serious behavioral problems in schools, and these factors, like the problems themselves, are related. They include such things as a poor family life, perhaps because children are being brought up in a social setting in which violence is accepted as a way to resolve problems, or have respectable but hard-working parents who do not dedicate enough time to being good, loving parents. In addition to social factors, there are physical factors that can lead to behavioral problems. For example, many studies show that lead poisoning from vehicle exhausts and other sources significantly reduces IQ and directly increases aggressive tendencies. It is very likely that there are many other physical factors, such as additives and pesticide residues in food, that have undesirable effects on people, especially children, but which have not yet been identified.

So what are the solutions? Psychological counseling and education for students, parents and teachers can play a constructive role in helping people understand and control undesirable forms of behavior. But the only long-term answer is the evolution of a culture in which the full range of human needs, C like the needs for love, a happy family life, satisfying employment, exercising creativity, acceptance no matter who or what one is are satisfied.

分析

文章采用三段论的写作方法，分别提出问题，分析问题和解决问题。

第一段话指出问题的不同表现形式。当我们想到学生行为不端的时候，绝大多数人都首先会想到暴力，比如近年来的在美国学校尤为严重的枪击案。当然，问题不仅仅在于暴力。学生对学习失去兴趣，破坏公共财产和偷窃也是严重的问题。但这些问题都是互相关联的。例如，厌学会导致挫败感和无聊乏味，而这些情绪又会导致反社会行为。

第二段话分析问题产生的种种原因，分成社会原因和物质原因。学生在学校里的行为问题的产生原因和这些行为问题本身一样，都是有关联的。如果学生家庭穷困，或者孩子从小生长在依靠暴力解决问题的环境里，或者学生家长虽然工作努力，令人尊敬，但却没有时间致力于关爱孩子等等。除了这些社会原因之外，还可能有一些其他因素。比如，汽车尾气排放等带来的铅中毒会大大降低智商，直接增加暴力倾向。也有可能有其他原因，比如食物中的添加剂和杀虫剂残留可能会对人们尤其是小孩造成不利影响。

第三段话提出解决办法。作者提出家长和老师可以对学生进行心理辅导和教育，帮助学生理解不端行为的危害并加以控制。但是惟一的长期的解决办法是文化建设。建设一个能够全方面满足人们需求的文化，包括爱，幸福家庭生活，成功就业，发扬创造性，宽容忍让等需求都能得到满足的文化。

范文二

Poor student behaviour seems to be an increasingly widespread problem and I think that modern lifestyles are probably responsible for this.

In many countries, the birth rate is decreasing so that families are smaller with fewer children. These children are often spoilt, not in terms of love and attention because working parents do not have the time for this, but in more material ways. They are allowed to have whatever they want, regardless of price, and to behave as they please. This means that the children grow up without consideration for others and without any understanding of where their standard of living comes from.

When they get to school age they have not learnt any self control or discipline. They have less respect for their teachers and refuse to obey school rules in the way that their parents did.

Teachers continually complain about this problem and measures should be taken to combat the situation. But I think the solution to the problem lies with the families, who need to be more aware of the future consequences of spoiling their children. If they could raise them to be considerate of others and to be social, responsible individuals, the whole community would benefit.

Perhaps parenting classes are needed to help them to do this, and high quality nursery schools could be established that would support families more in terms of raising the next generation. The government should fund this kind of parental support, because this is no longer a problem for individual families, but for society as a whole.

(257 words)

分析

文章开头首先提出问题：poor student behaviour（学生行为不端 = 题目中的 severe problems with student behaviour）。然后指出原因在于现代生活方式。

第二段话具体分析问题的原因，也就是把现代生活方式是如何造成学生行为不端的进行因果分析。在许多国家，出生率不断下降，导致家庭由于孩子数量的减少而规模缩小。这些孩子经常被宠坏，不是在所得到的爱和关怀方面，因为外出工作的父母没有时间给予这方面的照顾，而是在物质方面。孩子们可以不顾价钱想要什么就能得到什么，想怎么做就怎么做。这意味着在孩子们的成长过程中，他们不顾他人，并且也不知道他们的生活水准是如何得来。

第三段话指出问题的表现形式，也就是原因所导致的后果：当这些孩子到了上学年龄，他们没有学会自制力，不会遵守纪律。和他们父母相比，他们不那么尊重老师，也不遵守学校规章制度。

第四段开始提出解决问题的建议。老师们不断抱怨这些问题，为此应该采取措施加以解决。但是，作者提出，虽然问题是发生在学校，但起因却是在家庭。父母需要更加了解溺爱儿童造成的可能后果。如果家长在抚养小孩的时候，能够让小孩学会尊重他人，成为负责人的人，那么全社会都会受益。

第五段进一步提出建议。也许需要设立家长学校来帮助家长学习如何培养儿童，也应该建立高品质的托儿所来帮助家庭抚养小孩。而政府也应该对此进行资助，因为这不仅是个别家庭的问题，而是全社会的问题。

SPEAKING

E=Examiner C=Candidate

E：Good morning.

C：Good morning.

E：My name is Andrew. Can you tell me your full name please?

C：It's Zhang Ting. You can call me Angela.

E：OK. Thank you, Angela. And let's talk about what you do…Do you work or are you a student?

C：I'm a college student in Beijing Foreign Studies University and I major in English.

E：Hmm. What do you like about your studies?

C：I think it's OK. As is often said, English is a tool to communicate and to learn other things, especially the cultures and the societies of English-speaking countries.

E：Is there anything you don't like about your studies?

C：Well, How can I put it…I think on the whole it's quite satisfying, but sometimes there's too much work and too much pressure. We have to write a lot of papers, though my teachers told us that in the U.S., where they used to study, students have to write far more papers than we do.

E：When you graduate, what kind of job do you hope to get?

C：I hope I can get a decent job after graduation…you know, something like a civil servant, or a teacher in high school.

E：OK. Let's go on to talk about food and cooking. What kind of food do you like to eat?

C：Nothing in particular, really. But I love sweet food I have a sweet tooth.

E：What kind of food would you like to try?

C：Spicy food. (smiles)

E：Why?

C：Because I've never tried it. it's too much for me. But I really want to try the dishes in Sichuan restaurants. Most of my friends are crazy about spicy food. They can't live without it.

E：Do you like cooking?

C：Oh yes, very much. But I suppose I enjoy watching other people cooking even more.

E: Do you prefer home-cooked food or food from the restaurant?

C: I would go for home-cooked food 'cos it's more tasty and it's tailor-made. But most importantly, it' s clean.

E: OK. Let' s talk about traveling···er···do you like to travel alone or with other people?

C: Definitely I like to travel in a group because I'm terrible with directions. If I go to a place which is new to me, I can easily lose my way.

E: What kind of benefits does traveling have, do you think?

C: Benefits? Hmm···I think there are a lot. You can get to know more places, and people. But the best thing with traveling is that you can get away from your studies or your work. It' s really a good way to unwind.

E: Thank you. Now I' m going to give you a topic. I' d like you to talk about it for two minutes. B-efore you talk, you have one minute to think about what you're going to say. You can take some notes. Here is your topic.

Describe a useful website you have visited.

You should say:

What the website was

How you found the address for this website

What the website contained

And explain why it was useful to you.

E: All right, remember you have two minutes. I' ll tell you when time is up. You can speak now

C: Well, the first website comes up to my mind is "Goggle", one of the most famous search engines in the world. It's the first website I've ever known and also the most frequently visited. I got its address because it was contained in my computer, from this you can see how influential it is. It is just like the root of the tree of global internet, starting from here you can reach to all kinds of information you can think of. Open it, the front page is simple, well- designed and informative, and then fill the blank with what you need, In a few seconds, the whole world is on your computer screen. It's useful to me at the beginning is because it's not complicated, like an ATM machine. It's useful to me now is because, um , it's like a bus with no conductor, you can go anywhere and won't lose your way home. For example, when you want to find some materials for your thesis, you can go to "Google" because it's more brief and efficient than libraries, there are also flaws about "Google", sometimes the searching result is not accurate enough and some of them are even unavailable. Basically "Google" is a miracle.

E：What effect has the internet had on the way people generally communicate with each other?

C：Quite a lot, I think. For example, I'm now far away from my parents, but they can see me and talk to me simultaneously on MSN or Skyppe, we do not feel that far in geography anymore. Compare to the telegraph-years, it's a shocking change already.

E：Why do you think the internet is being used more and more for communications?

C：Once again take myself for example. Remember when people are expecting a very important terlet,they have to wait for days or even months. But now through internet, E-mail, or even QQ , it's a matter of seconds. And we have 6 girls in our dorm, and there are 5 lap-tops! From this number you can clearly see why we all think the internet is being used more and more for communications.

E：How reliable do you think information from the internet is? Why? What about the news on the internet?

C：Whether the information is trustworthy I think should be judged by different situations. Because people hide their identities on internet and speak freely for they are not supposed to be responsible for his or her remarks. Brighten your eyes and see clearly. About news I have not considered much about it, actually all forms of media would have false information, not only on internet. But I think choose big website with credit would reduce the possibility of getting wrong news information.

E：Why do you think some people use the internet for shopping? Why doesn't everyone use it in this way?

C：The group of people who buy things on internet must be with new ideas and have the will to try them out. The reasons of course would be it is efficient and sometimes the price is alluring. For myself I've never buy things on internet, though I want and anticipate how wonderful it would be for you to sit on your chair and wait till the goods to come. I think these people are just like, too lazy to register our bank cards. But, maybe recently I wanna try it.

E：What kind of things is easy to buy or see online? Can you give some examples?

C：I suppose things which are rarely see on the market or only can be bought in foreign countries, or digital products. For example, my friend bought a Barbie which has been set limit to producing on the internet from U.S. at a sky-high price, but she cried when she received the Barbie for she dreamed about it for so long.

E：Do you think shopping on the internet will be more or less popular in the future? Why?

C：Definitely it would be more prosperous in the future. For its priorities are clear to be seen. Efficiency, quickness and convenience. And as the credit system is completing gradually here in

China, we can foresee that internet would be more popular in the future.

E: Thank you.

C: Thank you.

General Training: Reading and Writing Test A

READING

SECTION 1

必背词汇

surrounding	*n.* 环境 *adj.*周围的	premier	*adj.* 第一的，首要的
deliver	*v.* 递送，交付	ultra-modern	*adj.* 超现代的
acre	*n.* 英亩	chef	*n.* 厨师
scenic	*n.* 风景，景色	specialty	*n.* 专业，特色
woodland	*n.* 森林地，林地	technique	*n.* 技术，技巧
license	*n.* 许可(证)，执照	gear	*n.* 齿轮
luxury	*n.* 奢侈，华贵	atmosphere	*n.* 空气，气氛
accommodation	*n.* 住处，膳宿	unthreatening	*adj.* 轻松的
landscape	*n.* 风景	confidence	*n.* 信心
cuisine	*n.* 厨房烹调法，烹饪	apprehensive	*adj.* 有理解力的
burger	*n.* 碎肉夹饼，各种夹饼	percussion	*n.* 打击乐器
steak	*n.* 肉片，鱼排，牛排	exotic	*adj.* 异国情调的，外来的
classic	*adj.* 经典的	rhythm	*n.* 节奏，韵律
takeaway	*n.* 外卖	magical	*adj.* 不可思议的
facility	*n.* 设施，设备	narration	*n.* 叙述
charge	*v.* 收费	proverb	*n.* 谚语
hygiene	*n.* 卫生，卫生学	essential	*adj.* 本质的，实质的
delicious	*adj.* 美味的	enthusiasm	*n.* 热情，狂热
constantly	*adv.* 经常地，不断地	guarantee	*v.* 保证，担保
anniversary	*n.* 周年纪念	choir	*n.* 唱诗班
snack	*n.* 小吃	variety	*n.* 变化，多样性

rehearse	v. 排练，预演	instruction	n. 指示，用法说明(书)
participation	n. 分享，参与	guidance	n. 指导，领导
desirable	adj. 值得要的，合意的	vegetarian	n. 素食者

试题分析

Questions 1—5

- 题型：Matching

Matching题即搭配题是雅思G类考试中必考题型的一种，属于典型的细节题。一般来说，matching 题考查的是考生带着需要获取的信息回原文快速找寻定位的能力，即快速找寻有用信息点的能力。因此，尽管在G类的第一部分文章较短，均为100－200字的短文章，但考生也没有必要精读全文，只需要将题目考查的信息点快速找出即可。考生可在平时多进行一些这方面的练习即scan reading(扫描性阅读)以提高做题速度。

- 题目解析

题号	定位词	文中对应点	题解
1	Monday evening	广告B倒数第2行及第3行	题目：此饭馆星期一晚上不开放。 原文：营业时间为周二至周六晚上。
2	country surroundings	广告A正文第1行	题目：如选择本餐馆，您就可以在优雅的郊区环境中用餐。 原文：座落在面积40英亩的森林景色之中。
3	Sunday night	广告E第2行	题目：您可以在周日晚上用餐。 原文：周日开放时间：5 － 11pm。
4	delivered for an extra fee	广告C正文第4至第5行	题目：支付额外费用可享受外卖(送餐上门)服务。 原文：本店4英里以内可以送餐上门(额外收费)。
5	stay the night	广告A小标题或正文第10行	题目：您在本店用餐之后还可以过夜。 原文：标题“THAI Restaurant and Hotel”(酒店表明可以住宿)；正文中“本店提供豪华住宿”。

参考译文

A

地道泰国风味

CHANGTOM

泰国酒店

营业时间：12－3，6－12 周日休息

- 座落在40英亩的森林景色之中
- 户外用餐区
- 总是使用新鲜农产品
- 接受信用卡
- 多达50个座位
- 特许酒吧
- 具备小型功能间
- 豪华住宿
- 停车方便
- 花园风景

提供最好的食物和服务

B

JACK'S

传统美国餐厅

为家庭聚会或特殊场合提供服务

- 上选美国汉堡和牛排
- 鱼，薯条并备有素食者和儿童菜单
- 特许酒吧
- 欢迎预定婚宴和聚餐
- 外卖服务

午餐营业时间：周二——周六

晚餐营业时间：周三——周六

C

MOGHUL EXPRESS

印度风味外卖

在家舒适地享用美味印度食物

全天营业

公共假期照常营业

便利的停车设施

4英里以内送货上门(额外收费)

电话：NORWICH 4209888/588980

开办两年来，我店获得了英国最佳外卖奖，最卫生和最优质奖

D

THE MARINA 餐厅

全天营业

以本地价格提供美味的国际餐饮

我们经常更换家常菜菜单

只选用本地上等原料

* 公务餐 * 周年纪念和婚礼用餐 * 所有的特殊场合用餐

小吃和零食，午晚餐，各式酒类供应

宜人港湾 船上用餐 闲情雅致 挪威顶级餐馆风格尊贵再现

周一至周六全天营业

餐厅对央有大型电子监控停车场

E

北京屋		午饭时间	晚上
餐饮和外卖	星期天	不营业	5 – 11pm
优质美食	星期一	不营业	5 – 11.30pm
地道中国美食由	星期二	不营业	5 – 11.30pm
经验丰富的大厨	星期三	不营业	5 – 11.30pm
在本店独一无二	星期四	不营业	5 – 11.30pm
超现代的厨房中	星期五	不营业	5 –午夜
精心为您烹调	星期六	不营业	5 –午夜
免费送餐上门—充足的停车位			
欢迎电话预定	**NORWICH(01603)571122**		
欢迎查询本店特色菜	挪威奇妍大街**40**号		

Questions 6－14

- 题型：Matching
- 题目解析

题号	定位词	文中对应点	题解
6	greeting	广告 C 最后一行	题目：为新成员提供热烈的欢迎。 原文：我们保证您会受到热烈的欢迎。
7	relevant skills are preferred	广告 D 最后一行	题目：具备相关技能者优先。 原文：有即兴朗诵才能和有合唱团演唱经验者优先。
8	cheer you up	广告 B 正文第二句	题目：cheer you up 原文：lift your spirits
9	a variety of ages	广告 B 最后一句	题目：此活动适合各年龄层者。 原文：一项适合全家的活动。
10	individual guidance	广告 E 倒数第二行	题目：提供个人化的指导。 原文：小班教学保证每个学生受到最大化的关注及指导。
11	public performance	广告 D 倒数第二行	题目：观众可参与公共表演。 原文：这个学期我们在为一场特别的音乐会排练，这场观众参与的音乐会将于12月1日，周日举办。
12	overcome shyness	广告 A 最后一句	题目：此活动有助于克服您的害羞感。 原文：学习氛围轻松活泼，聚焦于提高您的自信和能力(适合于起初在这些方面对自己有些担心的人)。

13	rapid progress	广告 B 正文第二行	题目：此活动承诺快速见效。 原文：你将立刻(in no time)创造出充满异域风情的韵律。
14	not held during the day	广告 D 正文第二行	题目：此活动不在白天举办。 原文：每周三晚上 7：30 到 9：30 碰头。

参考译文

A 里奇蒙体验剧院

学习全方位介绍别人的技巧。特别适合缺乏实际经验的人。学习氛围轻松活泼，聚焦于提高您的自信和能力(适合于起初在这些方面对自己有些担心的人)。

B 世界文化日

巴西的街道打击乐器

2:30 – 4:30

桑巴打击乐器工作室。狂欢节的氛围将使您的精神为之一振！无论你是经验丰富的音乐家或是初学者，都不重要，你将立刻创造出充满异域风情的韵律。

非洲讲故事

3:45 – 4:45

神奇的非洲讲故事的传统，运用叙述，诗歌和谚语等方式(主要起源于加纳和尼日利亚)，一项适合全家的活动。

C 苏格兰舞蹈

饶有趣味

很好的锻炼

- 我们有针对所有不同程度的舞者的课程。
- 是否有经验不重要。
- 你唯一要做的就是戴上一双柔软的舞鞋以及你的热情。
- 在很多地点，不同的时间我们都有课程。
- 我们保证您会受到热烈的欢迎。

D 新生代歌手

我们邀请新歌手加入我们的唱诗班，在剑桥演出多种不同风格的音乐。我们的唱诗班成立于1993年，每周三晚上7:30到9:30碰头。这个学期我们在为一场特别的音乐会排练，这场观众参与的音乐会将于12月1日，周日举办。

有即兴朗诵才能和有合唱团演唱经验者优先，但是这不是必须条件。

E 用颜色作画

针对初学者的密集研习

10月13日(周六)和10月14日(周日)

这个非同寻常的工作室提供用颜色作画的有效指导。活动将包括光线和阴影的研究，用颜色表达心情和情绪的方法。

小班教学(12个学生)保证每个学生受到最大化的关注及指导。95英镑的学费中包括了专业品质的原料的费用。

SECTION 2

必背词汇

independent	*adj.* 独立自主的，不受约束的	brow	*n.* 眉毛
mutual	*adj.* 相互的	artificial	*adj.* 人造的，假的
tutor	*n.* 家庭教师	nail	*n.* 指甲，
executive	*n.* 执行者	pierce	*v.* 刺穿,穿透
continuity	*n.* 连续性，连贯性	leisure	*n.* 空闲，闲暇
representative	*n.* 代表	maintenance	*n.* 维护，保持
belong to	*v.* 属于	colleague	*n.* 同事
entertainment	*n.* 娱乐，娱乐表演	graphic	*adj.* 绘画似的，图解的
ample	*adj.* 充足的，丰富的	visual	*adj.* 视觉的
cassette	*n.* 卡带	communication	*n.* 交通，通讯
subsidise	*v.* 消退，下沉，平息	composition	*n.* 作文，成分
refreshment	*n.* 点心，饮料，精力恢复	alongside	*adv.* 在旁 *prep.*横靠
refectory	*n.* (修道院，学院等处的)食堂	presentation	*n.* 介绍，陈述
modest	*adj.* 谦虚的,适度的	urban	*adj.* 城市的
allocate	*v.* 分派，分配	properties	*n.* 道具，物品
nursery	*n.* 托儿所	vocation	*n.* 职业
option	*n.* 选项，选择权	assignment	*n.* 任务,(课外)作业
pursue	*v.* 继续，从事	integrate	*v.* 使成整体，结合
potential	*adj.* 潜在的	reputable	*adj.* 著名的
thorough	*adj.* 十分的，彻底的	spreadsheet	*n.* 电子数据表
comprehensive	*adj.* 全面的，广泛的	accounting	*n.* 会计学
workload	*n.* 工作量	database	*n.* 数据库
salon	*n.* 沙龙	architecture	*n.*建筑，建筑学
massage	*n.* 按摩	secretarial	*adj.* 秘书的，书记的
lash	*v.* 鞭打	therapy	*n.* 治疗

试题分析

Questions 15－20

- 题型：TURE / FALSE / NOT GIVEN

TURE / FALSE / NOT GIVEN 题即判断题，是雅思 G 类考试中的一种必考题型，也是细节题的一种。这种题型难度较大，而且在 G 类试题中题量也极大。因此考生在平时应对此种题型多花费一些精力来复习。

- 题目解析

题号	定位词	文中对应点	题解
15	job experience placement abroad	第四段	题目：许多学生都会获得在国外工作的经验。 原文：坎特博雷学院多年来发展了较为紧密的国际联系，因此很多学生在学习期间都有机会去欧洲的一个国家进行访问和工作。
16	Union President, Executive Committee	小标题“Students’ Union and SRC”对应段落第2句和第3句	题目：执行委员会和学生会主席的选举一起进行。 此题根据大写字母 Union President, Executive Committee 很快定位到原文小标题“Students’ Union and SRC”对应段落第2句和第3句。原文中的表述是：这个非常活跃的学生会是由秋季学期学生选举产生的执行委员会进行管理。每年的夏季学期选举出学生会主席以便在下一学年使学生会的工作保持连贯性。原文当中很明确的指出两种选举一个在夏季进行，另一个在秋季进行，和题目的说法完全相反，因此答案为 FALSE。
17	LRC	小标题“LRC”对应段落	题目：LRC 中有一些工作人员帮助学生来使用设备。 此题根据大写字母 LRC 很快定位到原文小标题“LRC”对应段落，迅速扫描后发现没有提到题目中的内容，因此答案为 NOT GIVEN。
18	Nursery care	小标题“Children’s center”对应段落第2句。	题目：照看小孩的服务遵循先到先得原则。 此题根据核心词 nursery care 回原文定位，发现在文中虽然没有原词重现，但作者用小标题“Children’s center”做了 nursery care 的同义替换。原文在小标

题号	定位词	文中对应点	题解
			题"Children's center"对应段落第2句描述到"因为座位有限，所以如果你感兴趣，必须联系琳达·巴克进行提前预约"，和题目的表述一致，因此答案为TRUE。
19	Refectory	小标题"Refectory"对应段落	题目：食堂供应快餐。 此题根据大字字母Refectory迅速定位到到原文小标题"Refectory"对应段落，迅速浏览后发现没有提到题目中的内容，因此答案为NOT GIVEM。
20	Chapel View Restaurant	小标题"Chapel View Restaurant"对应段落	题目：Chapel View Restaurant只面向学生开放。 此题根据大写字母Chapel View Restaurant迅速定位到原文小标题"Chapel View Restaurant"对应段落，迅速浏览后发现没有提到题目中的内容，因此答案为NOT GIVEN。

参考译文

坎特博雷学院的学生生活

坎特博雷学院的大多数课程只占用一周之中的四天时间，剩余一天供学生独立学习。

学院为您提供一个成人化的环境，在这里，学院鼓励学生和导师之间建立一种互相尊重的关系。

坎特博雷是一个学生城，有着几个继续教育和高等教育机构。从学院步行到城市的中心只用5分钟，学生可在用餐和学习的间隙前往。

坎特博雷学院多年来发展了较为紧密的国际联系，因此很多学生在学习期间都有机会去欧洲的一个国家进行访问和工作。

学生会和学生代表委员会

所有的学生都自动成为坎特博雷学院

书店

校园内有水石书店的分店。在这里，你可以买到各类文具、绘画用品、艺术家用品和书籍。此外，这里也出售你可能需要的其他有用的东西。

儿童中心

学院的儿童中心为5岁以下儿童开放并为部分儿童提供补助，供学生申请。因为名额有限，所以如果你感兴趣，必须联系琳达·巴克进行提前预约。琳达的电话请查询学校电话簿。

学生会的成员，并可以参加会议。这个非常活跃的学生会是由秋季学期学生选举产生的执行委员会进行管理。每年的夏季学期选举出学生会主席以便在下一学年使学生会的工作保持连贯性。每个学区的代表组成了学生代表委员会，以保证每一个学生在学生会事务中都有发言权。坎特博雷学院学生会代表了在学院内部的学生，并在学院社团设有一个分支委员会。除此之外，它还属于全国学生联合会。这一联合会代表了全国学生的利益，并同时组织和支持娱乐活动，体育活动以及短途旅行。

学生设施

学习资源中心(LRC)

凯瑞学习资源中心提供大量的印刷的，视觉和听觉的学习资料，这些学习资料能帮助学生完成课程。中心有足够的安静的独立学习空间，同时还有供小组讨论的区域。收藏的学习资源包括图书，期刊，录像，录音卡带和CD。学生通过大英图书馆可以实现本地和全国范围内的馆际互借。中心鼓励所有学生使用位于一楼的开放通路信息技术中心。这个中心有很多计算和文字处理、桌面出版软件。

食堂

食堂在8点30分到19点之间提供点心。每天分三个时间段提供饭食。在这里，你可以享用健康的饮食。

咖啡店

咖啡店在正常的学院工作时间内营业，提供小吃和饮料。咖啡店的盈余归学生会掌管。

Crypt 餐馆

Crypt 餐馆是一个培训餐馆，提供美味佳肴和愉快的环境。饭菜价格相当便宜。当餐馆对外营业的时候，你还会被邀请尝试学生们制作的美味佳肴。

订餐电话：01227　511244。

Chapel View **餐馆**

这是另一个培训餐馆，是作为快速服务设施兴建的。它提供了小吃，菜价适中。

Questions 21 —27

- 题型：Matching
- 题目解析

题号	定位词	文中对应点	题解
21	advertising	课程 F 对应段落第 1 行及第 3 行	题目：广告 原文：这门课旨在提供一个图像和视觉交流的基础。获取桌面出版和陈述的第一手经验。
22	TV production	课程 A 对应段落第 1 行	题目：电视节目制作 原文：即使是初级水平的学生也能在这门课中体验媒体和表演艺术。
23	architecture	课程 G 对应段落第 1 行	题目：建筑学 原文：这门课旨在介绍建筑行业(Construction industry)。

题号	定位词	文中对应点	题解
24	company management	课程 B 对应段落第 1 行	题目：公司管理 原文：这门课的目标是为学生提供与商业相关的技能(business-related)和商业实践全面的知识方面比较透彻的基础。
25	disabled	课程 E 对应段落第 1 行	题目：残疾人护理 原文：这门课将为那些有志于从事儿童、老人和特殊人群(people with special needs)看护的学生建立职业方面的基础。
26	secretarial	课程 H 对应段落第 2 行	题目：秘书类 原文：在这门课上学到的知识和技能能够帮助学生获取办公室工作(office work)的机会。下句话中的 word processing 也可辅助判断。
27	beauty therapy	课程 C 对应段落第 2 行	题目：美容 原文：…提供面部按摩和肌肤保养，化妆品指导，修睫毛和眉毛，人工指甲构造，打耳洞。

参考译文

坎特博雷学院

课程表

课程 A

即使是初级水平的学生也能在这门课中体验媒体和表演艺术。这门课将给学生提供实践的经历。这些经历将帮助他们决定是否继续在这一领域发展，并培养他们为演出公司工作的潜力和适应能力，不管这一职位是表演角色还是技术角色。

课程 B

这门课的目标是为学生在与商业相关的技能和商业实践全面的知识方面奠定良好的基础。这门课专门针对有商业学习背景的学生。这些学生能够胜任繁忙的工作，进行更高程度的学术研究。

课程 C

这门课提供更高层次的培训。分为以下单元：包括保持雇佣标准，沙龙管理职责，提供面部按摩和肌肤保养，化妆品指导，修睫毛和眉毛，人工指甲构造以及打耳洞。

课程 D

这门课旨在提升休闲活动的技能，包括准备和开展身体活动，维护设备区域，在参与者和同事之间建立关系，处理运动设备和健康、安全事项。

课程 E

这门课将为那些有志于从事儿童、老人和特殊人群看护的学生建立职业方面的基础。核心单元包括计算、交流和信息技术。本门课的一个重要部分是工作布置。

课程 F

这门课旨在提供一个图形和视觉交流的基础。学生需要完成的单元包括：构图和遵循平面设计元素的摄像处理、并获取桌面排版和陈述的应用经验。

课程 G

这门课旨在介绍建筑行业。分为以下单元：热量、光线和声音，城市环境导论，交通步骤和技巧，道具原料。所有学生必须结合在著名公司工作的经验完成假期作业，并可获得著名公司的工作经验。

课程 H

在这门课上学到的知识和技能能够帮助学生获取办公室工作的机会。除了文字处理以外，这门课还包括电子数据表，电子会计学，数据库和桌面出版。所有的学生都有机会提升自信，并在找工作的技巧、陈述技巧和个人外貌方面获得建议和信息。

SECTION 3

篇章结构

题型 说明文

主题 早期电影的历史

结构 第一段：电影发展概况

第二段：电影业的先驱者

第三段：美国逐渐成为电影业的主导

第四段：好莱坞成功的主要原因

第五段：好莱坞之外的电影业存活的原因

第六段：电影的艺术形式

第七段：默片时代的电影发展

必背词汇

第一段

unparalleled	*adj.* 无比的，空前的	occasionally	*adv.* 有时候，偶尔
expansion	*n.* 扩充，开展	supersede	*v.* 代替，接替
handful	*n.* 一把，少数	opulence	*n.* 富裕
rival	*n.* 竞争者，对手	dominate	*v.* 支配，占优势

第二段

relatively	*adv.* 相关地	passionate	*adj.* 充满热情的
exploitation	*n.* 开发，开采，剥削		

第三段

vigorous	*adj.* 精力旺盛的	glory	*n.* 荣誉，光荣
competitive	*adj.* 竞争的	epic	*n.* 史诗
spectacular	*adj.* 引人入胜的，壮观的	isolation	*n.* 隔绝，孤立
collapse	*n.& v.* 倒塌，崩溃		

第四、五段

narrative	*adj.* 叙述性的	innovation	*n.* 改革，创新
dimension	*n.* 维(数)	correspond	*v.* 符合，协调

adventurous	*adj.* 喜欢冒险的，敢做敢为的

第六段

primitive	*adj.* 原始的，粗糙的	trick	*n.* 诡计，骗局
lantern	*n.* 灯笼，幻灯	animated	*adj.* 活生生的，活泼的
slide	*n.* 幻灯片	cartoon	*n.* 卡通片，动画片
sketch	*n.* 草图，概略	studio	*n.* 工作室，演播室，摄影棚
serial	*adj.* 连续的	newsreel	*n.* 新闻影片
episode	*n.* 一段情节，[音]插曲		

第七段

slapstick	*n.* 闹剧，趣剧	documentary	*n.* 记录片
thrive	*v.* 兴旺，旺盛	distinctiveness	*n.* 与众不同有特色

第八、九段

avant-garde	*n.* 先锋派，前卫	revolution	*n.* 革命
exclusively	*adv.* 排外地，专有地	flee	*v.* 逃避，消失
display	*n.& v.* 陈列，展览，显示	escape	*v.*逃脱，避开
uncertainty	*n.* 无常，不确定	undistinguished	*adj.* 未经区分的，平凡的
insignificant	*adj.* 无关紧要的，无意义的	fame	*n.* 名声，名望
explode	*v.* 爆炸，爆发	adapt to	适合
overshadow	*v.* 遮蔽，使…失色	proportion	*n.* 比例

难句解析

1. Beginning as something unusual in a handful of big cities —New York, London, Paris and Berlin — the new medium quickly found its way across the world, attracting larger and larger audiences wherever it was shown and replacing other forms of entertainment as it did so.

参考译文：这种新媒体形式新颖、独特，在纽约、伦敦、巴黎和柏林这些大城市中放映后，很快就风靡全球，不管在哪里放映都吸引了越来越多的观众，并取代了其他的娱乐方式。

语言点：表数量的特殊构词法

handful 指的是少量，一些的意思。以一个名词加上后缀 ful 组成一个表数量的新名词是英文中一种比较独特的构词法。(注意这样的数量词虽然以常见形容词后缀 ful 结尾，但其词性实际上是名词。)常以词组形式出现如 a handful of。

相关词还有：a mouthful of food 一口食物　a handful of raisins 一把葡萄干
a spoonful of sugar 一勺糖　a basketful of peaches 一筐桃子

a armful of flowers 一捧花　a houseful of guests 一屋子客人

a busful of children 一车孩子　a roomful of antiques 一房间古董

2. Hollywood films appealed because they had better-constructed narratives, their special effects were more impressive, and the star system added a new dimension to screen acting.

参考译文：好莱坞电影之所以吸引人是因为它们有结构缜密的故事，让人印象深刻的特技和能给银幕表演增添光彩的明星体系。

语言点：合成形容词(形容词或副词加上过去分词形式的构词法)

形容词better-constructed意为结构很好的，在此可翻译为结构缜密的，这也是英文当中的一种特殊构词法，即用一个形容词或副词加上一个动词的过去分词或带-ed词尾的词来组成一个新的形容词。

相关词还有：

well-received 受到欢迎的　well-done 做得好的，完全煮熟的

well-built 体格健美的，体型匀称的　most-watched 最常看的

3. None of this would have happened without technology, and cinema is in fact unique as an art form.

参考译文：电影是一种独特的艺术形式。但是如果没有科技，这一切都不会发生。

语言点：虚拟语气would have done的用法

这是英文当中常见的一种虚拟语气表达即表示过去情况的虚拟条件句。例如，

(1) I would have done more, if I'd had the time. 如果我有时间我就会做的更多些。

(2) If I had seen the advertisement, I would have applied for the job.
如果我看到了广告，我早就申请这份工作了。

(3) They would never have met if she hadn't gone to Annie's party.
要是她没有去参加安妮的聚会，他们就绝不会相遇的。

(4) What would you have done if you'd been in my position?
如果你处于我的位置你会怎么办？

试题分析

Questions 28—30

● 题型：多项选择题

多项选择题是雅思G类试题中的一种非必考题型，题量较小，因此考生只需大体熟悉此类题型即可。

● 题目解析

该题问的是美国在电影工业中占据统治地位的三个原因。根据文章结构定位到第四段，发现该段第二句用原因状语从句告诉我们美国占主导地位的几个原因，分别为“had better-constructed narrative, special effects were more impressive, the star system added a new dimension to screen acting,"分别对应的是备选答案中的 D 和 F，下一句则指出了另一个原因"If Hollywood did not have enough of its resource, it had a great deal of money to buy up artists and technical innovations from Europe to ensure its continued dominance over present or future competition"即充足的资本，于是我们可以据此选出第三个答案即选项 A。

Questions 31—33

- 题型：Short Answer Questions

Short Answer Questions 也是雅思 G 类试题中的一种非必考题型，题量较小，也属于典型的细节题。

- 题目解析

题号	定位词	文中对应点	题解
31	not...made in major studio	原文第 6 段倒数第 2 句	题目：那两种类型的电影不是在主要工作室中制作的？ 原文："The making of cartoons..., generally practiced outside the major studios, and the same was true of serials."答案为 cartoons, serials。
32	America, in both short and feature film	原文第 7 段第 1 句	题目：美国的哪种电影形式在短片和故事片中均有所发展？ 此题根据大写字母美国及 short and feature film 定位到原文第 7 段第 1 句"From early cinema, it was only American slapstick comedy that successfully de veloped in both short and feature format."答案为 slap stick comedy。
33	profitable, "silent"	原文第 7 段最后一句	题目：那种类型的电影开始在无声电影时期获利？ 此题根据引号中"silent"一词定位到原文第 7 段第二行，然后快速往下浏览并找到该段最后一句"It was also at this time that the avant-garde film first achieved commercial success, ..."答案为 the avant-garde film。

Questions 34—40

- 题型：Matching
- 题目解析

题号	题目定位词	文中对应点	题解
34	help other countries	第 2 段第 4 行	题目：帮助其他国家发展自己的电影工业。 原文：法国人在推广电影的过程中热情最高，美国人紧随其后，在他们的帮助下，中国、日本、拉丁美洲和俄国建立了自己的电影院。因此答案为 A。
35	biggest producer	第 3 段第 1 句，第 2 句及第 4 句	题目：最大的电影制造商。 原文：最终，美国成为了全球电影的最大单一市场，现在仍是如此。通过保护自己的市场及积极进行电影的海外推广，在一战开始时，美国人已经在世界电影市场取得了主导地位。电影制作的中心也向西移到了好莱坞。这些由新的好莱坞工作室出品的电影在一战后充斥着世界电影市场，并且从那以后一直如此。面对好莱坞的绝对主导地位，几乎没有任何其他国家的电影业能够与之抗衡。因此答案为 C。
36	first，feature film	第 3 段第 7 及第 8 行	题目：第一个发展故事片。 原文：意大利的电影业开创了故事片的先河，…然而面对好莱坞的竞争也败下阵来。由此判断答案为 H。
37	creating stars	第 4 段第 3 行	题目：负责制造明星。 原文：好莱坞电影之所以吸引人是因为它们有结构缜密的故事，让人印象深刻的特技和能给银幕表演增添光彩的明星体系。因此答案为 C。
38	avant-garde	第 7 段最后一句	题目：赚的大部分钱来自于先锋电影。 原文：…也就在这一时期，先锋电影开始取得了商业上的成功，这几乎完全归功于法国电影以及偶尔出现的德国电影。因此答案为 A。
39	own culture	最后一段第4行	题目：主要基于本国文化而非外部影响来制作电影。 原文：日本电影主要是在传统戏剧的基础上发展起来的，只是很少量的吸收了其他艺术形式并慢慢受到西方的影响。因此答案为 F。
40	silent movie	最后一段倒数第 3 行末尾至第 5 行开头	题目：尽管规模不大，但对默片产生了巨大影响。 原文：丹麦在默片时代占有和其稀少的人口不成比例的一席之地。因此答案为 D。

参考译文

早期电影的历史

在电影出现后的三十年里，迎来了一个主要的发展时期，其规模前所未有。它形式新颖、独特，在纽约、伦敦、巴黎和柏林这些大城市中放映后，很快就风靡全球，无论在哪里放映都吸引了越来越多的观众，并取代了其他的娱乐方式。当观众群越来越大的时候，放映电影的地点也日益增多，也创造了20世纪20年代的“大照片宫殿”时期。在此期间，电影的魅力可与剧院和歌剧院相媲美，有时甚至要更胜一筹。同时电影本身也有了很大的发展，从最初的几分钟的短小片段到今天的独占全球银幕的故事片大制作。

虽然法国、德国、美国和英国一直因发明了电影受到世人赞誉，但是英国人和德国人在电影的全球扩张中作用相对要小一些。法国人在推广电影的过程中热情最高，美国人紧随其后，在他们的帮助下，中国、日本、拉丁美洲和俄国建立了自己的电影院。在电影的艺术发展方面，法国人和美国人依然处于领先地位，尽管在一战之前，意大利、丹麦和俄罗斯也曾占据过一席之地。

最终，美国成为了全球电影最大的单一市场，现在仍是如此。通过保护自己的市场及积极进行电影的海外推广，在一战开始时，美国人已经在世界电影市场取得了主导地位。电影制作的中心也向西移到了好莱坞。这些由新的好莱坞工作室出品的电影在一战后充斥着世界电影市场，并且从那以后一直如此。面对好莱坞的绝对主导地位，几乎没有任何其他国家的电影业能够与之抗衡。意大利的电影业曾开创了故事片的先河，其代表作有1913年出品的*Quo vadis* 和1914年的*Cabiria*，然而面对好莱坞的竞争也败下阵来。在斯堪的纳维亚，瑞典电影业的史诗电影和喜剧片有过一段辉煌，但为时很短。甚至连法国的电影业都陷入了艰难境地。在欧洲，只有德国的电影产业值得一提。在日本和刚刚成立的苏联，尽管两国与外界经济隔绝，但电影在那里得到了一定的发展。

好莱坞在艺术和商业上都处于领先地位。好莱坞电影之所以吸引人是因为它们有结构缜密的故事，让人印象深刻的特技和能给银幕表演增添光彩的明星体系。如果好莱坞自身没有足够的资源，它会用大量的金钱从欧洲买入艺术家和技术创新，以保证它在现在和将来的竞争中能持续保持主导地位。

好莱坞之外的电影业能够存活的原因，部分是因为他们在向好莱坞学习，部分还因为观众持续地需要一种产品来满足他们的需要，而这部分需要是好莱坞不提供的。除了普通观众以外，还有一部分人数不断增加的观众，他们喜欢在艺术上更加创新的电影或者探讨外部世界问题的电影。

电影是一种独特的艺术形式。但是如果没有科技，这一切都不会发生。这种艺术早期形式非常粗糙，有些类似于17世纪法国人最初设想的用灯笼和玻璃幻灯片拍摄电影的想法。早期的电影程序是各种项目的一个混合体，包括滑稽梗概，自立的叙述，连续的情节，偶尔出现的恶作剧和美术片。随着达到了正片应有长度的故事片开始出现并成为了主要的吸引力，其他的电影形式就变得不那么重要了。卡通片的制作成为了电影制作的独立分支，通常都在非主要工作室完成。连续剧也是如此。

早期的电影，只有美国的闹剧在短片和长片中都获得了成功的发展。然而，在默片时期，喜剧、连续剧和戏剧都不断兴盛，记实电影或记录片也在不断发展。也就在这一时期，先锋电影开始取得了商业上的成功，这几乎完全归功于法国电影以及偶尔出现的德国电影。

在默片时代，有些国家发展和保持了有特色的本国影片。在这些国家中，最重要的是法国、德国和苏联。在这三个国家中，排除战争和战后经济的不稳定性因素，法国显示了最强的连贯性。德国电影在世界银幕上的兴盛始于1919年，在战前，德国电影相对来说不太重要。然而，即便是英国和德国的电影，和十月革命后的苏联电影相比也黯然失色。

电影变化非常大的其他国家还有：英国——在默片时代有着很有趣但普通的电影历史；意大利——其电影在战前有过短暂的国际声誉；斯堪地纳维亚国家，尤其是丹麦——在默片时代占有和其稀少的人口不成比例的一席之地；以及日本——日本电影主要是在传统戏剧的基础上发展起来的，只是很少量的吸收了其他艺术形式并慢慢地受到西方的影响。

WRITING

WRITING TASK 1

题目要求

You were hurt in a minor accident inside a supermarket, and you wish to complain to the supermarket.

Write a letter to the manager of the supermarket. In your letter

- ***say who you are***
- ***give details about the accident***
- ***suggest how the supermarket could prevent similar accidents***

范文

Dear Sir or Madam,

I am writing this letter to inform you of the accident I had at 3:45 pm yesterday.

I was pushing my shopping cart down the aisle by the frozen meats when I slipped on the wet floor and broke the scaphoid bone in my right wrist as I tried to stop my fall. Your staff were very helpful, and your assistant manager drove me to St. Martin's Hospital, where my arm was put in a cast that will stay on for about six weeks.

I am a self-employed canteen owner, and will not be able to work for at least two months. My insurance will only cover my medical costs, not my lost earnings, which, as you can see from the attached photocopies, average 450 pounds a week. Given that the accident was due to the dangerous condition of the floor, I trust you will arrange for me to be compensated with an amount equal to my average weekly earnings for the time that I am unable to work.

May I suggest that you instruct your staff to pay better attention to safety, and have a sign that clearly warns customers of such dangers as a slippery floor.

Yours sincerely,
John Smith

分析

这是一封投诉信。题目分两部分。第一部分是背景交待：你在超市受了轻伤，要向超市投诉。第二部分是题目要求，需要表明作者身份，具体说明投诉的原因，并且提出建议。

在这里，考生只能写在超市发生的问题，而且受轻伤是因为超市某方面问题所引起。理由需要考生自己编，只要基本合理即可。本文作者写的是在超市推购物车的时候由于地板湿滑导致右手腕骨折。

既然是投诉，就需要提出要求对方加以解决，比如医药费误工费之类的。其次，可以对超市提些建议，以避免今后发生类似问题。

考生还需要注意的是语言要礼貌得体。虽然是投诉，但依然要坚持礼貌，以反映事实为主，不要进行抒情或是控诉。用词和句型上最好尽量正式。

WRITING TASK 2

题目要求

In the past, many people had skills such as making their own clothes and doing repairs to things in the house. In many countries, nowadays, skills like these are disappearing.

Why do you think this change is happening?
How far is this situation true in your country?

题解

过去，许多人都会各种技能，比如自己做衣服，自己在家里进行修理。而现在在许多国家这些技能正在消失。要求分析导致这个变化的原因，并且结合本国实际加以说明。

这篇文章要求分析原因，但注意：不需要提出解决问题的建议，只要分析原因即可。另外，考生还应该结合本国实际，也就是中国的实际情况进行说明，也就是要求运用举例论证的写作方法。

本题从内容上看，属于传统的丧失这一类题目。考生可以从科技发展，社会变化，文化演进等角度进行分析。

范文

There is no doubt that as a society modernizes many skills that were once commonly possessed by most of its members gradually disappear. These skills include such things as making clothes, basic carpentry and home repairs.

There are a variety of interrelated reasons for this phenomenon, many of which are related to industrialization and the increasing division of labor that goes with it. With industrialization, many things that were once produced by individual households become so cheap when mass-produced that people think it is not worth the time and trouble to make them themselves. This applies to many things used in daily life. Take food, for example. Many people with gardens used to grow some of their own food, but the availability of relatively cheap food produced by industrialized agriculture persuades most people to go to the supermarket, rather than dig the garden. It is the same with cooking. Many things that used to normally be prepared at home are now purchased as frozen foods or in a can or bottle: I think, for example, of Chinese dumplings and cleaning a chicken.

At the same time, the increasing technical sophistication of everything from motor cars to lawn mowers means that repairing them requires ever more specialized skills, skills that the ordinary person either cannot or does not wish to acquire.

Another important factor is the increasing availability of home entertainment, such as television, DVDs and computer games. Many people would rather enjoy these things than peel potatoes or make wooden toys for the kids it's much simpler to buy a plastic toy.

All the above factors apply to my country, China, especially its cities. And so does another: The cities are now home to many former farmers who have come to escape poverty. These are a cheap source of labor for tasks, like home painting and decorating that are normally used to be done by the home owner.

分析

文章第一段提出问题。先泛泛说明，然后指出具体表现形式。毫无疑问，随着社会的现代化，许多本来人们拥有的技能在逐渐消失，比如制作服装，基础木工和家庭修理。

然后文章用三段话来具体分析这个现象出现的各种原因。在第二段指出，最重要的原因是工业化和随之而来的劳动分工。工业化使得原本由家庭制作的东西在经过大规模生产后变得非常便宜，因此人们就觉得不值得付出时间和精力来自己制作。比如食物。许多有院子的人原本自己种点蔬菜，但是由于工业化农业的出现，使得食物售价低廉，于是绝大多数人去超市购买，而不是自己在院子里耕种。烹调也是如此。原来许多由家庭制作的食物现在都可以买到，无论是速冻的还是罐装的。比如包饺子和自己杀鸡。

与此同时，技术越来越先进，随着汽车和割草机的出现，要修理这些机器需要更加专业的技能。而这些技能普通人不会或不愿去学。

另外一个重要因素是家庭娱乐方式的日益多样化，比如电视，影碟，和电子游戏。许多人宁可玩这些而不愿自己削土豆或者给小孩做木制玩具。与其做木制玩具，不如买塑料玩具方便得多。

文章结尾把这些因素和中国实际相结合。指出，所有以上这些因素在我们中国，尤其是中国城市都存在。现在城市越来越成为农民为了脱贫而向往的地方。这些民工成了主要的劳动力，在城市从事家装等工作，而本来家庭装修这些事情是家庭成员自己亲手做的。

General Training: Reading and Writing Test B

READING

SECTION 1

必背词汇

cottage	*n.* 村舍，小屋	sufficient	*adj.* 足够的
brochure	*n.* 小册子	furniture	*n.* 家具
alternative	*n.* 可供选择的办法；*adj.* 选择性的	damage	*n.* 损害
		overseas	*adj.* 海外的，国外的
availability	*n.* 可行性，有效性	delight	*v.* 高兴，乐意
reservation	*n.* 保留，(旅馆房间等)预订，预约	meter reading	*n.* 读表器
		conclusion	*n.* 结论
available	*adj.* 可用到的，可行的	fixed	*adj.* 固定的
provisional	*adj.* 临时的	coin meter	*n.* 硬币收费表
reference	*n.* 提及，涉及，参考	linen	*n.* 亚麻制品
deposit	*n.* 存款，押金，保证金	duvet	*n.* 棉被
credit card	*n.* 信用卡	pillow	*n.* 枕头
cheque	*n.* 支票	cot	*n.* 吊床
cancel	*v.* 取消，删去	query	*n.* 疑问
confirm	*v.* 确定，确认	accountant	*n.* 会计师
attach	*v.* 配属，隶属于，附上	professional	*adj.* 专业的
outstanding	*n.* 负债	audit	*n.* 审计
departure	*n.* 离开	accountancy	*n.* 会计
arrival	*n.* 到达	taxation	*n.* 税务
property	*n.* 物品，财产	at all times	在任何时候
caretaker	*n.* 管理员	insurance	*n.* 保险

respray	*n.* 重新喷漆	limo	*n.* 豪华轿车
restoration	*n.* 修复	occasion	*n.* 场合
victim	*n.* 受害人	express	*n.* 速递
solicitor	*n.* 法律顾问，律师	reliable	*adj.* 可靠的
claim	*v.* 索取	estate	*n.* 不动产
compensation	*n.* 赔偿	surveyor	*n.* 估价人
specialist	*n.* 专家	commercial	*adj.* 商业的
freephone	*n.* 免费电话	surrounding	*n.* 氛围
cater	*v.* 备办宴会	freshly	*adv.* 新鲜地
quote	*n.* 报价	desktop	*n.* 桌面
budge	*n.* 预算	localisation	*n.* 地方化，本土化
venue	*n.* 地点		

试题分析

Questions 1—7

- 题型：TURE / FALSE / NOT GIVEN
- 题目解析

题号	定位词	文中对应点	题解
1	Saturdays in February	小标题 21st October to 30th March 下第一段	题目：2 月份每周六照常营业，但会比平常提早一点关门。 本题考查的是时间，因此定位起来较容易。迅速定位到小标题 21st October to 30th March 下第一段，原文中的表述是："平时下午 5 点关门而周六 4 点 30 分关门"，与原文的表述完全一致，因此答案为 TRUE。
2	deposit, confirm your booking	小标题 Arrival 上面 1 段第 1 句	题目：收到您的定金收据后，维斯特小屋将会电话确认您的预订。 原文：从我们收到您的约定表格和保证金的那一刻起，您的预约将被确认。由此可见并不是电话确认，所以答案为 FALSE。虽然下一句提到了 telephone number，但其意思是"同时我们将寄给您一份约定确认单和如何到达您的假日小屋的建议以及一个当地的电话号码"，与题干中的电话确认无关。

题号	定位词	文中对应点	题解
3	ten weeks	小标题 Arrival 上面一段最后 1 句	题目：英国境内预定必须在缴纳保证金后的10周内支付剩余费用。 此题根据题干中的时间 ten weeks 可以很快定位到原文小标题 Arrival 上面一段最后 1 句，原文的表述与题目完全一致，因此答案为 TRUE。
4	departure, arrival	小标题 Departure 对应段落第 1 句	题目：在头一个旅客离开和下一个旅客到来之间，我们会检查和准备好物品。 此题根据题干中的 departure 和 arrival 很快定位到原文小标题 Departure 对应段落第 1 句，原文中的表述是：请在上午10点之前离店，以保证管理员能够有充足的时间为下一位游客做好物品的准备。因此答案为 TRUE。
5	last-minute booking	小标题 Last-Minute Bookings 对应段落	题目：如果您想临时订房，价格会相对便宜一些。 此题根据题干中的 last-minute booking 很快定位到原文小标题 Last-Minute Bookings 对应段落，原文中的表述是：用房前十周可以临时订房，但预定时需付全款。因此很明显答案为 FALSE。
6	Electricity	小标题 Electricity 对应段落第 1 句	题目：在大多数维斯特小屋中，电费都包含在房租中。 此题根据题干中的 Electricity 很快定位到原文小标题 Electricity 对应段落第 1 句，原文中的表述是：在大多数维斯特小屋中，电费不包含在房价中，需要额外支付。(...electricity must be paid for in addition to the holiday price.)因此答案为 FALSE。
7	beach towels	小标题 Linen 对应段落倒数第 3 至第 4 行	题目：游客可以租用在海滩使用的毛巾。 定位到原文小标题 Linen 对应段落倒数第 3 至第 4 行，原文中的表述是：你可以选择租用亚麻制品，这其中包括床上用品(即：床单和/或被套、枕套)、浴巾、手巾、抹布，但游泳或在海滩使用的毛巾不包含在内。因此很明显答案为 FALSE。

参考译文

预订维斯特小屋假期

如何预订你的假期

如果您已经浏览过我们的小册子，并挑选了您愿意入住的二到三个备选小屋，请致电假日预订处。

电话：01225 892299

5 月 31 日 — 10 月 20 日

周一，周二，周三，周五，早上 9 点到下午 5 点，周四上午 9 点 30 分到下午 5 点。

周六、周日休息

10 月 21 日 — 3 月 30 日

周一，周二，周三，周五，早上 9 点到下午 5 点，周四上午 9 点 30 分到下午 5 点。

周六上午 9 点 30 分到下午 4 点 30 分

周日休息

我们将核查您的选择的可行性，预订人员将帮助您做出决定。如果您的任一选择都无法实现，我们将尽全力给您推荐合适的代替方案。

您的临时预订将保留 7 天。我们将给您一个假日参考电话，并要求您填写假日预订表格并回收。同时，您还需交付相当于 1/3 租金的保证金，地址如下：

WESSEX COTTAGES HOLIDAY BOOKING OFFICE

PO BOX 675

MELKSHAM

WILTSHIRE SN12 8SX

保证金接受当场信用卡支付或支票支付(抬头请写“维斯特小屋有限公司”)

如果在 7 天内没有收到您填写并签名的表格和保证金，我们很抱歉您的预约将被取消。

从我们收到您的预订表格和保证金的那一刻起，您的预约将被确认。同时我们将寄给您一份预订确认单和如何到达您的假日小屋的建议以及一个当地的电话号码，如果您想了解更多关于假日小屋的详情，请在出发之前和这个号码联系。随预定确认单一同附上的短信将会显示您应支付的费用及付款日期。英国境内预订必须在保证金交纳的 10 周内支付剩余费用。

抵达

请不要在下午 3 点 30 分之前或晚上 7 点之后到达您的假日小屋。

离开

请在上午 10 点之前离店，以保证管理员能够有充足的时间为下一位游客做好物品的准备。请您不要带走本店的物品。请勿移动家具以免造成家具和物品的损害。

国外预订

我们非常高兴接受国外预订，请电话或传真联系我们：+44 (0)1225890227。必须用信用卡或支付。国外旅游者的临时预订将保留 14 天。在

14天内，如果没有收到填写并签名的预订表格和保证金，预约将被取消。

临时订房

如果您想临时订房(马上预订并立即获得房间)，请致电假日预订中心查询。

用房前十周可以临时订房，但预订时需付全款。

电费

在大多数维斯特小屋中，电费不包含在房价中，需要额外支付。在假期结束后，我们将检查您的电表或额外收取固定费用。此外，一些小屋设有硬币收费表，在您预订的时候，我们会告知您这一情况。我们还提供一些电费包含在租金内的小屋和少量不供电的小屋。

日用织品

在大多数小屋，你可以选择租用日用织品，收费标准为每人每周6英镑，或者您可以选择自带。部分小屋配有日用织品，少数小屋则不提供。如果您选择租用日用织品，这其中包括床上用品(即：床单和/或被套、枕套)、浴巾、手巾、抹布，但游泳或在海滩使用的毛巾不包含在内。我们不提供供帆布床使用的日用织品。如果您有任何问题，请咨询假日预订处。

Questions 8—14

- 题型：Matching
- 题目解析

题号	定位词	文中对应点	题解
8	car，broken	广告B标题及正文	题目：我出了事故，汽车尾灯损坏。我需要换一个。 原文：广告B标题“圣保罗修车行”及正文“故障修理服务”(breakdown service)。
9	provide the food	广告D标题	题目：我在帮忙筹备一场婚礼。婚宴将设在新娘家中，想找人提供食物。 原文：广告D标题为“MELROSE BUFFET CATERING”。此题考查词汇量，考生须知“catering”一词的含义为“宴会承办、备办酒席”。
10	lawyer	广告K标题及正文第一行	题目：我找到一处想买的房子，需要律师来帮助我处理相关文件。 原文：此题依然考查词汇。广告K的标题中“Solicitor”一词意为“律师，法律顾问”。另外正文第一行中的legal service即法律服务也可作为辅助判断。

题号	定位词	文中对应点	题解
11	Thailand, understand recipe	广告 L 标题	题目：我刚从泰国度假归来，在那里买了一本泰国菜谱，准备在自己的餐馆中使用。但我需要有人帮我理解它们。 此题目实际告诉我们需要找的是翻译人员，因此迅速定位到广告 L，其标题为“优美诗句翻译有限公司”。
12	find somewhere to live locally	广告 G 正文第 1 行	题目：我刚找到一份新工作。我需要找个地方住。 原文：房地产代理(ESTATE AND PROPERTY AGENTS)
13	find somewhere for them to stay	广告 J 正文第 1 段	题目：周末一些朋友要过来拜访我，但我的房子太小容纳不下他们。我想给他们找个地方住。 原文：大小适中的家庭房(ENSUITE FACILITIES WITH GOOD-SIZED FAMILY ROOMS)
14	organise our finance	广告 A 标题及正文	题目：我在本地一家律师行工作。现在快到财年年底了，我想找人为我们提供财务方面的服务。 原文：STEADMAN & CO 特许会计师，全方位专业服务包括为大小公司提供审计，会计和税务服务。

参考译文

A

STEADMAN & CO 特许会计师

全方位专业服务包括为大小公司提供审计，会计和税务服务。

我们随时竭诚为您服务

Ely 教堂路 12 号

电话：(01353)562547/561331

B

圣保罗修车行

全机械化车身修理服务

保险公司担保

重新喷漆 修复

紧急故障修理服务

6，River Lane，Ely，Cambs CB6 4BU

Telephone:Ely 552247

C

意外事故受害者?

在意外事故中受伤?有没有其他责任人?专业律师向您提供免费咨询,告诉您是否可以获得赔偿。

致电:

免费电话 0800 8760831(24 小时)

全国意外事故热线服务

D

MELROSE BUFFET CATERING

具有 15 年经验的专业宴会承办者

在您预定之前,我们会给您提供一个报价

我们将在您的预算之内做到最好

我们为大小仪式备办食物。

在您的家里,办公室、花园、市政厅、教堂

事实上,你所希望的任何地方,我们都竭诚为您服务。

您提供地点,我们提供菜单——份适合您预算的菜单。

剑桥密尔顿市拜瑞路 28 号

电话 01223 640789

E

L M 豪华轿车租用

我们提供婚礼和其他特殊场合用车等服务

约翰和苏主教

The White House, 12A Fair Street, Ely CB6 1AE

电话:01353 667184

F

机票速递

是您通往全世界的热线

如果您在全世界任何一个地方,如果您对航班预订十分慎重,如果您看重可信赖的服务和低廉的价格

请立即拨打我们的电话:

0990 320321

25, Union Road, Bishops Stortford,

Herts CM23 2LY

G

Barton Hill & Knight

房地产代理

特许鉴定估价人

商业资产

家庭用品及艺术品出售

一家独立的房地产服务公司,提供专业知识

BURY ST EDMUNDS

01284 800717

15, DISS ROAD

BURY ST EDMUNDS

SUFFOLK IP33 3AA

H

PASCAL'S

法国餐馆 / 啤酒屋

特许经营

一杯酒就着新鲜准备的食物真是难得的乐事。

就餐氛围轻松

营业时间：

午餐—啤酒屋风格—周三—周日

晚餐—周三—周六—每餐三个菜—价格固定

本餐馆为无烟餐馆

2, Fen Road, Littleport,

Cambridgeshire 01353 565011

抱歉不接受信用卡

I

全球旅行

外币兑换服务

每周营业六天

我们保证最好的汇率

收取最低的佣金

14, March Road, Ely, Cambs. Tel: 01353 551136

J

THE PARKLANDS

- 大小适中的家庭房，设施包括：彩电，茶 / 咖啡制作设备
- 特许经营的餐厅和酒吧
- 供会议、婚礼、聚会和所以特殊场合使用的会议室

电话：(01440)862581

Mount Pleasant, Haverhill

K

BAKER, STEWART & YOUNG

法律顾问

提供多方面的法律服务

2, High Street, Ely, Cambridgeshire CB7 4JY

电话：(01353)552918

L

优美诗句翻译有限公司

领先的翻译专家 始于 1984 年

笔译和口译

超过 3,000 名职业翻译家

翻译　小型出版

口译　本土化

画外音　媒体分析

编辑服务

电话：++44(0)1223 856732

Fax：(0)1223 821588

5, Castle Court, Cambridge, CB12PQ

SECTION 2

必背词汇

specialist	*n.* 专家	degrade	*v.* (使)降级，(使)退化
rural	*adj.* 乡下的，农村的	pathway	*n.* 路，径
renowned	*adj.* 有名的，有声誉的	marine	*adj.* 海的，海产的，航海的
tropical	*adj.* 热带的	prepaid	*adj.* 先付的，已支付的
module	*n.* 模数，模块	photocopier	*n.* 影印机
bushfood	*n.* 灌木果实	representative	*n.* 代表
macadamias	*n.* 澳大利亚坚果	unique	*adj.* 惟一的，独特的
veterinary	*n.* 兽医 *adj.* 兽医的	account	*n.* 计算，账目
correspondence	*n.* 通信，函授	initially	*adv.* 最初，开头
tutorial	*n.* 指南	refund	*v.* & *n.* 退还，退款
workshop	*n.* 研讨会	denomination	*n.* 命名
traineeship	*n.* 受训者，实习生的地位	purchase	*v.* 买，购买
promotion	*n.* 促销	automatically	*adv.* 自动地，机械地
community	*n.* 公社，团体，社区	receipt	*n.* 收条，收据
fitness	*n.* 适当，瘦身	optional	*adj.* 可选择的，随意的
therapy	*n.* 治疗，疗法	allocate	*v.* 分派，分配
awareness	*n.* 知道，意识	identification	*n.* 辨认，鉴定，证明

试题分析

Questions 15 —21

- 题型：Matching
- 题目解析

这 7 道题目比较简单，每道题的题干当中均有大写字母出现，因此只需在原文中迅速定位到各题位置，然后在附近找寻答案，与选项列表一一对应选出正确答案。

题号	定位词	文中对应点	题解
15	Wollongbar	第一段第2句	原文“Tropical Fruit Growing”对应B选项“banana cultivation”。
16	Grafton	第一段最后1句	原文“offers traineeships in agriculture including Beef and Dairy”对应H选项“cattle farming”。
17	Tweed Heads	第2段最后1句	原文“Fitness Instruction courses”对应K选项“recreation program”。
18	Lismore	第3段第1句	原文“Aged Support program”对应E选项“elderly care”
19	Port Macquarie	第3段第1句	原文“Early Childhood Nursing program“对应D选项“infant illness”。
20	Ballina	第4段最后1句	原文“The Environmental practice course, which include Coastal Management”对应I选项“beach protection”。
21	Coffs harbour	最后一段最后1句	原文“Marine Industry Management program”对应F选项“fishing farming”。

参考译文

北海岸学院校园课程

农业

北海岸学院的农业中心专家开设的课程包括农业技能，牛肉加工，马匹研究和乡村管理。沃伦巴校区以热带水果种植课程著名，并引进了关于澳大利亚坚果，灌木果实和咖啡生产的一系列学习模式。塔瑞校区开设兽医助理课程并介绍农业研究。这门课程能使学生灵活学习，学习方式包括学习向导，电话辅导，信息会议和研讨会。M校区有着最受欢迎的乡村商业管理课程。这一课程也可以通过函授形式学习。G校区为学生提供进行农业活动的实习机会，包括牛肉业和奶制品业。

健康课程

社区内持续升温的健康生活见证了瘦身的增长和瘦身和运动行业对培训人员的需求。TH校区提供瘦身指导课程，并教授学生如何安全瘦身。

L校区开设老年支持课程，PM校区开设婴幼儿护理课程。这些课程将教给你理论技能、知识和实践经验，而这些是在社区健康护理机构工作的必要条件。对于那些对健康治疗看护行业工作有兴趣的学生，K校区有一个为自然疗法文凭而设的专家培训指导中心和一个健康诊所。

环境研究

北海岸学院提供的环境研究课程旨在帮助学生提高对环境问题的意识和加深对其的理解，并使他们能够决定他们对环境的影响。B 校区提供包括海岸管理在内的环境实践课程。

针对对恢复退化的自然森林工作感兴趣的学生，北海岸学院在 Casino 校区开设了森林再造课程。这门课程为学生进入大学取得自然资源管理学位提供了途径。Coffs Harbour 校区开设了海产业管理课程。

Questions 22 －27

- 题型：TURE / FALSE / NOT GIVEN
- 题目解析

题号	定位词	文中对应点	题解
22	Prepaid Service Cards, three locations	第 1 段	题目：预先付费服务卡可以在三个地方使用。 原文：此卡可以在图书馆， B Block 及学生代表委员会使用。因此答案为 TURE。
23	Prepaid Service Cards, Library	第 2 段第 2 句	题目：你只能在图书馆购买预先付费服务卡。 原文：学生和其他使用者都要到位于图书馆和 B Block 计算机实验室的贩卖机上去买一张预先付费服务卡。原文中很明显的表明至少可以在两个地方购买预先付费服务卡，因此答案为 FALSE。
24	$5	第3段最后一行及第 4 段倒数第 2 行	题目：在图书馆给校园服务卡充值，每次至少充5美元。此题根据货币符号迅速定位到原文第 2 至 4 段中包含货币符号的几个句子，迅速扫描后发现均未提及题目中的内容，因此答案为 NOT GIVEN。
25	library fines		题目：预先付费服务卡可以被用来支付图书馆罚款。带着罚款这个题目核心词回原文中找寻，发现原文中根本没有提及此内容，因此答案为 NOT GIVEN。
26	Notes and coins	第 4 段最后一句	题目：所有自动贩卖机上都能使用纸币和硬币。 原文：原文中的表述是 “coins only”，即学生代表委员会有一个只能接受硬币的贩卖机，因此答案为 FALSE。

题号	定位词	文中对应点	题解
27	PIN	最后一段第 1 句	题目：一旦你购买预先付费服务卡，该卡就会自动给你分配一个密码。 此题根据大写字母 PIN 很快定位到原文最后一段的第一句，原文中的表述是："为了增加安全性，卡片持有者可以选择给预先付费服务卡添加密码…"，由此可见密码是由用户自己来选择是否添加而非由预先付费服务卡分配，所以答案为 FALSE。

参考译文

影印信息

信息服务处为学生和老师提供了预付费服务卡系统，以便他们使用复印机、图书馆联系设备和 B Block 的激光打印机。这个系统最近已经在学生代表委员会安装了，以便使用那里的复印机。

这个系统采用了类似于钥匙卡的塑料卡，这个卡片被称为预付费服务卡。每一张卡都有一个惟一的 6 位数的账号，以便进入系统。学生和其他使用者最开始都要到位于图书馆和 B Block 计算机实验室的贩卖机上去买一张预付费服务卡。这张卡片价值 2 美元。重要的是，你要记录好你的六位数账号，并在卡上签上你的名字或写上你的学号。

通过往预付费卡上加钱，使用者就对图书馆、计算机实验室或学生代表委员会预先付费了。这个卡不能退款，所以只能按照你想要使用的次数来加款。一张卡最多能加 50 美元。

两个自动贩卖机都已经装好了程序，一个在图书馆 2 楼的影印室，另一个在 B Block 计算机实验室。这些自动贩卖机能接受 50 美元以内的任何纸币和硬币。学生代表委员会有一个小的，只能接受硬币的贩卖机。

购买一张新卡的同时，图书馆和 B Block 的贩卖机会自动打印一张收据给使用者。但是当你往卡里加钱的时候，可以选择是否打印收据。

为了增加安全性，卡片持有者可以选择给预付费服务卡添加密码或者个人识别数字。在每次使用的时候，必须输入密码。

SECTION 3

篇章结构

体裁 说明文

主题 蜜蜂如何通过舞蹈向同伴传达信息

结构 A 段：蜜蜂语言的特殊地位
B 段：Von Frisch 发现了蜜蜂之间的交流方式
C 段：蜜蜂舞蹈的三种类型
D 段：介绍前两种舞蹈的含义
E 段：蜜蜂如何通过舞蹈来表达食物的距离
F 段：在蜂巢外时蜜蜂如何通过舞蹈来表达方向
G 段：在蜂巢内时蜜蜂如何通过舞蹈来表达方向

必背词汇

seed	*n.* 种子，萌芽	waggle	*v.* 来回摇动，摆动
encode	*v.* 破译	troop	*n.* 群，组，军队
behavioural	*adj.* 动作的，行为的	sniff	*v.* 用力吸，嗅
witness	*v.* 目击，为…作证	horizontal	*adj.* 地平线的，水平的
unravel	*v.* 拆开，解开…之谜	platform	*n.* 平台
astonishing	*adj.* 令人惊奇的	portion	*n.* 一部分，一份
derive	*v.* 起源，来源	remarkable	*adj.* 不平常的，非凡的，显著的
syrup	*n.* 糖浆	gravity	*n.* 地心引力，重力
hive	*n.* 蜂巢	represent	*v.* 表现，描绘
scout	*n.* 侦察	vertical	*adj.* 垂直的，直立的
scamper	*v.* 奔跳	revolutionise	*v.* 宣传革命，大事改革
alternate	*v.* 交替，轮流	chase	*v.* 追赶，追逐
occasionally	*adv.* 有时候，偶尔	source	*n.* 来源，源
regurgitate	*v.* (使)涌回，(使)反刍	direction	*n.* 方向，指导
sickle	*n.* 镰刀		

难句解析

1. A bee's brain is the size of a grass seed, yet in this brain are encoded some of the most complex and amazing behavioural patterns witnessed outside humankind.

参考译文：蜜蜂的大脑只有草籽那么大，那然而就是在这么微小的脑子里，储存了一些除人类以外的最复杂和最神奇的行为模式。

语言点：状语提前引起的句子倒装

在英文中，如果谓语提到主语前面，则句子为倒装语序(Inverted Order)。在这里状语提前引起句子倒装，目的是起强调作用。例如，

① Only in this way can our honour be saved. 只有这样才能保住我们的荣誉。

② In vain did he try to open the locked door. 他设法打开那扇锁着的们但没有成功。

2. Von Frisch knew from experiments by an earlier researcher that if he put out a bowl of sweet sugar syrup, bees might at first take some time to find it but, once they had done so, within the hour, hundreds of other bees would be eagerly taking the syrup.

参考译文：芬奇从一个早期研究者的实验知道，如果他放一碗糖浆在外面，蜜蜂最初可能要花上一段时间找到糖浆，但是一旦它们找到了，在一个小时内，成百上千的其他蜜蜂都会急切地来获得糖浆。

He found that, once the scout bees arrived back at the hive, they would perform one of three dance types.

他发现，侦察蜂一旦返回了蜂巢，它们将表演三种舞蹈中的一种。

语言点：Once 的用法

once 意为“一旦”，是书面英语及口语中的常见词。例如，

① Once she arrives, we can start the party. 她一到，我们就可以开始举行晚会了。

② Once in bed, the children usually stay there. 小孩一旦上了床，通常就待在那儿了。

3. Experimenting further, von Frisch unraveled the mystery of the first two related types, the round and the sickle dances.

参考译文：在进一步的实验中，芬奇解开了前两种相关类型舞蹈之谜：圆舞和镰刀舞。

语言点：代替主句的现在分词短语

如果主语同时做出两个动作时，通常其中的一个动词可以由现在分词来表示。这时分词既可以放在动词不定式之前，也可以放在之后。如果主语所做的一个动作紧接着所做的另一个动作，第一个动作常用现在分词来表示，而且分词必须放在前面。例如，

① Holding the rope with one hand, he stretches out the other to the boy in the water.

他一只手拉着绳子，另一只手伸给水中的男孩。

② Opening the drawer he took out a revolver. 他打开抽屉，拿出了一把左轮手枪。

③ Raising the tapdoor she pointed to a flight of steps.

她把翻板活门拉开，指着一段台阶。

④ Taking off our shoes we creep cautiously along the passage.

我们脱了鞋，小心地、偷偷地沿着走廊走过去。

后三个例句好像用分词的完成式更合乎逻辑，如 Having opened, Having raised, Having taken off 等。但除了使用现在分词的一般式可能使意思含混不清的时候以外，没有必要使用完成式。这里举一个必须使用分词完成式的例子：Eating his dinner he rushed out of the house 会给人这样一种印象，好像他手里还拿着菜盘子就走出了房子。因此，这里最好用 Having eaten his dinner he rushed out of the house.

4. If he placed the feeding dish over nine meters away, the second type of dance, the sickle version, came into play.

参考译文：如果他把饲养盘放到超过 9 英里远的地方，侦察蜂开始跳起了第二种舞蹈，镰刀形舞蹈。

语言点：come into play 的用法

come into play 意为(开始)积极活动或起作用。例如，

Personal feelings should not come into play when one has to make business decisions.为公事做决策不应掺杂个人情感。

试题分析

Questions 28－34

- 题型：List of Headings

List of Headings 即段落大意题或标题匹配题是雅思阅读考试中为数不多的主旨题，旨在考查考生把握文章段落整体含义的能力。其主要形式是在文章之前给出一个标题列表(其中包含多个段落标题，一般多于文章段落数，因此有一些标题是迷惑选项)，要求考生根据文章各段落内容找出与其相匹配的段落标题。

● 题目解析

题号	段落主题句	题解
28	For bees are arguably the only animals apart from humans which have their own language.	此题有些难度。虽然乍看起来主要在讲蜜蜂行为，但实际上第2句话“蜜蜂是除了人类以外被证实的具有自己语言的惟一动物”告诉我们蜜蜂行为的秘密所在及语言。此外结合对末句“现今大多数的关于蜜蜂之间语言的知识都是起源于芬奇的工作”的分析，也可发现实际上本段主要强调的是蜜蜂语言的重要性。因此答案为选项 vi。
29	Von Frisch realized that, in some way, messages were being passed on back at the hive, messages which said,“Out there, at this spot, you' re going to find food.”	此题较难，B 段末句的意思是：芬奇认识到，通过某种方式，信息被传回了蜂巢。信息的内容是这样的：在外面，在那个地方，你们将会找到食物。再结合前面内容，发现该段主要讲述的是蜜蜂之间的交流及信息的传达，因此答案为选项 iv。
30	He found that, once the scout bees arrived back at the hive, they would perform one of three dance types.	该段主题句的表述是：他发现，侦察蜂一旦返回了蜂巢，它们将表演三种舞蹈中的一种。接下来该段就分别具体描述了这三种舞蹈，因此答案为选项 x。
31	Experimenting further，von Frisch unraveled the mystery of the first two related types, the round and the sickle dances.	该段主题句的表述为：在进一步的实验中，芬奇解开了前两种相关类型舞蹈之谜。迅速扫描下面内容，发现都是围绕这两种舞蹈进行的具体阐述，因此答案为选项 viii。
32	The measurement of the actual distance too, he concluded, was precise.	此题较难，通过主题句“他总结到，蜜蜂对实际距离的测量是准确的”并结合前面内容，可以看出E段主要讲述蜜蜂是如何通过舞蹈类型来说明食物的距离的，因此答案为选项 vii。
33	The outside dance was fairly easy to decode: the straight...their food.	F 段主题句即末句的表述为：室外的舞蹈是相当容易破译的：舞蹈的直线部分指出了蜜源的方向，所以蜜蜂只需要破译距离信息并沿着这个方向去寻找它们的食物。该段主要讲述室外舞蹈指明蜜源方向，因此答案为选项 ii。

题号	段落主题句	题解
34	But by studying the dance on the inner wall of the hive, von Frisch discovered a remarkable method which the dancer used to tell sisters the direction of the food in relation to the sun.	G段主题句即首句的表述为：通过研究在蜂巢内壁上的舞蹈，芬奇发现了一个不同寻常的方法：跳舞的蜜蜂以太阳为参照(in relation to the sun)向它的同伴指示取食的方向。首句话告诉我们该段主要讲蜂巢内的舞蹈，如不确定，结合第二句'在蜂巢内的时候，舞蹈蜂不能使用太用，所以，取而代之，它使用了重力'进行理解，依然描述的是蜂巢内的舞蹈情况，因此答案为选项v。

Questions 35－37

- 题型：Completion

这种类型的填空题形式与列举题比较接近，难度较低，是雅思G类考试中较少出现的一种题型。

- 题目解析

根据题干中的关键词"三种类型的蜜蜂舞蹈"在原文中快速浏览，发现原文D段中出现了"three dance types"及具体的序数词"first, second, third"，因此答案较为简单，分别为round，sickle，waggle三词。

Questions 38－40

- 题型：Sentence Completion
- 题目解析

题号	定位词	文中对应点	题解
38	difference between dance types	E段第4句至第6句	题目：Von Frisch通过改变什么的位置发现了蜜蜂舞蹈类型间的区别。 此题根据段落大意定位到原文E段第4句及第5句，原文中的表述是："…在预感下，他开始逐渐将饲养盘(feeding dish)移得越来越远，与此同时，他观察到回巢的侦察蜂的舞蹈也开始改变。如果他把饲养盘放到超过9英里远的地方，侦察蜂开始跳起了第二种舞蹈，镰刀形。但是一旦他把饲养盘移到超过36英里远的地方，侦察蜂就开始跳第三种舞蹈，差别很大的摇摆舞。"由此可见签案应为feeding dish即饲养盘。

题号	定位词	文中对应点	题解
39	out side the hive	F段第2句至最后一句	题目：蜂房外部的舞蹈指明了什么东西的位置。 此题根据段落大意定位到原文F段的第2句至最后一句，原文中的表述为："当侦察蜂回到家中，告诉它的姐妹蜜源(the food source)信息，有时候它们会在蜂巢水平的入口平台上跳舞，有时候会在巢内垂直的墙上跳。根据跳舞的位置，摇摆舞中直线的部分指向不同的方向。室外的舞蹈是相当容易破译的：舞蹈的直线部分指出了蜜源的方向，所以蜜蜂只需要破译距离信息并沿着这个方向去寻找它们的食物。"由此可见答案应为the food source及蜜源。
40	angle	G段第1句	此题根据定位词angle定位到原文中出现角度的段落及G段，原文中的表述是："通过研究在蜂巢内壁上的舞蹈，Frisch发现了一个不同寻常的方法：舞者以太阳为参照(in relation to the sun)，向它的同伴指示取食的方向。"因此答案为the sun。

参考译文

理解蜜蜂的行为

A

一只蜜蜂的脑子的大小和草的一粒种子是一样的。然而就是在这么微小的脑子里，储存了一些除人类以外的最复杂和最神奇的行为模式。一种说法是蜜蜂是除了人类以外具有自己语言的惟一动物。本世纪早期，卡尔·芬奇，慕尼黑大学的动物学教授，用了数十年的时间去体验"发现的最纯粹的乐趣"，解开了蜜蜂行为的秘密。因为芬奇令人吃惊的成就，他获得了诺贝尔奖。现今大多数的关于蜜蜂之间语言的知识都是起源于芬奇的工作。

B

开始是非常简单的。芬奇从一个早期研究者的实验知道，如果他放一碗糖浆在外面，蜜蜂最初可能要花上一段时间找到糖浆，但是一旦它们找到了，在一个小时内，成百上千的其他蜜蜂都会急切地来获得糖浆。芬奇认识到，通过某种方式，信息被传回了蜂巢。信息的内容是这样的：在外面，在那个地方，你们将会找到食物。

C

但是这是怎样发生的呢？为了观察蜜蜂，芬奇建了一个玻璃边的蜂巢。他发现，侦察蜂一旦返回了蜂巢，它们将表演三种舞蹈中的一种。在第一种舞蹈中，回巢的侦察蜂绕圈奔跑，交替着向左和向右，偶尔停下来并把采到的花蜜返吐出来，交给她兴奋的同伴们。第二种舞蹈中很明显是前一种圆圈舞的扩展版。在这种舞蹈中，侦察蜂表演8字形的镰刀舞。第三种舞蹈明显区别于前两种。开始的时候是沿着直线跑一小段距离，摇摆身体，半圆形回到起始点，再重复整个过程。它也会时不时停下来给那些乞求的蜜蜂一点食物。很快，其余的蜜蜂会兴奋地离开蜂巢去寻找食物。几分钟过后，芬奇做过标志的大部分蜜蜂就会吃上碗中的糖浆。

D

在进一步的实验中，芬奇解开了前两种相关类型舞蹈之谜：圆舞和镰刀舞。他总结到，这些舞蹈简单地告诉了蜜蜂，在离蜂巢非常短的距离内有值得获取的蜜源。侦察蜂跳的时间越长，越兴奋，表明食物越多。它所带回来的食物气味和它身上的味道传达给其他蜜蜂一个信息，即这就是它们正在寻找的食物。其他的蜜蜂则会成群离开蜂巢，呈螺旋形的圆圈飞行，按照气味去寻找食物。

E

最开始，芬奇以为蜜蜂只对食物的气味有反应。但是第三种舞蹈是什么意思呢？如果蜜蜂只对气味有反应，那它们如何能嗅到离蜂巢成百上千英里远的食物，而且有时这些食物处在下风带。在预感下，他开始逐渐将饲养盘移得越来越远，与此同时，他观察到回巢的侦察蜂的舞蹈也开始改变。如果他把饲养盘放到超过9英里远的地方，侦察蜂开始跳起了第二种舞蹈，镰刀形舞蹈。但是一旦他把饲养盘移到超过36英里远的地方，侦察蜂就开始跳第三种舞蹈，差别很大的摇摆舞。

他总结到，蜜蜂对实际距离的测量是准确的。比如，300英里远的饲养盘象征着在30秒内的15次完整跑。当盘子被移到60英里远的时候，数字下降到了11。

F

芬奇注意到了更多的一些东西。当侦察蜂回到家中，告诉它的姐妹蜜源信息，有时候它们会在蜂巢水平的入口平台上跳舞，有时候会在巢内垂直的墙上跳。根据跳舞的位置，摇摆舞中直线的部分指向不同的方向。室外的舞蹈是相当容易破译的：舞蹈的直线部分指出了蜜源的方向，所以蜜蜂只需要破译距离信息并沿着这个方向去寻找它们的食物。

G

通过研究在蜂巢内壁上的舞蹈，芬奇得出了一个不同寻常的发现——跳舞的蜜蜂以太阳为参照向同伴指示取食的方向。由于在蜂巢内的时候，舞蹈蜂不能利用太阳进行参照，所以它使用了重力作为替代。蜂巢顶部的墙代表了太阳的方向。如果它朝上直跑，就意味着太阳和蜜源在同一方向。例如，如果食物位于太阳左40°角的地方，舞蹈蜂就朝着与重力线呈40°角的方向爬。这就是芬奇的重大发现之一。很快，他发现了其他很多关于蜜蜂如何交流的事实并且给动物行为的研究带来了一场革命。

WRITING

WRITING TASK 1

题目要求

You want to sell some of your furniture. You think a friend of yours might like to buy it from you.

Write a letter to your friend. In your letter

- ***explain why you are selling***
- ***describe the furniture***
- ***suggest a date when your friend can come and see the furniture***

范文

Dear John,

As you know, I am a very lazy letter writer. What prompts me to write this is that Jane and I are selling the house and going to work in Hong Kong for a few years. The last time you were here you said how much you liked a lot of our furniture, so we decided to let you have the first opportunity to buy some of it. We would love to give it to you, but our finances don't allow us this luxury.

In case you don't remember, the dining room suite is in traditional Chinese style, and made of a hard reddish wood. I forget the name of the wood, but it will last forever.

The bedroom furniture is very different. It's a traditional New England style and made of white pine. We hate to part with it, but that's life!

So why don't you all come over this weekend for a barbecue and a look at the furniture. Anytime Saturday or Sunday would be fine with us.

Cheers,

Fred

分析

文章的背景提示是说你想要卖一些家具。你觉得有个朋友可能会想买。题目要求给这个朋友写一封信。在信中，解释为什么要卖家具，描述家具，提议一个时间，让朋友过来看看家具。

写这封信的时候要注意这封信的文体特点。这封信不是写给某个机构或者某个不知姓名人士的。虽然题目没有提供姓名，但考生应该自己编个名字。由于是给朋友写信，所以要直呼其名（given name），写的时候使用非正式文体。也就是说，通过使用一些非正式的口语化表达和缩略语来表现非正式的文体风格。

本文按部就班，逐一按照题目要求写作。先是解释卖家具原因：要到香港工作几年，而由于知道对方对家具感兴趣，所以有意出售。但由于经济状况，无法完全奉送。接下来对要卖的家具进行描述。有红木制作的中式餐厅家具，有白松质地的卧房家具。最后提出建议，让对方周末过来吃烧烤，顺便看家具。

WRITING TASK 2

题目要求

Some people believe that children should be allowed to stay at home and play until they are six or seven years old. Others believe that it is important for young children to go to school as soon as possible.

What do you think are the advantages of attending school from a young age?

题解

一些人认为小孩应该在家玩耍到六七岁。另一些人认为小孩应该尽可能早上学。你觉得尽早上学的优点是什么？

这道题由两部分组成。陈述部分表明两种针锋相对的观点。争论焦点是小孩是否应该尽早上学。但是应该引起考生注意的是，不需要详细分析两种观点各自的理由。因为这不是discuss题型。考生所需要做的是说明尽早上学的优点。注意：题目不是要求分析优缺点(advantages and disadvantages)，而是只要求分析优点(advantages)。

范文

There are many advantages of attending school from a young age for a child, and often for the parents. By young, I mean as soon as possible after the age of three.

Probably the most important one, especially in this day and age when many couples are deciding to have only one child, is that the child mixes with other children and acquires social skills that he or she might not acquire as readily at home. These skills include learning to help others and sharing things with them, becoming patient and learning to accept different ideas and differences of opinion.

Another advantage is that kindergarten and nursery teachers are trained in child development, and more capable than the average parent of providing an environment and activities that will promote the all-round development — physical, mental and emotional — of children.

A kindergarten or nursery school will usually have more space and exercise facilities than the typical home. With specially trained staff, this can foster the development of coordination and motor skills, as well as the social skills that come from playing with other children.

Finally, there is the question of the relationship between the parents and their young child or children. Having to look after a child all day and provide a stimulating environment is a full-time, and often tiring task. It is usually the mother who has to do this, and many mothers find that they can be much better mothers if they have a break from the demands of looking after a child.

So overall, I believe that, attending school from a young age is good for most children. They still spend plenty of time at home with their parents, so they can benefit from both environments.

分析

第一段话点题，指出小孩尽早上学对小孩本人以及家长都有许多好处。所谓尽早，我指的是从三岁就开始。

从第二段开始分析小孩尽早上学的好处。注意，除了列举好处以外，还需要对好处进行分析和论证。可以通过举例、解释、对比等方法论证。让小孩尽早上学的最主要原因是随着每家每户只生一个小孩，如果小孩尽早上学的话，就可以和其他孩子交流，获得在家里所得不到的社交技能。这些社交技能包括学会帮助别人，和他人分享，学会耐心，接受不同观念和容忍观点差异。

另一个好处是，托儿所和幼儿园的老师受过儿童教育方面的专门培训，和普通家长相比，更加能够为小孩提供一个身体、精神和情感上全面发展的环境。

托儿所和幼儿园和家里相比，通常空间更大，设施更齐备。在受过专门训练的老师帮助下，小孩可以培养平衡能力和运动技巧，以及通过和其他小孩玩耍学习社交技能。

最后，还有家长和小孩的关系问题。整天照料小孩，给小孩提供优良的成长环境是个全日而又劳累的任务。这项任务通常是由母亲承担，而许多母亲觉得，如果能够从照料小孩的任务中部分解脱出来，她们可以成为更好的母亲。

最后总结观点。因此，我认为，尽早上学对绝大多数小孩有好处。他们在上学之余依然可以和父母在一起，从学校和家庭两种环境中同时受益。

《剑桥雅思考试全真试题解析》（2、3、4）听力场景分布

《剑桥雅思考试全真试题解析 2》

	SECTION 1	SECTION 2	SECTION 3	SECTION 4
TEST 1	关于音像图书馆使用的对话	关于登山活动的采访	新学期开始学生讨论自己的课程	体育系主任介绍课程设置
TEST 2	申请个人财产保险的对话	对某学生公寓的介绍	关于各种媒体在儿童教学中使用的讨论	有关英国农业的讲座
TEST 3	有关新电视频道的市场调查	学校官员对校内外各种服务和设施的介绍	导师回答学生关于论文的问题	有关澳洲水资源问题的讲座
TEST 4	学生向租凭中介反映房屋问题	雨林导游介绍游览项目	学生与学校里的学习顾问谈论自己的问题	学生介绍自己对"汽车安全"问题进行的调查

《剑桥雅思考试全真试题解析 3》

	SECTION 1	SECTION 2	SECTION 3	SECTION 4
TEST 1	向中介查询租房事宜	邻居间有关医疗的咨询	工作面试	有关 back pain 的医疗健康讲座

TEST 2	入学第一天活动安排	校园咨询热线介绍会	有关工作面试的讨论课	关于在某中学进行的帽子制作活动的陈述
TEST 3	商讨圣诞之夜活动	介绍校内体育场馆	填写参加某设计比赛申请表的对话	有关鸵鸟饲养的讲座
TEST 4	两人商量如何祝贺朋友喜得贵子的对话	有关四样生活用品介绍的讲座	师生关于论文项目的讨论	有关环境噪音对住房设计的影响的讲座

《剑桥雅思考试全真试题解析 4》

	SECTION 1	SECTION 2	SECTION 3	SECTION 4
TEST 1	旅游咨询	工业村庄游览介绍	师生讨论作业延期及参考书目	有关树木对城市地貌影响的讲座
TEST 2	两位游客讨论旅游安排	校内咨询服务的介绍	三人讨论作业	有关公司犯罪的讲座
TEST 3	申请 homestay 的对话	电台有关 summer festival 的介绍	学生就短期课程的选择问题向老师咨询	学生代表就新的学生会楼的建设发表陈述
TEST 4	John 的告别派对	旅游公司自动应答电话	两个学生讨论在孩子间进行的5个科学实验	关于澳大利亚鲨鱼的讲座

INTERNATIONAL ENGLISH LANGUAGE TESTING SYSTEM

Test Report Form

ACADEMIC

NOTE *Admission to undergraduate and postgraduate courses should be based on the ACADEMIC Reading and Writing Modules. GENERAL TRAINING Reading and Writing Modules are not designed to test the full range of language skills required for academic purposes. It is recommended that the candidate's language ability as indicated in this Test Report Form be re-assessed after two years from the date of the test.*

Centre Number: CN001 | Date: 23/OCT/2004 | Candidate Number: 002853

Candidate Details

Family Name: HE

First Name: GANG

Candidate ID:

Date of Birth: 20/08/1972 | Sex (M/F): M | Scheme Code: Private Candidate

Country of Origin: China (People's Republic of) | First Language: Chinese

Repeating IELTS (Y/N): Y | Previous Test Date: 13/SEP/2003 | Previous Test Centre: BRITISH EMBASSY, BEIJING

Test Results

Listening  Reading  Writing  Speaking  Overall Band Score 

Administrator Comments

Centre stamp

Validation stamp

Writing Examiner Number: 003246 | Administrator's Signature:

Speaking Examiner Number: 997892 | Date: 03/11/2004 | Test Report Form Number:

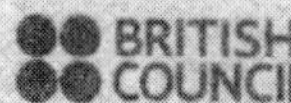

UNIVERSITY *of* CAMBRIDGE ESOL Examinations

新东方 NEW ORIENTAL

读者反馈表

尊敬的读者：

您好！非常感谢您对新东方大愚图书的信赖与支持，希望您抽出宝贵的时间填写这份反馈表，以便帮助我们改进工作，今后能为您提供更优秀的图书。谢谢！

为了答谢您对我们的支持，我们将对反馈的信息进行随机抽奖活动，当月将有20位幸运读者可获赠《新东方英语》期刊一份。我们将定期在新东方大愚图书网站 www.dogwood.com.cn 公布获奖者名单并及时寄出奖品，敬请关注。

来信请寄： 北京市海淀区海淀中街6号新东方大厦750室 北京新东方大愚文化传播有限公司

图书部收

邮编：100080　　E-mail：club@dogwood.com.cn

姓名：______　年龄：______　职业：______　教育背景：______　邮编：______

通讯地址：______　联系电话：______

E-mail：______　您所购买的书籍的名称是：______

1. 您是通过何种渠道得知本书的（可多选）：
□书店 □新东方网站 □大愚网站 □朋友推荐 □老师推荐 □其他______

2. 您是从何处购买到此书的？ □书店 □邮购 □图书销售网站 □其他______

3. 影响您购买此书的原因（可多选）：
□封面设计 □书评广告 □正文内容 □图书价格 □新东方品牌 □新东方名师 □其他______

4. 您对本书的封面设计满意程度： □很满意 □比较满意 □一般 □不满意 □改进建议______

5. 本书配哪种音像资料更适合您？ □磁带 □光盘 □MP3 □其他______

6. 您认为本书的内文在哪些方面还需改进？ □结构编排 □难易程度 □内容丰富性 □内文版式

7. 本书最令您满意的地方：□内文 □封面 □价格 □纸张

8. 您对本书的推荐率：□没有 □1人 □1－3人 □3－5人 □5人以上

9. 您更希望我们为您提供哪些方面的英语类图书？
□四六级类 □考研类 □雅思考试类 □GRE、GMAT类 □NEW SAT类 □实用商务类
□休闲欣赏类 □初高中英语类 □其他______
您目前最希望我们为您出版的图书名称是：______

10. 您在学习英语过程中最需要哪些方面的帮助？（可多选）
□词汇 □听力 □口语 □阅读 □写作 □翻译 □其他

11. 您最喜欢的英语图书品牌：______
理由如下（可多选）：□版式漂亮 □内容实用 □难度适宜 □价格适中 □对考试有帮助 □其他______

12. 看到“新东方”三个字，您首先想到什么？______

13. 您的其他意见和建议（可附在本页背面）：______